Would you like to...

- **Protect...**
  yourself
  your assets and
  your business
  from the IRS?

- **Solve your tax troubles...**
  for less than you ever
  thought possible?

- **Avoid future IRS hassles?**

If you answer "<u>YES</u>" read...

How to settle with the
IRS
...for pennies on the dollar

How to settle with the IRS

...for pennies on the dollar

Arnold S. Goldstein, J.D., LL.M., Ph.D.

Published By:

GARRETT PUBLISHING, INC.
384 South Military Trail • Deerfield Beach, FL 33442

How to Settle with the IRS for Pennies on the Dollar

Arnold S. Goldstein, J.D., LL.M., Ph.D.

First Edition Copyright ©1993 by Garrett Publishing, Inc.
Second Edition Copyright ©1997 by Garrett Publishing, Inc.

Published by
Garrett Publishing, Inc.
384 South Military Trail
Deerfield Beach, FL 33442
Tel. 954-480-8543
Fax 954-698-0057

This publication is designed to provide accurate and authoritative information in regard to the subject matter covered. It is sold with the understanding that neither the publisher nor the author is engaged in rendering legal, accounting, or other professional service. If legal advice or other expert assistance is required, the services of a competent professional should be sought. *From a Declaration of Principles jointly adopted by a Committee of the American Bar Association and a Committee of Publishers.*

Library of Congress Cataloging-in-Publication Data

ISBN:1-880539-43-8 : $19.95

Printed in the United States of America
10 9 8 7 6 5 4 3

★ABOUT THE AUTHOR

Dr. Arnold S. Goldstein is a veteran attorney with nearly thirty years of experience representing taxpayers with serious tax problems.

He is also president of Arnold S. Goldstein & Associates, P.A., a national law firm that offers tax representation, asset protection and debt restructuring to individuals and businesses nationwide.

He has written more than 100 books on law, business and finance. His titles include: *Asset Protection Secrets; The Business Doctor; Offshore Havens; How to Protect Your Money Offshore; How to Save Your Business from Bankruptcy; Commercial Transactions Deskbook; and The Small Business Legal Advisor.* Major media reviewers cite these and his other publications as complete, practical and enjoyable.

Dr. Goldstein's tax, financial and legal strategies have been featured in more than 350 magazines, journals and newspapers. A popular speaker on taxes, the IRS, asset protection and related subjects, Dr. Goldstein gives nationwide workshops and lectures on these topics. His distinguished academic career includes being a professor emeritus at Boston's Northeastern University and research scholar at the London School of Economics. He also has taught law, finance and management at several other colleges and universities and has appeared on numerous radio and television talk shows, including *CNBC* and *The Today Show.*

Dr. Goldstein is a graduate of Northeastern University (B.S., 1961) and Suffolk University (MBA, 1966, and LL.M., 1975), and he received his law degree from the New England School of Law (J.D., 1964) and a doctorate from Northeastern University (Ph.D. in business and economic policy, 1990). He is a member of the Massachusetts and Federal Bars and various professional, academic and civic organizations. He enjoys hearing from and assisting his many readers and can be reached at (954) 420-4990

ACKNOWLEDGMENT

Nearly 50,000 Americans have followed my tax-busting strategies in the first edition of *How to Settle with the IRS... for Pennies on the Dollar.*

This second edition is greatly improved thanks to the tireless effort of Nicole Ofstein, Esq., who heads the tax resolution department of Arnold S. Goldstein & Associates, P.A. She brings to this new edition her vast experience in successfully resolving tax problems for clients nationwide. Her many contributions to this new edition are acknowledged and appreciated.

TABLE OF CONTENTS

INTRODUCTION

What this book will do for you!

DO YOU OWE THE IRS?

1

HOW TO LEGALLY PROTECT YOUR ASSETS FROM THE IRS

2

FOUR ALTERNATIVES TO THE OFFER IN COMPROMISE

3

THE OFFER IN COMPROMISE PROGRAM IN A NUTSHELL

4

PLANNING YOUR OFFER

5

HOW TO PREPARE AND SUBMIT YOUR OFFER TO THE IRS

6

IF THE IRS REJECTS YOUR OIC

7

WHEN THE IRS ACCEPTS YOUR OFFER

8

HOW TO GET THE PROFESSIONAL HELP YOU NEED

9

STRAIGHT ANSWERS TO THE 50 MOST ASKED QUESTIONS ABOUT THE OFFER IN COMPROMISE PROGRAM

10

APPENDIX A

- IRS OFFER IN COMPROMISE PROGRAM
- IRS COLLECTION MANUAL
- UNDERSTANDING THE COLLECTION PROCESS
- QUICK AND EASY ACCESS TO TAX HELP AND FORMS
- YOUR RIGHTS AS A TAXPAYER

APPENDIX B

- IRS FORMS
- DO YOU NEED HELP SOLVING YOUR TAX TROUBLES?
- GREAT BOOKS TO FURTHER ASSIST YOU

WHAT THIS BOOK WILL DO FOR YOU

Few problems cause people such fear and worry as owing the IRS. These fears are justified. Countless stories abound of individuals, families and businesses who have been financially wiped out by the IRS. Tax problems are not unusual. About ten million Americans are known tax delinquents and another seven to ten million Americans haven't filed tax returns for years. Many are naturally reluctant to start now and risk detection and a crushing tax liability.

The fact that millions of Americans are in deep trouble with the IRS should hardly be surprising. There are simply too many opportunities to run afoul of the tax laws. As the tax laws become increasingly complex and taxes escalate, more and more Americans will end up with big bills due the IRS.

But there is one item of good news: It is now *easier* than ever before to resolve tax matters with the IRS. The IRS's "Offer In Compromise" (OIC) program now encourages delinquent taxpayers to settle their back taxes... often for pennies on the dollar!

Tens of thousands of Americans have discovered they can legally and easily solve their tax problems with an OIC. And many of these tax claims will be forgiven for as little as five or ten cents on the dollar, or even less.

Who are these people? Taxpayers with too little earnings and too few assets to fully pay their taxes. Some will be executors of tax-burdened estates, or a business owner hoping to compromise withholding taxes due from their business. The taxpayer may be going through a costly divorce, have health problems or for one of 101 other reasons simply have tax obligations he or she can't fully pay. Yes, the OIC program can also help you solve your tax problems whether you are unemployed, a wage earner, a business owner or a professional. It can work for you whether you are poor, enjoy modest wealth or are even a millionaire!

Moreover, you can compromise virtually any type of tax liability. It doesn't matter if it's ordinary income taxes, corporate income taxes, payroll taxes or estate taxes. With few exceptions, you can rid yourself of any tax liability due Uncle Sam. You can compromise a tax for $1,000 or less... or a whopping liability measured in the millions. Nor does it matter whether the tax is years old or is currently due.

A tax is a tax is a tax... and all can be compromised for pennies on the dollar... once you know how!

This doesn't mean that you're in for a free ride or that the IRS has suddenly turned into a charity. That is not the case. Instead, the IRS's newly liberalized policy acknowledges that a pennies-on-the-dollar settlement may be best for them as well as you, particularly when they won't gain more by seizing your assets or forcing you into an unrealistic installment arrangement that you can never pay.

It also costs the IRS far less to settle quickly for what you can afford to pay rather than endlessly chase you for what you can't pay. And the IRS knows you will be a more productive, tax-generating American if you can live and work free of IRS pressures. In a word, the IRS has become pragmatic and realistic in dealing with its errant taxpayers and this is best seen in its new policy in making Offers in Compromise easier to obtain.

Can the OIC program work for you? It can if you can convince the IRS that your offer in settlement of your delinquent taxes is more than they could obtain through seizure of your assets plus what you can reasonably afford to pay over the next five years under a full payment installment agreement. The IRS will welcome your *reasonable* offer that is logical for them to accept given your present and foreseeable financial circumstances. So the OIC is hardly a matter of beating the IRS. Instead, it's a win-win situation that gets the IRS the most money with the least hassle not only for them but also for you by your paying the IRS only what you can afford and wiping the slate clean.

Still, the OIC program is only one alternative when you owe the IRS. You do have other options this book will explore. For instance, it may make more sense *not* to compromise. Instead, convince the IRS to suspend collection by considering you "uncollectible." Or you may discharge your taxes in bankruptcy, or an installment agreement may be your fastest, most practical answer. This book will help you determine and pursue your best option.

It is not difficult to prepare your own OIC. Nor should you be so intimidated by the IRS that you don't try. I will carefully guide you, explain the law, work you through each step of the OIC process and show you how to complete the required forms.

I will then give you the tips you need to negotiate your very best deal – and, yes, contrary to what you may think, you really *can* bargain with the IRS! An Offer in Compromise *is* hard bargaining – often a long and exasperating process before you reach your deal with the IRS. But don't let this discourage or frustrate you. It's the price you pay when you owe taxes and want the opportunity for a fresh, tax-free start.

You'll have many other questions as you work your way to and through an Offer in Compromise. How do you stop the IRS from grabbing your assets or your wages? How do you position yourself financially so you have the least wealth exposed and can then negotiate your best settlement? What do you do if the IRS turns down your OIC? What do you do if you default on your OIC or you also have overdue state taxes? The answers to these and many other questions commonly asked by troubled taxpayers can be found in this book.

The Appendix contains every form you will need to complete your Offer in Compromise. For your guidance, you'll also find many other helpful forms for resolving your tax problems.

The IRS also offers considerable assistance and information to taxpayers. You will find several sources to obtain forms, publications and additional information in the Appendix and even a toll-free phone line for free tax information, a toll-free phone line for ordering forms and publications, a FAX line from which you can receive forms, internet addresses and mailing addresses.

As a special bonus, you will find the *Official IRS Collection Manual.* This hard-to-find publication is the bible for every collection officer... and now you can be forewarned and forearmed when dealing with the IRS.

Finally, you will find a full glossary of tax terms to hopefully take the riddle out of the IRS vocabulary.

While you can handle your own OIC, do carefully consider hiring a qualified professional firm, such as Arnold S. Goldstein & Associates, P.A. A qualified professional can help you to better assess your options, design the most advantageous offer and negotiate your best deal. Taxpayers can seldom muster the courage to bargain as hard as they must with the IRS and that's why I devote an entire chapter to finding the *right* professional and how you can work with your advisor for the best result. But even if you do hire a professional, this useful guide will familiarize you with the OIC program, make you more comfortable with the process and more knowledgeable in working with your advisors.

So if you have paralyzing tax problems, consider this book your passport to a new beginning. I'll provide you with all you must know. *You,* however, must provide the determination, sincerity and willingness to tackle your tax problems so they are finally behind you.

As so many other taxpayers have happily discovered, your tax troubles may soon vanish... for pennies on the dollar!

Wishing you every success!

Arnold S. Goldstein, Ph.D.

CHAPTER 1

Do You Owe the IRS?

Is the IRS chasing you? Do you suffer nightmares of losing your home, savings, business and all you worked for? It can happen! No threat to your financial security is as serious as owing the IRS because only the IRS has such awesome powers to extract money from you.

The IRS collection division is tough (it has a tough job to do) but can also be cooperative and reasonable – if *you* are cooperative and reasonable. While the IRS has powerful collection laws, you as a taxpayer have equally powerful laws to protect yourself from the IRS. You must understand and assert those rights as your first-line defense against the IRS.

How The IRS Tracks You Down

Hiding is never the answer when the IRS is after you. The IRS will find you no matter where you hide or how often you move. Its weapon? A powerful IRS computer linked to 50 state computers as well as to Social Security and every other federal agency that ever came in contact with you. You are also easily tracked through your state tax agencies, motor vehicle departments, unemployment offices, public welfare agencies, professional licensing boards, and even your voter registration records. It's impossible to hide.

Despite their vast network, the IRS computers work slowly. It can take the IRS years to find you. So while moving around can forestall your day of reckoning, it is not the way to avoid it.

If you owe taxes, then deal with the IRS as soon as possible. Delay will only cost you additional interest and penalties and even more aggravation and anxiety. You will also then face a more hostile IRS. But before you confront the IRS, you must protect your assets and position yourself so you can bargain with the IRS more on your terms – not its terms! You will learn these and many more essential survival strategies in the next chapter.

A WORD TO NON-FILERS

Are you one of the estimated ten million Americans who have not filed tax returns for several years? The bad news is that you have little chance of escaping detection. Eventually the IRS catches its scofflaws, and as the IRS computer becomes even more sophisticated, avoidance will become all but impossible.

Don't let the IRS catch you! File your delinquent returns before the IRS discovers you're a non-filer. Voluntarily file and you virtually eliminate the possibility of criminal prosecution. On the other hand, if the IRS catches you, it may criminally prosecute you, particularly if your delinquent returns involve sizeable taxable income.

It may take you time to get your tax returns prepared, so at least *notify* the IRS of your delinquency and your intent to file. In this notification, consider requesting a "statement of your account" for all delinquent years and a record of any "earned income" for any years in which you did not file. The IRS should give you a reasonable opportunity to file, and your notification will usually protect you from criminal prosecution. Do not let your inability to pay stop you from filing. File your tax returns even without the tax payment. You will be assessed interest and penalties for late filing, but you will avoid those more costly penalties imposed on non-filers.

If you do file several years of delinquent returns, then file them about one week apart so the IRS can't easily detect the scope of your non-filing. However, preparing all your returns simultaneously will allow you to determine the total amount due the IRS and to more intelligently cope with the tax liability. Deal with your delinquent returns collectively and never pay any one IRS return unless you know how all past returns will be paid or discharged.

Once your unpaid returns are processed or you otherwise incur a tax liability, the IRS will start the collection process. Expect four increasingly threatening notices from the IRS, each about one month apart. Your unpaid account is then considered delinquent and forwarded to the IRS Automated Collection System (ACS). An IRS collection officer, whose job is only to collect the taxes you owe, will then phone or visit you.

WHAT THE IRS KNOWS ABOUT YOU

The IRS officer will initially want you to complete a *Collection Information Statement*, IRS Form 433-A or 433-F (both for individuals) and/or 433-B (for businesses) which require you to disclose your assets and income. Their purpose? To uncover property and wages available to the IRS for seizure and levy or to give the IRS the information it needs to work out an installment plan with you if you can't immediately pay.

If the IRS asks you for additional information and you are unsure of their legal right to the information, be aware of the Privacy Act of 1974. This Act says that when the IRS asks for information, it must first tell you its legal right to ask for the information, why it is asking for it, how it will be used, what could happen if you do not provide it and whether you must respond under the law.

If you refuse to cooperate, the IRS can summons you to an IRS office conference, and even have the federal court summons you to appear, as the court can jail you and/or impose a fine for your failure to comply.

The IRS can compel your appearance to answer questions, but it *cannot* compel you to disclose financial information or documents. Taxpayers may legally refuse to disclose financial information. It is not even necessary to invoke your rights under the Fifth Amendment. This involves technical questions of law, so always follow the advice of your legal counsel in this situation. You certainly can refuse information if you have good reason to suspect you are under criminal investigation by the IRS or any other federal or state law enforcement agency.

Most importantly, protect your assets *before* you give financial information to the IRS. The IRS quickly liens and seizes assets, so timing is critical. Also, observe this important rule: Never falsify financial information. Be truthful to the IRS because false statements are perjurious. Remember: It is generally legal to *refuse* information but illegal to *falsify* information. If you refuse information, the IRS can then reconstruct your finances from other sources. While the IRS may not find everything, few items will go undiscovered.

The IRS will want updated financial information about once a year. An IRS officer will meanwhile independently track your financial condition and your ability to pay. You may unknowingly trigger renewed IRS collection efforts with increased income on your tax return. The IRS computers reveal much about your financial affairs.

The IRS also obtains other financial information about you from your own and other taxpayers' tax returns. For instance, your own tax return reveals your:

- wages
- interest income
- dividend income
- tax refunds
- rental income
- royalty income
- capital gain distributions

- moving expense payments
- vacation allowances
- severance pay
- real estate taxes
- travel allowances

The tax returns or mandatory reports filed by others reveal:

- mortgage interest received
- funds received from barter and broker exchanges
- unemployment income
- tax shelters
- fringe benefits received from your employer
- distributions from pension and profit-sharing plans
- cash payments of over $10,000 made to your bank account
- cash payments of over $10,000 received in your business
- gambling winnings above $600
- insurance payments made to you as a health care provider
- fees paid to you as an accountant, attorney or entertainer

This vast database enables the IRS to reconstruct, with considerable accuracy, your financial past and present. A diligent IRS officer will independently check these and other sources to discover your assets and income. Few agents rely solely on what you voluntarily disclose so review your tax records and the information others will provide the IRS. What does the IRS *really* know about you?

WHAT IF YOU IGNORE THE IRS?

Now that you see how information arms the IRS, you may wonder what the IRS can do to collect from you if you ignore your problem? If you do not contact the IRS to resolve your tax bill, the IRS can assert these "enforced collection actions":

1) File a Notice of Federal Tax Lien (which attaches all your property, all your rights to property, and all future property).

2) Serve a Notice of Levy (to take your property in the hands of a third party to satisfy a tax debt).

3) Seize and sell your property (personal, real estate, and business property).

4)   Notify employers and other income sources to begin backup withholding.

5)   Assess a trust fund recovery penalty (for employment taxes).

Even if you cannot pay, never ignore the IRS! Options are indeed available for a taxpayer indebted to "Uncle Sam."

HOW TO DELAY THE TAX COLLECTOR

Once you understand the IRS's awesome powers, you may wonder how you can delay the tax collector.

Start with the IRS's massive Automated Computer System (ACS). To stop or suspend further collection action against you, you must act to have a "freeze code" entered into the ACS. Simply ignoring the IRS never stops the collection process.

There are several freeze codes. Each signifies a specific reason for suspending collection, and each code halts collection for a specific time interval, but never for more than one year.

To stall the tax collector, try these three little-known strategies:

1)   Challenge the accuracy of your tax bill. You do not have to explain why you disagree with the bill, only that you consider it incorrect. This tactic can suspend collection for weeks, or even months, while the IRS determines whether you have a reasonable defense; if not, your account in the ACS is simply reactivated.

2)   If you cannot complete your return by April 15th, you will get an automatic four-month extension by simply filing Form 4868, and if you find out later that you still need more time, you may get an additional extension by filing Form 2688.

3)   You can also request that your tax file be sent from the local office to the IRS District Office. This automatically suspends collection and also offers two other important advantages:

   a)   Revenue officers at the District Office level usually grant more lenient installment plans than will collection officers at local IRS offices, and

   b)   A District Office is also less familiar with your finances and, may then, be slower to garnish your wages or levy your bank accounts. The downside? A District revenue officer may more diligently investigate your finances.

To transfer your tax file to the District Office, you need only question your bill and request transfer. Should your tax officer refuse to transfer your case, you can appeal to the supervisor. Persistence is necessary.

HOW TO COPE WITH A TAX LIEN

The tax lien is a very serious IRS collection remedy. A tax lien attaches, or encumbers, all your property (i.e., house, car, or boat) and to all your rights to property (such as accounts receivable). The IRS must meet several legal requirements prior to filing a Federal Tax Lien:

1) The IRS must first assess the tax liability,

2) The IRS must then send you a notice and demand for payment, and

3) You must neglect or refuse to fully pay the tax liability within 10 days of said demand and notice of intent to file a lien.

A tax lien is not valid against the claims of other creditors until the IRS files a Notice of Federal Tax Lien with the appropriate official (in the county where you own property or state where you conduct business), this establishes their priority status amongst your creditors.

A tax lien will greatly affect you, your credit and your lifestyle. Its immediate effect is to automatically encumber your property. Its practical consequence is to prevent you from selling or borrowing against your major assets. It also makes it virtually impossible to get the credit you need to finance larger purchases, such as a car or home. Because the tax lien supersedes later encumbrances, a new lender cannot obtain proper security for a loan. One solution: Have your spouse take title, assuming he or she is free of tax problems. This underscores a big benefit to filing separate tax returns. Another strategy: Set up a corporation to own new acquisitions, with others. Avoid becoming the corporate stockholder.

These maneuvers won't solve your problems because a tax lien also destroys credit. Bottom line: a tax lien means you can not hold any asset in your name and must instead rely on others for financing.

Tax liens may also encourage foreclosure by existing lenders who would be concerned that the IRS may seize assets they now hold as collateral. This commonly occurs with accounts receivable because the IRS gains a superior lien against existing lenders on receivables generated more than 45 days from the lien date. This problem is critical for business people with pledged receivables since their lenders would eventually lose their priority rights to those receivables. These lenders naturally expect immediate release of the tax lien, which can happen only if the taxes are fully paid, other collateral substituted for the receivables, or by filing a Chapter 11 or Chapter 13 bankruptcy. Otherwise, the lender must foreclose upon the pledged receivables to protect itself. This one reason explains why many tax-burdened companies are forced into Chapter 11.

It is nevertheless possible to obtain a tax lien release, and the IRS will release the lien, usually within 30 days, if:

1) You satisfied or settled the tax debt (including interest and penalties), or

2) The IRS accepted a bond to guarantee payment, or

3) The IRS has not refiled the lien before the statutory period of collection expires (usually 10 years). In this case, the lien is released automatically.

To request a release of the tax lien, request IRS Publication 1450 *Request for Release of Federal Tax Lien.*

If you are selling your home or other ownership in other property while a tax lien is in effect, you may apply for a *Certificate of Discharge* if any of the following circumstances apply:

1) The equity in other property, also subject to the lien, is worth at least twice the total tax owed, plus any additions.

2) The IRS receives the liened equity in the property.

3) The IRS determines the property has no current value to the IRS at the time of sale.

4) There is a dispute as to who is entitled to proceeds from the sale, and such proceeds are escrowed while the dispute is resolved.

For such a discharge, request IRS Publication 783.

You may instead want the IRS to *subordinate* its Federal Tax Lien, which allows the IRS lien to have lower priority over a lien filed after the IRS. You must then

1) Give the IRS the dollar value of their lien, prior to subordination (the value of what they are giving up), or

2) Show the IRS how the subordination would facilitate tax collection.

3) Request IRS Publication 784 for more information on lien subordination.

THE COLLECTION POWER OF AN IRS LEVY

A levy gives the IRS the ability to attach all monies held by third parties. While a lien is *security* for a tax debt, a levy seizes (takes) property to partially or fully satisfy the tax. A levy can be used to seize:

- Checking and savings accounts
- Wages (salary), commissions, and other income (see table at end of chapter to determine amounts exempt from levy)
- Cash value life insurance
- Property (i.e., your vehicle, boat or house)
- Licenses and franchises
- Securities
- Contracts
- Promissory notes
- Accounts receivables
- Inheritances due to be received
- Interests in partnerships and certain trusts
- Claims against third parties
- State income tax refunds
- Keoghs and IRAs
- Social Security benefits and benefits under the G.I. Bill of Rights
- Retirement pensions to veterans
- Pension and Profit Sharing Plans (note: the IRS can not force distribution from a pension plan if the employee can not obtain a lump-sum payment)
- All other property not exempt (see Chapter 2 for a complete list of property exempt from seizure (levy) under Federal law)

The IRS must also provide you advance notice of its intent to levy. Unless you pay your taxes or reach an installment agreement, become "temporarily uncollectible," file an Offer in Compromise (which may not necessarily stop a levy), or file bankruptcy, the IRS can levy these assets without further notice. If the IRS believes your assets are in jeopardy of concealment or transfer, it can levy *without* prior notice. This is a "jeopardy assessment."

The IRS may seize or levy your assets in any order or sequence. If levied assets do not fully discharge your taxes, other assets can be levied until your tax is fully paid. But, you can convince the IRS to release its levy if:

1) You fully pay the tax, including penalties and interest.
2) The statute of limitation (time for collection) expires before the levy is served.
3) You convince the IRS that releasing the levy will help collect the tax.
4) You enter into an installment agreement.
5) The IRS determines that the levy will cause you extreme or undue financial hardship.
6) The value of the property levied greatly exceeds the taxes, and releasing a part of the seized property would not impair collection.

7) You file bankruptcy.

8) You submit an Offer in Compromise. (Note: this alone seldom stops enforced collection.)

Seizure of your assets rarely comes as a surprise because three legal requirements must be met:

1) The IRS must first assess the tax and send you a "Notice of Demand" for payment,

2) You must then neglect or refuse to pay the tax, and

3) The IRS must send you a Final Notice of Intent to Levy, at least 30 days before the Levy.

This seizure notice may be given to you in person, sent certified or registered mail to your last known address, or left at your home or workplace. Never ignore this notice! It is your one final opportunity to submit your OIC or otherwise resolve matters with the IRS *before* you lose your valuable assets through enforced collection.

THE FIVE WAYS YOU CAN RECOVER SEIZED PROPERTY

Unless your tax liability is discharged through bankruptcy, or resolved through an OIC or installment arrangement, the IRS will eventually seize and sell any type of real or personal property that you own (or have an interest in), at public or private sale.

The IRS can seize your home but will do so only as a last resort. Still, the IRS cannot immediately evict you. You have about 90 days between seizure of your home and public auction or sealed bid sale, and another 180 days to stay in possession after your home is sold. Within this six-month period you can redeem or reacquire your home for whatever price the buyer paid, plus interest. Once this 180-day redemption period passes, you lose all rights to your home and the buyer can then evict you, which can add several months. You may have about a year of rent-free living once your home is seized, indeed a small consolation to losing your home.

You have no similar right to continued possession of other seized personal property. The IRS can immediately seize cars, boats and other personal property. Nor have you the right to redeem or reacquire personal property, as with your home.

That brings us to the five ways to recover seized property from the IRS:

1) *File an Offer in Compromise or enter into an installment agreement.* The purpose of many seizures is only to prod taxpayers to resolve their tax problems. Lax taxpayers respond when they are about to lose valued assets.

2) *Show the IRS that release and return of the seized property will facilitate collection.* Business assets, for example, in operation may generate more money for the IRS than they would yield at auction. This would justify their release.

3) *Your tax liability is satisfied or no longer enforceable.* Full payment obviously discharges your obligation, as will expiration of the ten-year statute of limitations. In either instance, the IRS must release seized property in its possession.

4) *File bankruptcy* (Chapter 7, 11, 12 or 13). Any bankruptcy will automatically stop further action by the IRS, unless the bankruptcy court approves proceeding with the seizure.

5) *You give the IRS a bond or substitute collateral equal in value to the seized asset.*

SIX DEADLY TAXPAYER MISTAKES

Dealing with the IRS is a mine field of booby traps. You usually discover your fatal error only when it's too late. While no book can uncover all such mines, beware these six ticking time bombs:

1) *Putting up with an unreasonable or incompetent revenue officer.* If you think you're being overly mistreated or victimized by an incompetent or overbearing revenue officer, then demand transfer of your case to another revenue officer. While revenue officers must be tough to be effective and collect, they must also act reasonably.

2) *Know where you stand.* Ask the revenue officer what further action you must take and what you might expect from the IRS. Never assume you know where matters stand or what will happen next. Avoid nasty surprises. And when the IRS says something – get it in writing!

3) *Never admit violating tax laws.* If a revenue officer tries to get incriminating statements from you, then terminate the interview and hire an attorney. If interviewed by a *special agent* or recited your Fifth Amendment rights, stop talking and run to an attorney.

4) *Never ignore the IRS.* Reply to all IRS correspondence and promptly return phone calls. Your willingness to communicate will help win IRS cooperation. But don't needlessly volunteer information.

5) *Pay your taxes if you can afford to pay the entire tax liability.* The IRS will incessantly pressure you to sell or borrow against your assets and this will be cheaper than having the IRS as a creditor. However, don't let

the IRS coerce your spouse to sell assets or lend you money to pay your bill. Pay only to the extent the IRS can seize *your* assets or income. But, if you cannot afford to pay *all* of your taxes by selling or borrowing against your assets, consider an Offer in Compromise before paying only part of your liability.

6) *Never extend the statute of limitations.* The IRS has only ten years from the date of tax assessment to collect your delinquent taxes. This was extended retroactively in 1991 from six years. Once the statute of limitations expires, your liability also expires. However, the statute of limitations is extended by:

- *Waiver:* When you sign a waiver, you voluntarily agree to extend the statutory period for collection to the date specified on such waiver.

- *Offer in Compromise:* Processing your Offer in Compromise extends the statute of limitation for the time period your OIC is under IRS consideration, plus one year.

- *Bankruptcy:* Bankruptcy extends the statute of limitations on non-dischargeable taxes for the pendency of the bankruptcy, plus six months.

- *Application for Taxpayer Assistance Order (ATAO):* This application extends the statutory period by the time it is under review by the IRS.

- *Absence from the Country:* The statutory period will be extended by the period of time you are outside the country for six or more continuous months.

- *IRS Lawsuit:* When the IRS starts a lawsuit to enforce collection prior to the expiration of the statute of limitations and later secures a judgment, the statutory period becomes extended to the same period as would other judgments in that jurisdiction.

Never voluntarily extend the statute of limitations. The IRS will try to get you to sign a Form 900 Waiver. When the statute of limitation is almost expired, the IRS may become overly aggressive in its collection efforts and offer you a "lenient" payment plan in exchange for the waiver. *Don't sign!* If the IRS couldn't collect from you during the preceding years, why will it succeed in the short time remaining? Once the statute of limitations expires, you are finished with the IRS. Extending the statute of limitations only extends your IRS problem!

Despite IRS collection powers, thousands of tax claims do expire each year. When *your* statute of limitations has expired, have the IRS abate the tax liability which then acknowledges that you are liability-free. Until you receive your abatement, continue to keep property out of your name. Becoming wealthy at the last moment may be the fatal mistake the IRS patiently awaits.

ASSERT YOUR TAXPAYER BILL OF RIGHTS

As a taxpayer, you gained several important rights against the IRS in 1988 when the IRS first adopted a Taxpayer Bill of Rights. On July 30, 1996, the second *Taxpayer Bill of Rights* was enacted. The purpose of this law is to educate taxpayers and to let them know in plain English what the IRS can and cannot do with taxpayers. The new law increases protection for taxpayer rights in dealing with the IRS. Publication 1, *Your Rights as a Taxpayer,* explains some of the taxpayer's most important rights. This publication is in the appendix – read it carefully.

You can also get help with your tax problems through the IRS Problem Resolution Program if you have a tax problem that you cannot resolve through normal channels. Reach the Problem Resolution Office by calling the IRS taxpayer assistance number in your area or request Publication 1546, *How to Use the Problem Resolution Program of the IRS.* See Appendix for requesting Forms and Publications.

There are two ways the Problem Resolution Office can help you. They may suggest that you submit Form 911 Application for Taxpayer Assistance. This form is also in the Appendix. Or you can call (800) 829-1040 to directly speak to a taxpayer ombudsman. If they believe the IRS action is causing you undue hardship, it may issue a Taxpayer Assistance Order (TAO) to suspend or modify further IRS action against you. Unfortunately, these are seldom issued.

The Appendix also includes various sources of assistance to the taxpayer in trouble with the IRS. Knowledge is critical when you deal with the IRS.

1. Table for Figuring Amount Exempt from Levy on Wages, Salary, and Other Income (Forms 668-W, 668-W(c), & 668-W(c)(DO)) 1996 (Amounts are for each pay period.)

Filing Status: Single

Pay Period	Number of Exemptions Claimed on Statement						
	1	2	3	4	5	6	More Than 6
Daily	25.19	35.00	44.81	54.62	64.42	74.23	15.38 plus 9.81 for each exemption
Weekly	125.96	175.00	224.04	273.08	322.12	371.15	76.92 plus 49.04 for each exemption
Biweekly	251.92	350.00	448.08	546.15	644.23	742.31	153.85 plus 98.08 for each exemption
Semi-Monthly	272.92	379.17	485.42	591.67	697.92	804.17	166.67 plus 106.25 for each exemption
Monthly	545.83	758.33	970.83	1183.33	1395.83	1608.33	333.33 plus 212.50 for each exemption

Filing Status: Married Filing Joint (and Qualifying Widow(er)s)

Pay Period	Number of Exemptions Claimed on Statement						
	1	2	3	4	5	6	More Than 6
Daily	35.58	45.38	55.19	65.00	74.81	84.62	25.77 plus 9.81 for each exemption
Weekly	177.88	226.92	275.96	325.00	374.04	423.08	128.85 plus 49.04 for each exemption
Biweekly	355.77	453.85	551.92	650.00	748.08	846.15	257.69 plus 98.08 for each exemption
Semi-Monthly	385.42	491.67	597.92	704.17	810.42	916.67	279.17 plus 106.25 for each exemption
Monthly	770.83	983.33	1195.83	1408.33	1620.83	1833.33	558.33 plus 212.50 for each exemption

Filing Status: Unmarried Head of Household

Pay Period	Number of Exemptions Claimed on Statement						
	1	2	3	4	5	6	More Than 6
Daily	32.50	42.31	52.12	61.92	71.73	81.54	22.69 plus 9.81 for each exemption
Weekly	162.50	211.54	260.58	309.62	358.65	407.69	113.46 plus 49.04 for each exemption
Biweekly	325.00	423.08	521.15	619.23	717.31	815.38	226.92 plus 98.08 for each exemption
Semi-Monthly	352.08	458.33	564.58	670.83	777.08	883.33	245.83 plus 106.25 for each exemption
Monthly	704.17	916.67	1129.17	1341.67	1554.17	1766.67	491.67 plus 212.50 for each exemption

Filing Status: Married Filing Separate

Pay Period	Number of Exemptions Claimed on Statement						
	1	2	3	4	5	6	More Than 6
Daily	22.69	32.50	42.31	52.12	61.92	71.73	12.88 plus 9.81 for each exemption
Weekly	113.46	162.50	211.54	260.58	309.62	358.65	64.42 plus 49.04 for each exemption
Biweekly	226.92	325.00	423.08	521.15	619.23	717.31	128.85 plus 98.08 for each exemption
Semi-Monthly	245.83	352.08	458.33	564.58	670.83	777.08	139.58 plus 106.25 for each exemption
Monthly	491.67	704.17	916.67	1129.17	1341.67	1554.17	279.17 plus 212.50 for each exemption

2. Table for Figuring Additional Exempt Amount for Taxpayers at least 65 Years Old and/or Blind

Filing Status	*	Daily	Wkly	BiWkly	Semi-Mo	Monthly
Single or Head of Household	1	3.85	19.23	38.46	41.67	83.33
	2	7.69	38.46	76.92	83.33	166.67
Any Other Filing Status	1	3.08	15.38	30.77	33.33	66.67
	2	6.15	30.77	61.54	66.67	133.33
	3	9.23	46.15	92.31	100.00	200.00
	4	12.31	61.54	123.08	133.33	266.67

* ADDITIONAL STANDARD DEDUCTION claimed on Parts 3, 4, & 5 of levy.

Examples

These tables show the amount exempt from a levy on wages, salary, and other income. For example:

1. A single taxpayer who is paid weekly and claims three exemptions (including one for the taxpayer) has $224.04 exempt from levy.

2. If the taxpayer in number 1 is over 65 and writes 1 in the ADDITIONAL STANDARD DEDUCTION space on Parts 3, 4, & 5 of the levy, $243.27 is exempt from this levy ($224.04 plus $19.23).

3. A taxpayer who is married, files jointly, is paid bi-weekly, and claims two exemptions (including one for the taxpayer) has $453.85 exempt from levy.

4. If the taxpayer in number 3 is over 65 and has a spouse who is blind, this taxpayer should write 2 in the ADDITIONAL STANDARD DEDUCTION space on Parts 3, 4, & 5 of the levy. Then $515.39 is exempt from this levy ($453.85 plus $61.54).

Department of the Treasury

Publication 1494 (Rev. 1-96)
Cat. No. 11439T

*U.S. Government Printing Office: 1995 - 402-284/39050

CHAPTER 2

How To Legally Protect Your Assets From The IRS

A taxpayer with severe tax problems chased by an over-zealous tax collector must quickly learn how to protect his or her assets from lien, seizure or levy.

With few or no assets exposed, the IRS has few or no assets to seize. This not only protects your assets but also significantly reduces what you will eventually pay the IRS under your OIC because your offer to the IRS cannot be for less than your equity in assets exposed to the IRS. Wealth available to the IRS is wealth you must pay the IRS. Make "poverty on paper" your objective. Only when you have very little for the IRS to seize can you win a pennies-on-the-dollar settlement.

There are many strategies to *legally* shelter your assets from the IRS. You can also quite easily *improperly* shield your assets so the IRS can recover them and impose serious criminal sanctions or civil fines. Faulty asset protection will also destroy IRS cooperation on your Offer in Compromise.

Timing is critical. Protect your assets at the first hint of a tax problem or preferably earlier. You can't afford to wait. Delay only jeopardizes your assets.

Hire An Asset Protection Professional

The most important rule: Never try to protect your assets on your own. To avoid trouble the job must be done correctly. Nor should you rely upon your tax professional for asset protection advice. Tax advisors are seldom experts in sheltering wealth. And because they constantly deal with the IRS, they may be too timid and ineffective in what they will do to protect you. You need a good asset protection lawyer who is bold and creative and will aggressively, but legally, shelter your assets using strategies unknown by others less experienced in asset protection.

HOW TO FIND YOUR ASSET PROTECTION PRO

Talk to a few bankruptcy lawyers. They usually have good asset protection skills. Estate planning specialists are also usually skilled in this area.

My own firm, *Arnold S. Goldstein & Associates, P.A.,* specializes in domestic and offshore asset protection. Our firm is staffed with highly qualified professionals with considerable experience shielding taxpayer assets from the IRS as well as other creditors.

The best place to start? Become knowledgeable yourself about asset protection. Even before you call a lawyer, read *Asset Protection Secrets.* This unique book, described in the Appendix, reveals over 200 perfectly legitimate and proven ways to protect everything you own from *any* financial threat... including the IRS! And don't think for a moment that you *can't legally* protect your assets from the IRS. You can. Read *Asset Protection Secrets* and you'll see how!

Why must you proceed knowledgeably? The IRS, like other creditors, can go to court to recover fraudulently transferred property. The IRS may also file a "nominee lien" against property wrongfully in the hands of the transferee. Of course, the IRS must prove in court that the property was fraudulently conveyed. Fortunately, the IRS as a giant bureaucracy seldom goes to such great lengths to recover fraudulently transferred property, unless the tax liability and the value of the transferred property is significant and the transaction a blatant fraud or sham. Asset protection in anticipation of a tax lien comes under the adage of "nothing to lose and everything to gain." Still, transfers best withstand scrutiny and challenge when handled by an asset protection specialist who can oversee the safest disposition of your assets and prevent serious problems for yourself or others involved in the transaction.

ASSET PROTECTION FUNDAMENTALS

There are several ways to protect your assets from the IRS:

1) Retitle your assets in the name of another individual or entity (but be careful of fraudulent transfers).

2) Convert your non-exempt (unprotected) assets into exempt (protected) assets.

3) Place your assets beyond the legal reach of the IRS, such as in a Family Limited Partnership, an Offshore Trust or a Limited Liability Company.

4) Decrease the equity in your exposed assets by encumbering those assets.

You must distinguish between these common tactics and those that are clearly illegal, such as concealing assets upon which a levy has been authorized, e.g., hiding an auto or boat.

A second serious mistake is committing perjury to conceal and thus protect your assets. You must never lie to the IRS, particularly when your statement is under oath. However, with sound asset protection, you *can* truthfully answer questions concerning your assets, confident the IRS can do nothing to seize them.

No law prevents you from selling, transferring or encumbering your assets. You can sell your property even when it has a tax lien against it. The IRS lien would continue to encumber the property, but the sale would protect any remaining equity from additional liens that may be filed against you after the transfer.

ASSETS THAT ARE SAFE FROM THE IRS

When the IRS wants payment, it doesn't have to leave you with much. But it still cannot seize everything that you own. Certain assets are automatically protected from seizure by federal law. These assets include:

- Clothing (furs and other luxury items are not included) and school books
- Fuel, food, furniture and personal effects for a head of household – up to $2,500
- Tools and books needed for your job, business or profession – up to $1,250
- Unemployment, worker's compensation, public assistance and job training benefits
- Undelivered mail
- Certain annuity and pension benefits
- Certain service-connected disability payments
- Income needed to provide court ordered child support
- Deposits to the special Treasury fund made by members of the armed forces and Public Health Service employees who are on permanent duty assigned outside the U.S.
- A minimum amount exempt from a levy on wages, salary, and other income (see Chart following Chapter 1)

Note that Social Security, Pensions, IRAs and Keogh plans are not automatically protected. The IRS seldom and only reluctantly seizes these assets, but if you have a large tax liability then be cautious and protect your IRAs or Keoghs. Property owned between husband and wife as tenants by the entirety may possibly be protected, depending upon your state law. Aside from these few assets, everything else you own can be seized by the IRS.

BEWARE OF STATE ASSET PROTECTION LAWS

Do you think your home is protected from the IRS by your state homestead laws? If so, you will be in for a rude surprise. The IRS is one creditor that can ignore your state homestead laws and seize your home.

The IRS can simply ignore other state exemptions designed to protect certain personal property from creditors. Why does the IRS have this unique power? Because the IRS is a *federal* agency whose authority supersedes state debtor protection laws. So don't count on your state laws for help. Other asset protection strategies are essential to protect your assets.

YOUR MOST VULNERABLE ASSETS

IRS collection officers enjoy wide discretion when deciding which assets to seize to satisfy a tax claim. In practice, they usually consider three factors:

1) The amount of the tax liability versus the property needed to pay the tax.

2) The ease of seizure and disposal of the various assets.

3) The importance of each asset to the taxpayer.

Now you can see why the IRS usually targets these assets, in descending order:

- Bank and checking accounts
- Cars, boats, airplanes, and other recreational vehicles with a high equity
- Cash value life insurance
- Accounts receivable
- Stocks and bonds
- Wages
- Collectibles
- Investment and vacation real estate
- Pensions, IRAs and Keoghs
- Home

The IRS will seize a taxpayer's home, Pensions, IRAs, Keoghs and wages when the taxpayer is uncooperative or no other assets are available to satisfy the tax. Still, the IRS may threaten these assets to spur the taxpayer into borrowing or selling assets to pay the tax. IRS officers know that no threat spurs taxpayers to find money faster than the spectre of losing their home or other treasured assets.

TWO WAYS TO SAFEGUARD YOUR BANK ACCOUNTS

You must quickly protect your bank account and safe deposit box because the IRS normally targets these first.

The IRS has a record of your checking and savings accounts and *will* levy these accounts. Any bank account in your name is unsafe as long as you owe the IRS. The IRS routinely and continuously levies bank accounts of delinquent taxpayers. To outflank an IRS levy, you must protect your money using two simple strategies:

1) Set up a corporation to hold your personal funds. From this account pay your personal debts. You may transfer money to the corporation as a loan and withdraw it as repayment without incurring a tax. Do keep good records to properly report all income at tax time.

2) Alternatively, transfer your money to banks the IRS doesn't know about. Small, distant banks are best because the IRS will "shotgun" or levy major banks in your area. Since the IRS periodically makes you submit a new financial statement and disclose *new* bank accounts, you must immediately thereafter open new accounts. This tactic is absolutely legal because you were truthful about your bank accounts when you answered!

Your safe deposit box is no safer than your bank accounts. If the IRS suspects you have cash or other valuables in your safe deposit box, the IRS will want to inspect it. This is automatic under an Offer in Compromise. If you refuse, the IRS will seal the box. To gain access to your box, you must permit IRS inspection or the IRS can patiently wait for your rental contract to expire, at which time a bank officer can legally open the box for IRS inspection.

This is why you must store cash or other valuables elsewhere. If you need a safe deposit box for your valuables, then set up a corporation to rent one in its name. Since your corporation is a separate legal entity, the IRS cannot demand access to its safe deposit box for *collecting* your personal taxes. There's another advantage even if you are not a tax delinquent. The IRS can seal and inspect *your* safe deposit box upon your death. But a corporate box has perpetual life. Your death will not bring IRS inspection of the corporate box, which can be opened by your spouse or another trusted individual.

Aside from collecting overdue taxes, the IRS snoops for cash in safe deposit boxes because the IRS considers such cash as undeclared, fully taxable income. *You* must prove the money is either tax-free or previously reported income.

TRUSTS AND JOINTLY OWNED PROPERTY: TWO DANGER ZONES

Property held in trust cannot be seized by the IRS to pay the tax liability of the grantor except under two circumstances:

- The grantor fraudulently conveyed the property to the trust, or

- The grantor retains control over the trust property or the right to revoke the trust.

If you convey property to the trust before you incur a tax liability, you have well-sheltered assets provided you use an irrevocable trust and adequately relinquished control over the assets. The IRS will closely examine your irrevocable trust. If it finds you retained sufficient control over the trust, it will be considered your alter-ego and your trust assets will be in jeopardy. Living trusts are popular because these trusts let you avoid probate. They do not, however, protect assets from the IRS or other creditors because they are *revocable* trusts. Cautiously use trusts to protect your assets. Few are trustworthy protectors of your wealth.

Similar problems arise with jointly owned property. If a husband and wife, for example, own a home in joint tenancy, instead of tenancy by the entirety, the IRS can usually seize and sell the interest of the spouse with the tax liability. However, since the Taxpayer Bill of Rights was passed, the IRS may only seize a personal residence with the approval of the District Director. If your property is held as tenants by the entirety, which can only exist between husband and wife (each spouse owns 100% of the corpus), your property may be protected from the creditors of any one spouse, but not creditors of both spouses. This protection usually also applies to the IRS. Do you own property under a tenancy by the entirety? Verify its protection with your attorney. And beware, the IRS is gaining rights over these properties.

Legal complications usually discourage the IRS from seizing jointly owned marital property when only one spouse owes taxes. But don't take a chance. Protect jointly titled property *before* a lien is filed. While the IRS may have difficulty seizing the interest of only one spouse, a tax lien will cloud title to the entire property and make it difficult or impossible to sell or refinance.

Joint bank accounts are particularly vulnerable because the IRS levies *all* joint account funds. The non-liable joint-owner must then prove what he or she contributed to the account to recover his or her share. Never participate in a joint account or joint tenancy unless you are absolutely certain your co-owner is free of tax and other creditor problems. However, since you can't be certain whether your joint-owner has or will have legal or financial problems, it is best to avoid these arrangements altogether.

You may now see why you should *not* file joint tax returns with your spouse. You will pay slightly higher taxes when you file separate tax returns, but the IRS cannot seize jointly owned property as easily as individually owned assets when only one spouse has the tax liability. With joint returns you cannot easily protect your assets since neither you nor your spouse can serve as a safe harbor. You must absolutely file individual returns when:

- One spouse has ongoing tax problems, continuing audits, or recurrent tax liabilities.

- One spouse's tax returns may cause serious civil or criminal problems.

- One spouse has most of the marital assets in his or her name and the other spouse has the greater likelihood of tax problems.

HOW TO WORK FOR THE IRS FOR BELOW MINIMUM WAGE

The wage levy is the IRS's most devastating power and particularly devastating when you consider the IRS can take everything you earn, except for your paltry personal exemption which can be as low as $113.46 depending on your filing status and the number of exemptions claimed on your statement (see Table for Figuring Amount Exempt from Levy on Wages, Salary, and Other Income at the end of Chapter 1). One IRS levy automatically garnishes all future wages until your tax liability is fully paid or the wage levy is released.

Because the wage levy is such an extreme IRS collection weapon, it is used only when the taxpayer is uncooperative after several notices, including a Notice of Intent to Levy and a Final Notice. Not even the IRS can realistically expect a single wage earner with a net salary of $500 a week to give the IRS almost $400 and continue to work forever for just over $100 a week. The wage levy therefore chiefly prods the taxpayer to respond when other efforts fail. Avoid this embarrassment and aggravation. File bankruptcy, negotiate an installment plan, or submit an OIC with the IRS *before* it resorts to a wage levy. Take the initiative and you will find the IRS more lenient. But you can take two steps to combat an IRS wage levy:

1) If you own your own business, you can divert your income to your spouse or adult children who work in your business. They can then gift or loan the funds back to you. Be prepared to prove that your spouse and children actually perform services for the business and can justify their income.

2) You can also set up another corporation to subcontract to your primary business, and you can get paid from this subcontractor corporation. The IRS will eventually find out about your new employer, but this can take a year or more. You can then repeat the process with another corporation. This strategy is perfectly legal and workable!

You forfeit this ability to sidestep the wage levy if you work for a large company that must honor the levy. If that's you and you owe a small tax that several paychecks can handle, then just grin and bear it. If your tax liability is too large to be quickly paid, then, for release of the levy, you must either file bankruptcy, submit an OIC, or negotiate an installment plan (these alternatives are fully explored in Chapter 3). Filing an OIC should release the wage levy; however, it may be necessary to set up an installment plan during the pendency of your offer. Your final alternative? Quit your job. It's not the solution for most taxpayers but is an option if you have other sources of income unknown to the IRS. Collecting unemployment will give you more money each week than what the IRS will leave you.

TIPS TO STALL THE IRS FROM SEIZING YOUR BUSINESS

Do you realize the IRS actually favors certain tax-delinquent businesses? What are they?

- Businesses financed by the SBA or other federal agencies. It's foolish for one federal agency to collect its money at the expense of another federal agency that will, by its action, lose its loan.

- Minority-owned businesses or those that employ a high number of minorities.

- High-profile businesses within the community, such as a major employer.

Is yours such a favored business? Highlight these points to your tax collector. You will see greater restraint. No, it is not official IRS policy to favor these businesses, but it is unofficial policy! Leniency still should not be construed as immunity. No matter how important the business, the IRS eventually expects payment of overdue taxes from *everyone*.

If you own such a favored business, you should be able to work out a more lenient installment plan or more easily negotiate an Offer in Compromise.

Another tip: The IRS never seizes businesses with hazardous waste problems. If you have such a problem, let it work for you!

Why else would it be unpleasant for the IRS to seize your business? Would your equipment be difficult to remove? Is vandalism a potential problem? Would your customers hound the IRS for the return of stored goods? Is your business so heavily encumbered there's no equity for the IRS?

Be sure to highlight the positive benefits that result from not seizing your business. Are there important customers counting on your future shipments? Will your assets increase in value with time, perhaps by turning raw material into finished products or receivables? Wouldn't this enhance the value of the business if the IRS waited to enforce its rights?

IRS officers only want *one* good reason for *not* going through the strenuous job of liquidating your business. Find one!

THE FIVE MOST POWERFUL ASSET PROTECTION STRATEGIES

Always assume you won't resolve your difficulties with the IRS. Prepare for the worst by following these five powerful strategies to protect your assets when the IRS is chasing you:

1)   Transfer your assets to family limited partnerships.

Although unfamiliar to most Americans, a family limited partnership is one of the safest ways to title your assets to protect them from creditors and to save yourself taxes. As the general partner, you (or your corporation) can continue to enjoy complete control over the partnership property while the majority of the interest in the partnership can be safely owned by other family members, corporations, or trusts as limited partners (with no decision-making power). The limited partnership can hold virtually any asset: real estate, CDs, savings, stocks, bonds, and even cars and boats. You will, however, want to isolate your "dangerous" or "liability-creating" assets, such as a business, in a separate corporation so these assets cannot endanger your "safe" assets in the limited partnership.

What can the IRS get by chasing your partnership interest? The weak judgment collection remedy known as a "charging order," which gives the creditor the right to wait for only your share of the distributed profits and your share of the net proceeds upon liquidation, both of which events remain entirely up to the managing general partner - you! A limited partnership protecting your assets leaves the IRS with no meaningful recourse. Discuss this with your lawyer, or see how it works in *Asset Protection Secrets,* by Garrett Publishing. Savvy lawyers rank the family limited partnership America's No. 1 asset protector. They're right!

2)   Transfer your assets to an Offshore Trust.

A taxpayer's assets are safest from IRS seizure only when they are sheltered offshore. An Offshore Trust is a special trust established in a foreign country with strict laws that protect the trust assets from lawsuits and creditors. An Offshore Trust will not enforce an IRS levy or summons or cooperate with other IRS efforts to discover or seize trust assets. The trust also enforces secrecy concerning the trust and provides a platform for international investing. Further, included in the trust are many features which make it less vunerable to creditor attacks so that creditors can almost never reach its assets. For instance, an *anti-duress provision,* so that if a U.S. court compels the grantor to repatriate trust assets, the trustee must refuse this request, and a *flight provision,* which compels or authorizes the trustee to relocate the trust to another trust haven if the trust became endangered in its present location.

Taxpayers with serious IRS problems frequently sell or mortgage their assets and then transfer their liquidated wealth to their Offshore Trust, often steps ahead of a tax lien. As with bankruptcy, all asset transfers to the trust and legal or beneficial interests in the trust *must* be honestly disclosed to the IRS when it attempts enforced collection. Looking for more information on the Offshore Trust, be sure to read *How to Protect Your Money Offshore,* also by Garrett Publishing.

3)   Encumber the equity in your property.

Can you borrow another $50,000 on your home, $10,000 on your car or $100,000 on your business? When the IRS is after you, borrow heavily so the smallest possible equity remains exposed. Do you owe a relative or a friend? Secure the debt with a mortgage on your property. Your goal must be to encumber the equity in your assets until there is absolutely no equity available for the IRS to seize. Encumbered assets will also help reduce your OIC settlement because you have less equity.

4)   Liquidate your life insurance cash value, savings, CDs, IRAs, Keoghs, stocks, bonds, annuities or other securities.

Sitting-duck assets are as good as cash to the IRS. Liquidate them *before* the IRS grabs them. What do you do with the cash proceeds? You'll soon find answers. But before you liquidate these assets, check with your attorney. These assets may already be protected by existing laws or easily sheltered in other ways. For instance, life insurance put into a life insurance trust may protect it against the IRS and keep your insurance intact.

5)   Collect what you are owed.

Your next step? Coax those who owe you money to pay now even if you must heavily discount their bills. It's obviously smarter for you to get less cash now rather than have the IRS collect more later. Similarly, settle your lawsuits against others, even if at a bargain price. Your claims against others lose all value to you once levied by the IRS. Finally, are you due a tax refund? File your tax return before the IRS computers are fed the fact that you owe *them* money!

HOW TO MAKE CASH DISAPPEAR QUICKLY AND LEGALLY

Sell or refinance your assets and you may wind up with a wheelbarrow full of cash. How do you protect this cash from the IRS?

1) *Buy exempt assets:* You can take the cash proceeds from a non-exempt asset and buy an *exempt* asset, such as tools of the trade or furniture (discussed earlier in this Chapter).

2) *Pay "friendly" creditors:* Do you owe your father for your college tuition? A brother for a past loan? You see the idea. Why not use your cash to pay these "friendly" creditors? If it's a *bona fide* debt, the IRS can't complain.

3) *Prepay expenses:* Did you know you can prepay your child's education, even years in advance? Many colleges offer prepayment arrangements. You can also prepay alimony, child support, insurance, medical care and even the legal fees necessary to combat the IRS. Your lawyer will like that. What bills can you prepay?

4) *Use offshore accounts, trusts or companies:* When you owe the IRS big money and have big money to shelter, then an offshore haven may be your answer. Nevis and Isle of Man are two havens whose principal industry is to safely shelter money from the IRS and other American creditors. Your money is even safer when titled in a foreign-based asset protection trust or an Offshore Limited Liability Company, popularly used in these two havens. Offshore banking is also perfectly legal, totally effective and neither as difficult nor inconvenient as it sounds. If you have $100,000 or more to protect, then investigate an offshore haven.

5) *Give a gift:* You can gift up to $10,000 per year, per donee without a gift tax. A gift to hinder creditors is a fraudulent transfer; however, the IRS rarely chases small cash gifts to your children or other family members who are logical beneficiaries of your generosity.

HOW TO PHYSICALLY PROTECT YOUR PROPERTY FROM THE IRS

Although the IRS code makes it a felony to remove, deposit or conceal property upon which an IRS levy has been authorized with the intention of defeating the collection of taxes, this doesn't mean you must docilely turn over to the IRS those assets subject to seizure. For all their power, IRS officers do not have the authority to force a taxpayer to produce property for seizure.

If you do volunteer the location of your assets to an IRS officer, your disclosure must be truthful. As with relocated bank accounts, a car, boat or other tangible asset may be similarly moved to defeat seizure. Still this tactic is not recommended, no matter how desperately you may want to keep your property. The

IRS will eventually find and seize your more significant assets. The safer strategy is to sell or encumber your assets *before* the collection process reaches the point of lien and seizure. For example, if you sell your car and lease another, the IRS has no car to chase and you avoid a "hide-and-seek" game you will lose. More importantly, you have cash from the sale which, as you have seen, is so much more easily protected.

Nor can the IRS enter your residence or business premises to seize property unless you voluntarily consent to such entry or the IRS officer has a warrant or a "writ of entry" court order.

You may examine the writ of entry and confine the officer to those premises described in the writ. But this applies only to private premises. The IRS needs no writ of entry to seize assets on public property. An automobile in a public garage, for instance, can be seized by the IRS without a writ of entry, while the same auto in your garage cannot.

Property located in another state can also slow IRS seizure as the local IRS officer must usually transfer your file to an officer in the state where the asset is situated.

As you can see, there are ways to protect your assets from the IRS. This chapter revealed only a few of the more basic examples. With the many other possible strategies, there are other potential pitfalls and dangers. That's why you must read *Asset Protection Secrets* and get the advice of an asset protection specialist at the very first round in your battles with the IRS. Remember, your goal is to *legally* protect your assets, not illegally violate the law.

CHAPTER 3

FOUR ALTERNATIVES TO THE OFFER IN COMPROMISE

Before you proceed with an Offer in Compromise (OIC), decide whether an OIC is your best remedy or whether another solution to your tax problems would make more sense in your circumstances. Consider four alternatives to the OIC:

1)   An abatement

2)   An installment agreement

3)   Remaining "uncollectible"

4)   Bankruptcy

You also have the option to pay the liability in full or to fight the determination of liability in court.

HOW TO ABATE YOUR TAX LIABILITY

Under an abatement, the IRS cancels all or part of the accrued penalties and/or interest, but not the under-lying tax liability. The OIC, in contrast, compromises the total tax plus interest and penalties for an amount that coincides with your assets, income and general ability to pay.

Apply for an abatement if you can pay the tax liability but believe you should be excused from penalties or interest for good cause. Most abatements extend to penalties (about 40 percent are granted). Interest abatements are far less common.

You have good reason for an abatement if your tax problems were at least partly due to:

- Illness

- Destruction of your records

- Family problems, such as divorce or death in the family

- Incarceration or other significant disruption to your life

- Improper advice from a tax professional

- Erroneous written advice from the IRS

In sum, an abatement may be granted if you were victimized by factors beyond your control which caused your tax delinquency and the penalties.

There are abatements for acts of non-compliance, including:

- Civil fraud penalties

- Negligence penalties

- Penalty for failure to pay estimated tax

- Failure to file penalties

- Late filing penalties

- Dishonored check penalties

Don't consider an abatement if you can't pay the abated amount (usually the amount owed less penalty). In most cases, this is about 75 percent of the unabated or present tax bill.

How do you file for an abatement? Use IRS Form 843 *Claim for Refund and Request for Abatement;* available in the Appendix. Include, with your request, copies of all documents that support your case. You will need strong and convincing documentation and you can't overbuild your case. Send this form to the IRS Center where you filed your return.

Should you pay the underlying tax in the meantime? If the IRS thinks you will have difficulty paying even that amount, they may be prompted to abate rather than risk receiving less under an OIC or bankruptcy. On the other hand, you will continue to accrue interest (and possibly penalties) while your abatement application is pending. If you foresee the possibility of an OIC or bankruptcy, then it is probably more sound to make no payment until your abatement is acted upon.

The IRS should reply to your abatement request in about 60 days. Call or write the IRS to follow up and then send a copy of your original letter and documentation. Don't drop your guard during this period. The IRS will continue collection activity until the abatement is granted and the abated amount is fully paid.

You may appeal a rejected abatement request. This appeal must be in writing and made within 30 days of the rejection. IRS brochures are available on how to appeal an abatement.

PAYING YOUR TAXES IN INSTALLMENTS

You may owe the IRS more than you can immediately pay but have sufficient assets or income to fully pay the taxes over time. Many taxpayers are too financially strapped to handle one whopping tax bill. If you're among these taxpayers the installment agreement may be your answer.

If you are filing your return and don't have the money to fully pay the IRS, you can request an Installment Agreement. The IRS has a new Form 9465, *Installment Agreement Request,* which you must attach to your return (see Appendix for form). This indicates the amount you can pay each month. The IRS does not require that you disclose any additional financial information to support your request, nor do you have to show the IRS there's no other way for you to make the payment now due. Further, the IRS does not specify what it considers an acceptable minimum monthly payment, nor the duration of the tax payments. Each individual IRS office determines by its own policies whether a proposed payment plan is acceptable or not. If your installment proposal is approved, you will be charged a $43 fee. The IRS will then send you a letter informing you that your request was approved, how to pay the fee, and how to make your first installment payment. If your installment proposal is unacceptable, the IRS will contact you and tell you what they do want as a payment schedule.

If you filed your return without the new form, you should send a letter to the IRS explaining your situation and propose a monthly payment schedule. Keep in mind that spreading your payments over time will cost you more interest, currently calculated at 9 percent annually. You may also incur late payment penalties of 1/2 of 1 percent of the unpaid amount for each month or partial month the tax is not paid (the penalty cannot be more than 25% of the unpaid amount). Combined, they equal about 15 percent annual interest, so borrow money elsewhere at a lower rate, if possible.

When you owe delinquent taxes for past years and cannot fully pay, an Installment Agreement can often be negotiated verbally by phone. When a taxpayer is sent a notice from the IRS regarding delinquent taxes, the notice typically states either, "For Assistance Call: (phone number)", "Please call us at (phone number)" or "If you can't pay TODAY, call us at (phone number)." Many offices prefer Installment Agreement negotiated by telephone. Before calling the IRS, be sure to have completed the worksheets at the end of Chapter 5 so you will know what to expect from the conversation and how to set up an agreement that you can comfortably comply with.

Individual IRS offices can approve Installment Agreements up to $10,000. Requests for installment payments for amounts in amounts over $10,000 will trigger an IRS request for additional financial information (Form 433-A or 433-F for individuals and/or 433-B for businesses). Also, if you owe above $10,000, a tax lien is almost always filed. Be sure to pay timely. It is not enough that your payment is mailed by the due date. The IRS *must receive* your payment by the due date.

IRS guidelines recommend installment arrangements if it "facilitates collection" of the owed taxes. Once the IRS agrees to an installment arrangement, it must honor it unless:

- You miss or are late with a payment.

- You fall behind on other taxes due the IRS.

- Your ability to pay changes significantly.

- You fail to give the IRS requested, updated financial information.

- You gave the IRS false information when negotiating your installment plan.

- The collection of the tax is in jeopardy.

- You fail to meet any of the addition conditions set forth on a signed, formal installment agreement.

If you need more than a year to pay your taxes, then expect the IRS to take a hard look at your income and expenses. The IRS will cooperate – provided they get every dollar above what you absolutely need to support yourself and your family.

The IRS has two categories of allowable expenses: necessary and conditional. Necessary are those which must provide for a taxpayer's and their family's health and welfare and/or the production of income (see the Income / Expense Worksheet at the end of Chapter 5). Conditional expenses are those which are not necessary. They are allowable only if the tax liability, including projected penalty and interest accruals, can be paid in full within three years.

The IRS will expect a monthly installment payment that at least equals the monthly difference between the taxpayer's income and allowable expenses. And if both spouse's work and only one has the liability, the IRS will expect the spouse with the liability to pay at least the monthly difference between the delinquent spouse's income and their percentage of the total household allowable expenses, usually determined by the percentage this spouse contributes towards the total family income. For example, if the husband is the delinquent spouse and makes 45% of the total family income, he is responsible for 45% of the total expenses and the IRS should accept an installment plan based on his income minus 45% of the family expenses; the wife does not have a tax liability and cannot be required to pay towards her husband's liability with her separate property or income.

The IRS prefers agreements calling for equal monthly installments. Suggest payment dates that coincide with your payroll dates. An installment agreement for more than two years must be reviewed at its mid-point, but in no event less than every two years.

As a practical matter, installment agreements beyond three years are seldom sensible to the taxpayer. If you owe the IRS more than you can pay within three years, you should either submit an OIC (if you have few assets), sell or borrow against your assets to pay the taxes sooner, or file for Bankruptcy.

As with an abatement, you can appeal an IRS rejection of your installment proposal. This appeal may be made by letter and mailed to the officer's immediate supervisor. In fact, the officer must advise you of your right to appeal if you cannot agree on installment arrangements.

STOP COLLECTION BY BECOMING "UNCOLLECTIBLE"

Do you have negligible assets subject to levy by the IRS, and no income beyond that which is absolutely necessary to cover your living expenses? If so, the IRS may temporarily inactivate collection against you under the "undue hardship" rule. If you are "uncollectible," the revenue officer will prepare Form 53 to report your account as such. This is referred to as "53'ing an account."

You will continue to owe the taxes and interest will accrue, but once the IRS has earmarked you as "uncollectible," they will temporarily suspend further collection activity.

The IRS will periodically re-examine your finances to see if your financial condition has improved to the point that some payment can be demanded. This financial review will occur about once a year and you must then complete a new financial statement (Form 433A). The IRS may question you in conference about this updated financial information or simply request that you complete and return the form by mail. As with all information you give the IRS, make certain that what you say is completely truthful.

The IRS may also monitor your financial condition by computerized review of your tax returns. For example, the IRS computer may "trigger" your return if your reported gross income exceeds a pre-established amount.

Millions of Americans have remained "uncollectible" for years and completely avoided paying their back taxes. Obviously, these individuals could not title assets in their name or have significant income available for IRS levy. Still, many of these "uncollectibles" enjoyed relatively comfortable lifestyles.

If you have no valuable assets in your name, a small income and expect your bleak financial situation to continue, then remaining "uncollectible" may be your most practical remedy. And remember, the IRS only has ten years from date of assessment to collect delinquent taxes. Once the statute expires, so does your liability.

However, if you do not intend on remaining "uncollectible" for the next ten years, or you do not want the tax liability hanging over your head, you may want to file an Offer in Compromise while you are registered as "uncollectible." Taxpayers have been able to get offers accepted, while being "uncollectible," for as little as $1,000 to $2,000 when they have been able to borrow money "strictly for the purposes of settling their tax debt in an Offer in Compromise."

WILL BANKRUPTCY END YOUR TAX WORRIES?

If you have significant creditors other than the IRS or if the IRS is being totally uncooperative, bankruptcy may be your best option. There are essentially two types of bankruptcies and two types of taxes. The effect of bankruptcy on your tax obligations depends upon both the type of bankruptcy and the type of tax you owe.

First, let's consider the different types of bankruptcy. Chapter 7 is the chapter which provides for the liquidation of non-exempt assets and the discharge of dischargeable debts. Chapters 11 and 13 provide for repayment of debt in whole or in part.

Now, you may be liable for either personal income taxes or for withholding taxes (usually due from a business that you owned or managed). Withholding taxes are not dischargeable through any type of bankruptcy. Personal income taxes are dischargeable in Chapter 7 bankruptcy, but only if the tax is over three years old.

Income taxes, whether more or less than three years old, are not dischargeable under a Chapter 13 wage-earner plan or Chapter 11 reorganization. Under Chapter 13, you agree to make monthly payments over three to five years to pay either a portion or all of your taxes, and under a Chapter 11, you have up to six years from the assessment date of the taxes. Because taxes are a priority claim, you generally pay the entire tax claim under a Chapter 11 or Chapter 13.

A Chapter 7 bankruptcy can effectively rid you of old income tax claims, but you must move carefully:

- Make certain that the taxes are over three years old from the date the taxes became *due* (if extension was requested, use extension deadline as due-date). More recent taxes are not dischargeable.

- Make certain that the taxes have been *filed* at least two years prior to the petition.

- Make certain that the taxes have been *assessed* as an audit deficiency for at least 240 days.

- If you either negotiated a settlement (OIC) with the IRS, or had your tax claim adjudicated, the 240 day period is extended.

- Bankruptcy won't discharge taxes if you understated your income or filed false tax information for the years you want discharged. The IRS can still come after you for any deficiency discovered through audit, so make certain your taxes for these years are accurate.

- Filing bankruptcy does not affect liens presently against your property. The IRS can, with bankruptcy court approval, still sell and seize the property. Your remaining tax obligation will be discharged.

- Don't forget that a Chapter 7 bankruptcy will not discharge withholding tax liabilities - but the fact that you are bankrupt may influence the IRS to consider you "uncollectible."

A Chapter 11 or Chapter 13 may work well for you if you can fully pay your taxes over time. A Chapter 13 gives you three to five years to pay your taxes and the IRS cannot bother you during this time. In a business or profession? You can elect a Chapter 11 reorganization which generally gives you up to six years from the date of assessment to fully pay the IRS. A Chapter 13 or Chapter 11 bankruptcy is recommended only if you have assets you do not want to lose. If you have relatively few assets and a substantial income tax liability, then wait the three years and fully discharge the tax under a Chapter 7 bankruptcy.

As powerful as the IRS may be, the federal bankruptcy laws are considerably stronger. Once you file bankruptcy, the IRS must stop all further collection action. So, bankruptcy can be an effective way to save your assets and stretch out your payments to the IRS. But don't wait too long before you file for bankruptcy.

For example, if you are in business, the IRS may have levied your cash and your accounts receivable. Perhaps the IRS seized and closed your business as well. Under Chapter 11 or Chapter 13 you can compel the IRS to return these assets. That, however, can take time to enforce. Your attorney must first file a complaint against the IRS for turnover. The bankruptcy court may take weeks or even months to act. Meanwhile, your business remains closed, employees find new jobs, and customers flock to competitors. Customers who owe you money will find the IRS levy a convenient excuse not to pay. Few businesses can survive so serious a disruption.

Bankruptcy is probably not your best alternative if the IRS is your only significant creditor. If you have a few assets you will do as well with an Offer in Compromise (and probably resolve your claim for very little) and/or being classified "uncollectible," thus suspending all collection efforts.

Bankruptcy may be your right remedy if you have many other creditors also pressing for payment *and* your taxes are dischargeable under bankruptcy.

Finally, do not file bankruptcy unless you first review your situation with an experienced bankruptcy lawyer *and* a tax professional who can counsel you on whether another alternative may be preferable.

CHAPTER 4

THE OFFER IN COMPROMISE PROGRAM IN A NUTSHELL

Simply stated, the IRS Offer in Compromise Program (IRS code section 7122) authorizes the IRS to compromise outstanding tax obligations with financially burdened taxpayers for less than the full tax due. In essence, the IRS makes a deal with you to pay all you can reasonably afford and forgives any remaining balance.

The Offer in Compromise Program (OIC) is not new. The IRS has compromised tax liabilities for over 80 years. Historically, the IRS discouraged OICs, or at least did little to encourage their use, as seen by the fact that so few taxpayers over the years took advantage of the OIC program. For example, during the 1980s the IRS processed as few as 2,000 offers a year, yet millions of taxpayers who were ideal candidates for the OIC program never tried to compromise their taxes.

In 1992, the IRS adopted new policies and procedures to greater promote taxpayer use of OICs and to streamline the handling of such cases. IRS officers increasingly and more enthusiastically now advise delinquent taxpayers about the OIC program. Many tax professionals agree the IRS is now more lenient and willing to accept reasonable OICs than in the past. Apparently, the IRS has discovered that allowing taxpayers to voluntarily pay a portion of what they owe is preferable to chasing the taxpayer for the full amount and ending up with even less.

WHY THE OIC PROGRAM HAS BECOME SO POPULAR

It is not surprising that the IRS has found the OIC a more productive solution when dealing with tax-burdened Americans. Too many long-term installment agreements fell into default and too much IRS effort was lost enforcing those agreements. And the heavy hand of the IRS forced too many taxpayers into bankruptcy or made them impoverished to the point they were "uncollectible."

The Offer in Compromise Program, in contrast, provides a realistic way for the IRS to bring in revenue it otherwise would never collect, or at least not efficiently collect, while giving the taxpayer a fresh start.

The IRS's new attitude toward OIC's is best summarized in its own policy statement.

> "The Service will accept an Offer in Compromise when it is unlikely that the tax liability can be collected in full and the amount offered reasonably reflects collection potential. An Offer in Compromise is a legitimate alternative to declaring a case as currently not collectible or to a protracted installment agreement. The goal is to achieve collection of what is potentially collectible at the earliest possible time and at the least cost to the government.
>
> In cases where an Offer in Compromise appears to be a viable solution to a tax delinquency, the Service employee assigned to the case will discuss the compromise alternative with the taxpayer and, when necessary, assist in preparing the required forms. The taxpayer will be responsible for initiating the first specific proposal for compromise.
>
> The success of the compromise program will be assured only if taxpayers make adequate compromise proposals consistent with their ability to pay and the Service makes prompt and reasonable decisions. Taxpayers are expected to provide reasonable documentation to verify their ability to pay. The ultimate goal is a compromise which is in the best interest of both the taxpayer and the Service. Acceptance of an adequate offer will also result in creating, for the taxpayer, an expectation of and a fresh start toward compliance with all future filing and payment requirements."

The OIC program is detailed in the Appendix. While this and the following chapters highlight the law's key provisions, do turn to the Appendix for more complete and thorough information about the program.

WHO CAN BENEFIT FROM THE OFFER IN COMPROMISE PROGRAM?

Any taxpayer can file an Offer in Compromise. This includes:

* individuals

* married couples

* incorporated businesses

* partnerships

* non-profit organizations

- receivers

- trustees of trusts

- executors of estates

In sum, any person or entity that can in any way incur a federal tax liability can file an Offer in Compromise to settle that liability. That right also extends to the taxpayer's duly authorized agent or representative.

WHAT TAXES CAN BE COMPROMISED?

Just as any taxpayer can file an OIC, the OIC program compromises virtually any personal, estate or business tax, including:

- personal income taxes

- corporate income taxes

- estate taxes

- unemployment taxes

- withholding and employment taxes

- road taxes

These, of course, are taxes most commonly owed by taxpayers.

The IRS can further compromise any civil or criminal case related to the tax laws. It can compromise not only the tax but also all penalties and interest.

Nor does it matter how old the tax may be. The Offer in Compromise may extend to old taxes on which collection has been suspended, recent taxes currently placed for collection, or taxes for the present year which have not even been assessed. You may also combine the various tax obligations, regardless of tax type or age, into one Offer in Compromise. Finally, you can compromise taxes, regardless of the amount.

WHEN CAN YOU COMPROMISE YOUR TAXES?

There are only two circumstances when an Offer in Compromise may be legally compromised by the IRS:

1) When the taxpayer is unable to pay the full tax liability and it is doubtful that the tax, penalty and interest can be fully collected through the collection process within the foreseeable future *("doubt of collectability");* and/or

2)   Where there is doubt about the taxpayer's tax liability *("doubt of liability")*.

A case may involve both doubt of collectability and liability.

Compromises of civil liability do not compromise criminal liability in the same case, and vice versa. Criminal liability may be compromised if:

1)   the violations involve a regulatory provision of the Internal Revenue Code or associated statutes, and/or

2)   the violations are not premeditated with the intent to defraud.

WHAT YOU MUST PAY THE IRS

IRS policy is to accept an OIC only when it is in its best interests – as well as that of the taxpayer.

In doubt of collectability cases, the IRS will consider these three questions:

1)   Could the IRS collect more from you (through seizure and liquidation of your assets or through an installment agreement based on your present and future income) than you are offering? You must convince the IRS that it's more cost-effective for the IRS to accept your offer rather than enforce collection.

2)   Would the IRS be better off to wait for some future date when your financial position may improve? Keep in mind that the IRS will consider your possible *future* wealth, as well as your *present* wealth.

3)   Would the general public believe that accepting your offer was incorrect and improper?

Answer "no" to each of these questions and your offer stands a very good chance of being approved.

Many OICs are literally settled for "pennies on the dollar," but this does not suggest that the IRS works on the "something is better than nothing" principle. The IRS has ten years to collect – unless you discharge the taxes in bankruptcy – and the IRS frequently takes the chance it will collect more someday rather than settle for too little today.

HOW THE COMPROMISED AMOUNT IS PAID

You can pay the offered amount:

- In one lump sum payment – paid in full with offer, paid within 10, 30, 60, or 90 days of acceptance of the OIC, or other proposed, specific payment terms.

- In installments, but typically not beyond two years (rarely accepted by the IRS).

- Through a combination of a lump sum payment and installments (again, typically not beyond two years).

If you cannot pay the amount you are offering within 90 days or if you intend to pay in installments, you must include the specific dates and payment amounts in your offer. And, if the IRS, in reviewing your financial situation, determines that you can pay the amount you are offering sooner, they will require earlier payment or, in the alternative, will reject your offer.

You should also submit a small, refundable (if the OIC is not accepted) deposit with the OIC because it reflects your good faith effort at compromise; however, it is not required. The IRS may additionally ask for collateral agreements that obligate you to pay a portion of your future income or grant to the IRS other concessions. These agreements will be discussed in greater detail in the next chapter. Such agreements were often requested by the IRS in the past; however, they are rarely requested today.

THREE MORE KEY POINTS IN A OFFER IN COMPROMISE

Your Offer in Compromise also commits you to:

- Comply with *all* terms and conditions of the agreement.

- Give the IRS your tax refunds, for periods ending before or within or as of the end of the calendar year in which the offer is accepted. This is applied only to unpaid taxes not compromised.

- Comply with all IRS requirements (timely tax filings and payments, no extensions) for five years.

If you fail on any of these points, the IRS can rescind the OIC agreement and collect the balance due on the original tax liability or that amount remaining due under your OIC.

The IRS takes OIC compliance quite seriously. Many OIC's come from chronic tax delinquents and scofflaws, and OIC's are not intended to encourage people to disregard the tax laws. The aim of the OIC program is to help troubled taxpayers get back on a straight track with the IRS – *if* they can stay on a straight track. This explains why the IRS quickly revokes OIC's when the taxpayer continues to violate the tax laws.

REQUIREMENTS FOR FILING YOUR OIC

Filing an OIC requires you to complete and submit to the IRS:

•   Form 656 Offer in Compromise
•   Form 433-A *and/or* 433-B Collection Information Statements

With these forms you also submit your deposit and any additional documents that support your case. These forms, as well as corresponding instructions and worksheets, are contained in the Appendix.

For an OIC to be considered, all tax returns due from you must be filed and all years for which there is an outstanding tax liability must be included with the offer. This includes not only income taxes, but also other outstanding tax liabilities.

OIC'S AND CONTINUED COLLECTION

Filing an Offer in Compromise does not automatically suspend IRS collection. However, the IRS usually does not continue enforced collection if you have submitted a reasonable offer. The IRS *will* continue to enforce collection if it appears you are using the OIC only to delay collection, fraudulently transfer your assets, *or,* in some way, diminish the IRS's ability to collect. Notwithstanding a filed offer, the IRS will file a lien against your property and *will* not release the lien until your OIC has been fully paid.

ADVANTAGES AND DISADVANTAGES OF AN OIC

This overview of the Offer in Compromise Program should help you determine whether an OIC is *your* best solution to your tax problems.

The obvious advantage of the OIC is that it gives you the chance to begin your financial life anew without pressing tax claims. While you must pay the IRS something, this amount may represent a very small fraction of what you owe. The OIC provides a systematic and rational way for you and the IRS to agree on a fair, equitable, and realistic way for you to end your tax difficulties.

There are several minor disadvantages to an OIC:

- An accepted OIC is public record for one year. Anyone can examine considerable personal information about you and your finances. Such disclosures may hurt you in the future. Unaccepted offers remain confidential and are not public record.

- You must comply with all provisions of the Internal Revenue Code for filing your returns and paying your taxes for 5 years from the date the IRS accepts your offer; otherwise the full amount of the liability is reinstated. This does not apply to *"doubt as to liability"* offers.

- Filing the OIC extends the 10-year statute of limitations for collecting taxes one additional year *plus* the time the OIC is under IRS review, *including* the time you have not paid all of the offered amount or have not completed all terms and conditions of the offer. This extension occurs even if your OIC is rejected. This can be a disadvantage as OIC's frequently take a year for the IRS to review. This is particularly true when amended OIC's are filed. If you offer installment payments, this added year doesn't begin until your final payment is made.

- An OIC also requires you to agree not to contest in court nor appeal the amount of your tax liability *if* your offer is accepted. But this would become a disadvantage only if the OIC was later rescinded by the IRS because *you* violated the agreement, *and* the IRS tried to collect the original disputed amount.

- You will lose all tax overpayments (refunds), including interest, for tax periods extending through the calendar year that the IRS accepts the offer, to the extent such application of refunds is necessary to pay the uncompromised liability. You also may not designate a refund, to which the IRS is entitled, to be applied to estimated tax payments for the following year. The condition does not apply to *"doubt as to liability"* offers. Even without the OIC, the IRS could automatically offset and apply these refunds to your tax liability so this is not a true disadvantage.

- Finally, the OIC process requires you to fully disclose to the IRS your entire financial history. This, however, is no more information than is provided for an installment agreement. If your offer is rejected, the IRS *will* know more about your assets, and your disclosures may even prompt an IRS audit; however, this seldom occurs as a result of an OIC.

The opportunity to end your tax problems on terms you can afford should clearly outweigh the several disadvantages of an Offer in Compromise. The Offer in Compromise Program is an opportunity every troubled taxpayer must seriously consider!

Are You A Candidate For An Offer In Compromise?

Is an Offer in Compromise your best remedy or would another solution to your tax problems make more sense in your circumstances? You should consider these four alternatives to the OIC:

1)   An abatement

2)   An installment agreement

3)   Remaining "uncollectible"

4)   Bankruptcy

The following questions will help you to determine which remedy is best for you.

- Can you pay the tax liability?
  ❏ Yes ❏ No

- Should you be excused from penalties and/or interest for good cause?
  ❏ Yes ❏ No

- Were your tax problems at least partly due to: illness, destruction of your records, family problems or divorce, incarceration or other significant disruption to your life, OR improper advice from a tax professional?
  ❏ Yes ❏ No

- Can you pay 75% of the unabated tax bill?
  ❏ Yes ❏ No

  ◆   If you answered yes to the above questions, you are a candidate for an **Abatement.**

- Do you have enough income to fully pay the taxes over time?
  ❏ Yes ❏ No

- Are you too financially strapped to handle your tax bill with one payment?
  ❏ Yes ❏ No

- Can you repay the IRS within three years?
  ❏ Yes ❏ No

  ◆   If you answered yes to the above questions, you are a candidate for an **Installment Agreement.**

- Do you have negligible assets subject to levy by the IRS?
  ❏ Yes ❏ No

- Do you have no income beyond what is absolutely necessary to cover your living expenses?
  ❏ Yes ❏ No

- Do you expect your bleak financial situation to continue?
  ❏ Yes ❏ No

  ◆ If you answered yes to the above questions, you are a candidate for being registered **"Temporarily Uncollectible."**

- Are you liable for personal income taxes?
  ❏ Yes ❏ No

- Has the tax (1) been due, including extensions, for over three years, (2) been filed for at least two years, *and* (3) been assessed at least 240 days?
  ❏ Yes ❏ No

- Did you properly state your income and file true tax information for the years you want discharged?
  ❏ Yes ❏ No

- Do you have any significant creditors other than the IRS?
  ❏ Yes ❏ No

  ◆ If you answered yes to the above questions, you are a candidate for **Bankruptcy.**

- Are you unable to pay the full tax liability?
  ❏ Yes ❏ No

- Is it doubtful that the tax, penalty, and interest can be fully <u>collected</u> through the collection process within the foreseeable future, OR is there doubt about your tax <u>liability</u>?
  ❏ Yes ❏ No

- Are your taxes more than you can pay either through selling or borrowing against your assets or from income above what you need to support yourself and your family?
  ❏ Yes ❏ No

- Do you have too many assets and/or too much income to be classified as temporarily uncollectible?
  ❏ Yes ❏ No

- Do you have no other significant debts, OR are your taxes not dischargeable in bankruptcy?
❏ Yes ❏ No

- Is it doubtful that your financial position will improve, thus making it disadvantageous for the IRS to wait for some future date to collect?
❏ Yes ❏ No

- Would the general public believe that accepting your offer was correct and proper?
❏ Yes ❏ No

◆ If you answered yes to the above questions, you are a candidate for an **Offer in Compromise.**

NOTE: Use of one of these "remedies" does not preclude use of another! For instance, you can be registered "temporarily uncollectible" or have an existing Installment Agreement with the IRS and still file an Offer in Compromise.

CHAPTER 5

PLANNING YOUR OFFER

The success of your OIC rests on your ability to propose an offer that is:

1)   Acceptable to the IRS, and

2)   Within your ability to pay.

The IRS is very strict when considering the adequacy of an offer on doubt as to collectibility cases. An offer viewed as adequate and fair by the average taxpayer may not be acceptable to the IRS.

As an overview, an Offer in Compromise must represent the taxpayer's *maximum* capacity to pay. This means all that can be reasonably collected from the taxpayer's equity in assets and income, whether present or prospective. This also includes amounts that may be recoverable through transferee assessment, as well as exempt assets beyond the reach of the government and other income, such as inheritances, available to the taxpayer.

ESTIMATING YOUR MAXIMUM CAPACITY TO PAY

In "doubt as to collectibility" cases, the IRS focuses on your maximum capacity to pay. This is unlike doubt as to liability cases where your offer is based on the estimated degree of liability rather than the collectibility of what you owe.

In determining your maximum capacity to pay, the IRS totals the equity in all of your assets, which is determined by the "current market value" minus the "current amount owed" for each of your assets (page 3 of both 433-A and 433-B). In the instructions for an Offer in Compromise (revised January 1997), the IRS clearly defines 'Current Market Value' as follows:

"The amount you could reasonably expect to be paid for the asset if you sold it. Do not guess at the value of an asset. Find out the value from realtors, used car dealers, publications, furniture dealers, or other experts on specific types of assets. If you get a written estimate, please include a copy with your financial statement."

For offer purposes, the taxpayer's equity in assets represents the current market value of an asset less only those encumbrances which have *priority* over the federal tax lien (typically, only debts secured prior to an IRS lien).

If only one spouse has a liability, prepare the offer based on the equity in assets (or in partial interests in assets) owned by the liable spouse *unless* state community property laws allow for collection from a non-liable spouse. The nine community property states are: Arizona, California, Idaho, Louisiana, Nevada, New Mexico, Texas, Washington, and Wisconsin.

In determining your maximum capacity to pay, decide first whether your offer at least equals the current market value of your assets. There is no one formula to compute the current market value of an asset. These values vary depending upon supply and demand, availability of financing, the local economy and even the time of year. Unusual or hard to sell assets may have an exceptionally low current market values. These variables encourage the IRS to use considerable discretion when negotiating asset valuations with the taxpayer, and those values can be quite low if the taxpayer knows how to bargain effectively. The IRS will often allow a lower value to be accepted when the lower value can be shown to be in the best interest of the IRS. An example of this is hazardous waste property which makes the property difficult, if not impossible, to sell.

HOW TO VALUE SPECIAL ASSETS

Certain assets present special valuation problems. Use these IRS guidelines when valuating:

- **Joint Ownership Property:**

  If you own property with others, your offer must reflect the value of *your* interest in the property. Where a taxpayer owns property as a tenant by the entirety with an innocent (no tax liability) spouse, the IRS considers the taxpayer's interest to be no more than 50-percent and usually as low as 20-percent of the overall value of the property. Twenty percent is the amount that should be offered because the IRS will have difficulty reaching assets owned as tenants by the entirety.

  Joint tenancy and tenancy in common properties are normally valued on the full basis of the taxpayer's interest in the property because the IRS has full recourse to these ownership interests.

- **Pensions:**

  Pension plans also present special valuation problems. The IRS manual suggests the following guideline for valuating a taxpayer's pension plan:

  1) "Where under the terms of employment, a taxpayer is required to contribute a percentage of his/her gross earnings to a retirement plan and the amount contributed, plus any increments cannot be withdrawn until separation, retirement, demise, etc., this asset will be considered as having no realizable equity.

  2) Where the taxpayer is not required, as a condition of employment, to participate in a pension plan, but voluntarily elects to do so, the realizable equity for compromise purposes shall be the gross amount in the taxpayer's plan reduced by the employer's contributions. However, in these situations, each case should stand on its own merits.

  3) If the taxpayer is permitted to borrow up to the full amount of his/her equity in a plan, this should be taken into consideration in the computation of realizable equity.

  4) The current value of property deposited in an Individual Retirement Account (IRA) or Keogh Act Plan Account should be considered in the computation of realizable equity. Cash deposits should be included at full value. If assets other than cash are invested (e.g., stock, mutual funds), the IRA should be valued at the quick sale value, less expenses. The penalty for early withdrawal should be subtracted in computing net realizable equity." [IRC ß 57(10)13.4.]

  Because negotiations concerning the terms and requirements of pension plans will require extensive information from the employer, you should obtain this information as soon as possible.

- **Exempt Assets:**

  Exempt assets are technically protected from the IRS, but the IRS argues that since the taxpayer has access to them, they should be in the equation of what should be paid the IRS. This seems to contravene the intent in legislating these assets as exempt; however, it is IRS policy to count them, even if they cannot collect directly or immediately from the asset.

- **Closely Owned Corporations:**

  Taxpayers who own family owned corporations or unincorporated businesses will find them particularly difficult to value.

While a taxpayer should argue that the value of the business equals the liquidation value of its assets less outstanding liabilities, the IRS believes an offer should reflect the company's "going concern value" rather than the liquidation value of its assets.

To obtain the sales value of your business that will be acceptable to the IRS usually requires a professional appraisal. A written estimate of this value may be obtained from a local business broker if you own a small business. Larger companies should be appraised by a certified business appraiser. For the names of certified appraisers in your area, call the Institute for Business Appraisers at (561) 732-3202.

- **Jewelry and Collectibles:**

  The IRS will want to inspect your home for art, antiques, jewelry, coin and stamp collections and other collectibles. If these assets have a value above $1,000, they also should be professionally appraised.

- **Your Home:**

  It is not difficult to obtain a valuation on your home. Obtain several written appraisals from local real estate brokers and use the *lowest* appraisal.

OTHER FACTORS IN EVALUATING YOUR OFFER

While there is no formal IRS policy on these following points, the IRS does consider factors beyond the current market value of your assets when measuring your net worth and maximum capacity to pay.

- Do you have a close, wealthy relative, particularly an innocent spouse who is not responsible for your taxes? The IRS wants you to borrow what you can.

- Do you own exempt or unreachable property that can be mortgaged or sold to increase your offer?

- Do you have property that may rapidly escalate in value?

- Do friends or relatives hold mortgages against your property? The IRS will want you to ask them to accept less than the amount owed to increase the equity available to the IRS.

- Do you have recently transferred property that the IRS may consider a fraudulent transfer or conveyance?

- Do you anticipate a substantial inheritance within the next several years?

HOW TO MINIMIZE YOUR NET WORTH

You want to give your assets the lowest possible asset values because that is how the IRS mainly evaluates the adequacy of your offer. To minimize those values, try these three strategies:

1) *Get two or three appraisals on major assets and then submit the lowest appraisal.* You have no obligation to show the IRS the highest appraisals, so always build your case on the *lowest* appraisal. If the IRS wants to challenge your appraisal, it can hire its own appraiser.

2) *Deduct from the current market values all costs and necessary expenses of liquidation.* Will the IRS need to insure the property, protect it from vandalism, or heat it? What will it cost to advertise the property for sale? What about broker and auctioneer fees? These costs can reach 20-percent or more of the value of the property. Document and deduct these costs.

3) *Use convincing evidence to support your low value.* For instance, have comparable homes in your area been recently foreclosed upon? What did *they* sell for? What is the assessed value of your property for real estate tax purposes? Is this assessed value lower than your appraisals?

4) *Use photos to show defects in the asset or to substantiate its poor condition.* A home, boat or car may vary considerably in value based on its physical condition. Pictures can tell the story and inspection reports can confirm poor mechanical condition.

5) *Have you tried to sell the asset?* Can you show you were unsuccessful in obtaining a higher price than the amount used for your offer?

HOW TO FIGURE YOUR NET WORTH

It is not difficult to calculate your net worth if you use the convenient *Net Worth Worksheet* at the end of the chapter. If only one spouse has a liability, prepare the worksheet using only the assets (or partial interests in assets) belonging to the spouse with the tax liability.

WILL YOUR INCOME REQUIRE A HIGHER OFFER?

Your net worth is, of course, only one test on the issue of collectability. The IRS also considers the taxpayer's present or prospective income or earning capacity, or in the case of a business, its present and prospective profits.

Income analysis:

The IRS evaluates *all* sources of taxpayer income and deducts only those expenses that are reasonable and necessary. Those expenses are referred to as "necessary living expenses." The difference between your income and necessary living expenses over the next five years is added to what you can pay the IRS toward your offer.

Since the IRS will want to know about every source of income, use the *Income/Expense Worksheet* at the end of this chapter. If both spouses have income and only one has the liability, prepare the offer using only the liable spouse's income and expense information *unless* your state is a community property state and allows collection from a nonliable spouse. However, where community property laws do *not* apply, the IRS will require disclosure of financial information on the non-liable spouse during the investigation.

The IRS will also check whether your income matches your earning power, considering your age, education, occupation, health, and experience. If you are, for instance, a physician earning two-thirds less than similar physicians, then why? If your income dropped from a steady $80,000 a year to $30,000, the IRS will again ask why.

The IRS also estimates your prospective income. If your income may substantially increase, the IRS may want a collateral agreement to share in that increase; however, this is unlikely as collateral agreements are rarely used today.

Your goal is to underscore to the IRS why your earning capacity is low and will remain limited in the future.

- Is your health poor? If so, fully document your medical problems. Will your illness become progressively worse and further decrease your ability to work or force you to work fewer hours? Does it limit the type of work you can do? Is it a psychiatric problem? How does that translate into decreased earnings? Detailed and persuasive medical reports are critical to support your case.

- Do you work in a distressed business or occupation? Show the IRS why your job or business has an unstable income or future. If you own a business, then poor financial statements will be helpful. Do you plan to change jobs? Submit your OIC while you are unemployed. Remember: Poverty is your ally when you negotiate with the IRS.

- Do you have family or other problems? There are endless factors the IRS can consider, and contrary to popular belief, the IRS can be quite understanding and very lenient with taxpayers who have problems in life other than their tax troubles. You may, for example, be going through an emotionally draining divorce. Perhaps you have a sick spouse or child. If situations within your family impair your ability to earn money, then let the IRS know about them.

- Do you have criminal problems or serious lawsuits against you? Do you face the possible loss of a professional or occupational license? This shows economic instability which can also convince the IRS to accept less.

- What about your education level? Do you have a college degree? Do you have a high school degree? Perhaps your income potential is limited by your limited education.

- What about your age? The IRS seldom demands installment payments or collateral agreements from taxpayers over 60. Some IRS officers show age consideration to taxpayers over 50.

Expense analysis:

Taxpayers are allowed to deduct from their income "necessary expenses" (individuals only, not business entities). Necessary expenses are those which must provide for a taxpayer's and their family's health and welfare and the production of income. The expense amount must be reasonable. The total necessary expenses establish the minimum a taxpayer and family need to live. There are three types of necessary expenses: national standards, local standards, and other expenses. National expenses include clothing and clothing services, food, housekeeping supplies, personal care products and services, and miscellaneous. IRS expense amounts are determined by the Bureau of Labor Statistics Consumer Expenditure Survey. Local standards apply to housing and utilities and transportation expenses. The IRS also developed local standards for housing and utilities from information received from the Bureau of Census. Other expenses are those which have no nationally or locally established standards and are discretionary in determining if they are necessary and reasonable. Expenses which are not generally allowed include, but are not limited to, tuition for private elementary and secondary schools, public or private college expenses, charitable contributions, voluntary retirement benefits, unsecured debts (credit card debt is typically unsecured), and cable television charges.

For your calculations, include *all* expenses. If only one spouse has a liability and both have incomes, include only the liable spouse's expenses. This does not mean to include only the liable spouse's *individual* expenses. Include a percentage of the total family expenses. Use the *Income/Expense Worksheet,* at the end of this chapter, to determine total family expenses. Then transfer only the liable spouse's percentage of the expenses (usually determined by the percentage this spouse contributes towards the total family income) to the Form 433-A *Collection Information Statement.*

The IRS uncovers all sources of income but conveniently forgets many expenses. Form 433-A includes only the basic expenses and does not clearly itemize many smaller expenses we all have and must pay from our incomes.

That's why you must use the *Income/Expense Worksheet* to insure no reasonable and necessary expense is overlooked. Also, review your own records. What other necessary expenses do you have that are not covered in the worksheet?

Your goal is to have your expenses equal or even exceed your income. You can then show no excess income is available to the IRS. Expect the IRS to challenge many expenses to lower the exclusion, and thus raise the income available for collection. Your offer should always use the highest necessary expenses you can reasonably justify and document.

Since the IRS tries to disallow many expenses as unnecessary and decrease other expenses as excessive, you must be firm. Stand strong. Defend your expenses. Don't allow the IRS to intimidate you into a life of poverty. Make your strongest case. Be prepared!

- Why is each listed expense necessary? Are there less costly alternatives?

- What have you historically spent on each expense? Can your records prove this?

- Have you included all foreseeable expenses?

HOW WILL YOU PAY THE IRS

The total amount you offer the IRS may be paid in the following ways:

- a lump sum payment and/or
- installments.

Since the IRS will want to get paid as quickly as possible, it generally accepts a lower lump sum over a larger offer paid over time. The IRS wants to close its cases, not spend time monitoring long-term installment plans. Offers on installment will then require earlier payment or the IRS will reject your offer if they believe you can pay in a shorter time frame.

If possible, satisfy this important IRS objective and pay whatever you can as an immediate lump sum payment – while still paying as little as possible. Plus, if you pay the full amount of the offer within 90 days of acceptance, the IRS will discount your offer based on the "present value" of your offer (see table at the end of this chapter). For instance, if you had no assets and a monthly net difference of $200 left from your income after payment of your necessary expenses, the IRS will expect your offer to be at least $12,000 if you were paying "within six months," but only $9,714 if you were paying "within two months."

The IRS will often demand an up-front payment to match what you can immediately generate from your assets. For instance, the IRS will expect you to:

- Liquidate all cash, savings, CDs, cash value insurance and other easily cash-converted assets.

- Borrow whatever you can on any assets with equity – such as a home or car.

- Sell all luxury items – such as a vacation home, boat or recreational vehicle to extract all the equity from these non-necessities.

Convert as many assets as you possibly can into cash before you submit your OIC. This shows the IRS that you are serious about settling your tax bill. A larger down payment can also significantly reduce your overall settlement, and you will find it cheaper to borrow from other lenders rather than pay IRS interest rates. And, if the IRS does *not* settle, you will want your net worth in the form of more easily protected cash rather than more easily seized tangible assets.

An installment arrangement can sometimes be used to pay the "net worth" that cannot be sold or refinanced. Installment payments can sometimes be used to cover disposable income available to the IRS. However, the IRS is still much more likely to reject an offer with installment payments. But if your only possible offer includes installment payments, the payments should not exceed two years.

You can also discount an installment obligation through prepayment. For instance, if the IRS estimates it can collect $500 a month for the next two years, the IRS will accept less than $12,000 – if you pay today. Just as you must pay interest on your installment payments, the IRS will allow you a discount for prepayment. Such discounts are based on the "present value" of your offer (use the table at the end of this chapter).

COLLATERAL AGREEMENTS

The IRS may require an additional agreement (a "collateral agreement") which would require you to pay a percentage of future earning. Collateral agreements should *not* be part of your offer to the IRS. In the past, such agreements, especially the future income collateral agreement, were frequently required by the IRS as a condition to the overall OIC settlement. However, their new policy is as follows:

> "Collateral Agreements should not be routinely secured, but secured only when a significant recovery can be reasonably expected. For

example,future income collateral agreement would be appropriate where it was reasonably expected that the taxpayer would be receiving a substantial increase in real income. A Collateral Agreement should not be entered merely on unfounded speculation about real increase in income. A Collateral Agreement should not be secured to cover statistically impossible events such as lottery winnings. Securing a Collateral Agreement should be the exception and not the rule. Additionally, the expectation is that all collateral agreements except those designed solely to amend or clarify an Offer will be monitored for compliance. Therefore, agreements which require monitoring or which contain terms not in conformance with the outlines of the IRM will not be entered into unless approval is secured from the National office" [IRM 57(10)15.5].

Other provision within the Manual also discourage other types of Collateral Agreements.

HOW TO FORMULATE YOUR OFFER

Let's review the five basic steps for formulating your offer:

Step 1)   *Compile your information.*

Assemble all your financial records, including appraisals, deeds, titles, bills of sale, leases, mortgages, insurance policies, wage or other income statements (last month), bank statements (last 3 months), tax return, financial statements provided to any lending institution in the past 12 months and other documents you and the IRS will eventually review.

Step 2)   *Calculate your net worth.*

With the *Net Worth Worksheet,* list *al*l your assets. Estimate your net worth for each item based upon its current market value less prior encumbrances and liquidation expenses. Assign fractional values if you co-own property. Obtain appraisals to confirm the value of the key assets.

Step 3)   *Determine your disposable income.*

Use the *Income/Expense Worksheet.* Give yourself every benefit of the doubt to eliminate excess income and maximize estimated expenses.

Step 4)   *Add your net worth and disposable income.*

Your total offer should at least equal the total sum of:

a)   your net worth (*from the Net Worth Worksheet)* plus

b)   any monthly net disposable income projected ahead five years (60 months). If you are to pay the offer within 90 days of acceptance, instead of multiplying your monthly net disposable income by 60 months, use the "present value" figure, currently 48.57 (60 months discounted to present value at nine percent - see table at end of chapter). This sum represents the maximum amount to offer the IRS to settle *all* tax obligations now owed, irrespective of amount.

Step 5)   *Calculate how this amount will be paid.*

Offer to pay as much as possible upon acceptance by selling unessential items and borrowing against other assets. Installments necessary to pay the balance should be paid as soon as possible.

CASE EXAMPLES

Case No. 1

Mary and Sam, both in their early 70s, owed the IRS about $45,000. Having filed bankruptcy several years earlier because of a failed business, they had only a small equity in a modest home and lived on Sam's $1,200 a month pension.

Because they had only enough income to live on (Sam had health problems and couldn't work), Mary and Sam decided to offer the IRS $4,500 to settle their $45,000 tax liability. They correctly reasoned they had too little equity in their home for the IRS to seize it, and after nearly a year the IRS accepted the $4,500 cash offer.

Case No. 2

Charlie, a married 60 year-old man, had not filed taxes for the last 12 years. The IRS computer generated all but his last 3 years of taxes which were completed by his accountant and filed. Charlie owed the IRS over $50,000; the last three years totaled about $30,000 with penalties and interest. He also owed about $45,000 in credit card debt, which he had recently discharged in a Chapter 7. (Note: Chapter 7 did not discharge any IRS debt because the returns were not filed for at least two years or assessed for at least 240 days.)

Charlie had no major assets and his miscellaneous assets were valued at under $2,000. Further, the company he was working for recently downsized, leaving him currently unemployed with only his pension to support himself and his wife.

After disclosing his assets, income and expenses to the IRS, Charlie was registered "temporarily uncollectible" and no further collection actions were taken - he then filed an Offer in Compromise of $300 down as a good faith deposit and $1,700 payable within 60 days of written acceptance. After four months of investigation, the IRS accepted.

Case No. 3

Stan, a single attorney, owed the IRS about $35,000 in income tax liabilities from the last four years.

The equity in his vehicle was about $6,000, his miscellaneous assets totaled about $2,000, and he was currently not making enough income to cover his necessary living expenses.

Stan offered the IRS $8,000 in his Offer in Compromise ($500 refundable deposit, balance within 60 days of acceptance). After the investigation was complete, the investigating officer determined that he could not recommend acceptance of the offer unless the offer was increased to $11,500. Stan agreed to increase his offer to that sum, and his offer, as amended, was accepted.

Case No. 4

Sally, a retired 68-year-old schoolteacher, owed the IRS $16,000 arising from some disallowances of deductions on her tax return.

Sally had no assets except for her pension, household furniture, a used car and less than $500 in savings. Sally's offer to settle for $500 was rejected and the IRS officer suggested instead that Sally be classified as "temporarily uncollectible" because of her negligible assets and income. Sally never again heard from the IRS.

Case No. 5

Through numerous business adventures and misadventures, Greg ran up a $600,000 tax liability.

Greg's assets consisted of a $700,000 home with only a small mortgage, a fully paid Cadillac and investments worth $400,000.

Greg proposed to settle for $100,000 with $50,000 paid upon acceptance and $50,000 paid over five years. The IRS summarily rejected this as frivolous considering Greg's financial situation. He then amended his OIC to $150,000 in installments with the same $50,000 down. The IRS insisted upon the full $600,000 because Greg had the assets to fully satisfy the tax and there were no mitigating circumstances to either settle for less or accept payment over time. When Greg failed to satisfy the tax obligation, the IRS seized and sold his home and several other assets and fully collected the tax.

Case No. 6

Newman and Sally owed the IRS $90,000 from a failed business venture. Newman is presently employed as a government worker and Sally as a tutor. Together they earn about $60,000 a year. They have two children. Their income covers their necessary expenses and leaves them $200 a month for other expenses.

Their major asset is a $150,000 home with a $100,000 mortgage. Both of their cars are leased and therefore have no equity. Their miscellaneous assets total less than $10,000.

Newman and Sally figured they could borrow $20,000 against their home, and sell some of their remaining assets and/or borrow from his parents to raise another $15,000. This would give Newman and Sally about $35,000 toward the taxes. Plus, they figured they could scrimp by and pay the IRS about $400 a month from their future net earnings. This, they proposed, would be paid over the next year for a total settlement of $39,800. The IRS accepted.

Case No. 7
Pedro, a victim of "tax shelter deal-gone-wrong," owed the IRS about $200,000.

His only asset was his condominium worth $90,000. Moreover, Pedro had only sporadic earnings as a chef because he suffered from recurrent manic depression. He seldom earned more than he needed to live on.

Pedro offered and the IRS accepted $50,000 to settle. Pedro would raise this money by refinancing his condo with a 20-year mortgage. Pedro knew he could manage these payments and the IRS felt the $50,000 was close to what they would get through a forced sale of the condo. Considering Pedro's health problems and his sporadic earning, the IRS did not press for future installments or a collateral agreement.

DOUBT AS TO LIABILITY OFFERS

Unlike "doubt as to collectability" cases, offers based on "doubt as to liability" center on whether the IRS can sustain a claim against the taxpayer. This involves a careful assessment of the applicable law or the facts of the case – depending upon whether the dispute involves one primarily of law or facts.

You do not need to provide financial information (Form 433-A and/or 433-B) when submitting an offer based on "doubt as to liability."

The IRS can usually assess its chances of winning a disputed tax case with considerable accuracy. Therefore, an offer that does not coincide with the IRS case assessment is likely to be turned down.

It is almost always necessary to employ a tax professional to assess the merits of a tax case and suggest an appropriate offer. Moreover, the tax professional may correctly recommend that instead of an OIC to resolve the issue (invariably turned down by the IRS), the taxpayer instead pay the tax and then start refund litigation or even proceed to tax court where the taxpayer's odds are greatly improved.

INCOME/EXPENSE WORKSHEET

1. MONTHLY INCOME

List monthly income. Disclose all sources of income. Income should be monthly averaged when received in different periods. This information can later be transferred to Form 433-A, page 4.

To determine monthly income (when not paid monthly):

- if income received weekly, multiply by 52 and divide by 12
- if income received bi-weekly, multiply by 26 and divide by 12
- if income received bi-monthly, multiply by 2

	HUSBAND	WIFE
Salary/Wages	_____	_____
Commissions	_____	_____
Tips	_____	_____
Dividends	_____	_____
Interest	_____	_____
Alimony	_____	_____
Child Support	_____	_____
Annuity Income	_____	_____
Pension Income	_____	_____
Social Security	_____	_____
Business Profits	_____	_____
Veterans Adm. Payments	_____	_____
Royalties	_____	_____
Disability/Workers Comp.	_____	_____
Unemployment Benefits	_____	_____
Public Assistance Payments	_____	_____
Other income:		
_____	_____	_____
_____	_____	_____
_____	_____	_____

TOTALS   _____   _____

2. MONTHLY EXPENSES

Use the expense chart on the following pages to complete your monthly expenses. It is more complete than the IRS Form 433-A. This information can be summarized and included on Form 433-A.

MONTHLY NECESSARY LIVING EXPENSES WORKSHEET

Item:	Claimed:	Total Claimed:
42. National Standard Expenses:		(see Chart)
New clothing		
Laundry and cleaning		
Groceries		
Meals out		
School lunches		
Housekeeping supplies		
Personal care products / services		
Miscellaneous		
43. Housing and Utilities:		
Rent or Mortgage payment		
Second Mortgage payment		
Property Taxes		
Homeowner's or Renter's Insurance		
Parking		
Necessary Maintenance and Repairs		
Homeowner dues		
Condominium fees		
Utilities: gas_____, electricity_____, water_____, fuel_____, oil_____, coal _____, bottled gas_____, trash/garbage collection_____, wood/other fuels_____, septic cleaning_____, phone_____		
Other:		
44. Transportation:		
Lease or purchase payments		
Insurance		
Registration fees		
Normal Maintenance		
Fuel		
Public Transportation		
Parking		
Tolls		
Other:		

MONTHLY NECESSARY LIVING EXPENSES WORKSHEET (Continued)

45. Health Care:		
Doctors & Dentist		
Prescription		
Hospital bills		
Eyeglasses/contacts		
Health Insurance		
Other:		
46. Taxes: Income_____, FICA_____, Medicare_____, State _____, other _____		
47. Court Ordered Payments:		
Child Support		
Alimony		
Other:		
48. Child/Dependant Care		
49. Life Insurance		
50. Secured or Legally-Perfected Debts:		
51. Other Expenses:		
Employee Business Expenses: only those which are _unreimbursed_ by employer:		
• Business trips (travel, phone calls, 50% of meals & entertainment)		
• Business supplies & equipment (with a useful life of <1 year)		
• Dues (professional/business org.)		
• Car use for work (not to/from office)		
• Tuition (schooling required for job)		
• Other unreimbursed work expenses		
Job-hunting costs (resume, travel, job counseling, agency fees, phone calls, 50% of meals & entertainment)		
Retirement: (Pension/IRA/Keogh/other)		
Accountant_____, Attorney_____		
Other:		
52. TOTAL MONTHLY EXPENSES:		

PRESENT VALUE TABLE

Interest Rate

YEAR & MONTHS	13%	12%	11%	10%	9%	8%	7%
4 years	37.77	38.41	39.07	39.75	40.45	41.18	41.93
1 month	38.38	39.04	39.72	40.43	41.16	41.91	42.69
2	38.98	39.67	40.37	41.10	41.86	42.64	43.45
3	39.58	40.28	41.01	41.77	42.55	43.36	44.20
4	40.17	40.89	41.65	42.43	43.24	44.08	44.94
5	40.75	41.50	42.28	43.09	43.92	44.79	45.69
6	41.33	42.10	42.91	43.74	44.60	45.50	46.42
7	41.90	42.70	43.53	44.38	45.27	46.20	47.16
8	42.46	43.29	44.14	45.02	45.94	46.90	47.89
9	43.02	43.87	44.75	45.66	46.61	47.59	48.61
10	43.58	44.45	45.35	46.29	47.27	48.28	49.33
11	44.12	45.02	45.95	46.92	47.92	48.96	50.05
5 years	44.67	45.59	46.54	47.54	48.57	49.64	50.76

NET WORTH WORKSHEET

Use this worksheet to determine your equity (or net worth) in the various assets you own. When determining Current Market Value (FMV), if you own only a partial interest in that asset, then use that proportionate share; use a 20% value for property held as tenants by the entirety.

ASSET	Current Market Value	Current Amount Owed	Equity in Asset
Home			
Vacation			
Rental Property			
Vacant Land			
Farm			
Time Share			
Automobile			
Boats			
Profit sharing plans			
Pension plans			
Retirement accounts			
Individuals Retirement Account			
Life Insurance cash value			
Checking and Saving accounts			
Certificates of Deposit			
Money Market Funds			
Mutual Funds Annuities			
Stocks and Bonds			
Partnership Interests			
Closely Held corporations			
Trusts			
Antiques			
Art			
China and Silver			
Jewelry			
Furs			
Sporting or hobby equipment			
Collections			
Furniture and Furnishing			
Mortgages and notes receivable			
Contract rights			
Liens and judgements held			
Livestock and pets			
Tax refunds due			
Other			
TOTALS			

CHAPTER 6

How To Prepare And Submit Your Offer To The IRS

Read this chapter carefully *before* you complete and submit your OIC. Many OIC's are returned or rejected, not because the offer was unacceptable, but because the forms were improperly or inadequately completed. Sloppy preparation only delays the process and encourages the IRS to press collection while you scramble to correct the problem, often under undue stress.

The OIC forms are comprehensive but not too difficult to prepare. The key is to answer each question *fully and truthfully!* The IRS will closely scrutinize and investigate each point, so avoid false or incomplete statements. Even inadvertent errors can lead to serious civil or criminal fraud charges, and the IRS will automatically reject or rescind any OIC found to be materially incorrect, even if discovered years later.

ASSEMBLING YOUR DOCUMENTS

Begin by carefully assembling all your financial records. Don't guess or estimate amounts. Reconstruct your assets, liabilities, income and expenses from checks, deposits and other records. If your records were destroyed or lost, then document the reason for their loss, such as with fire, police or other casualty reports. Bear in mind that IRS officers, like Customs agents, have a keen sixth sense of when you're trying to hide something.

Later in this chapter, you will see the various documents that may be requested by the IRS. Assemble these documents in advance. It's even proper to submit many of these documents with your OIC. Never give the IRS your originals, only submit copies.

You will need Form 656 *Offer in Compromise.* A blank copy is in the Appendix. If you are using a substitute Form 656 that is computer generated or photocopied (for example, the blank copy in the Appendix is a substitute form), be aware that you are affirming that 1) the substitute form is a verbatim duplicate of the official form, and 2) you agree to be bound by all terms and conditions set forth in the official form. The terms and conditions are also found in the Appendix with Form 656. The official form and others can be requested from the IRS at (800) 829-3676. Along with Form 656, you must submit a Form 433-A *Collection Information Statement for Individuals* and/or Form 433-B *Collection Information Statement for Businesses,* both also found in the Appendix. Before using them, make certain that they are the most current forms by calling the IRS at (800) 829-1040, or ask your IRS Revenue Officer.

ENLIST THE IRS TO HELP YOU PREPARE YOUR OFFER

If an IRS officer has already been assigned to your case, you can request the officer's assistance in completing your forms. Do not be discouraged by an officer who suggests your OIC attempts will be unsuccessful. Whether your OIC succeeds is not the decision of the IRS collection officer but that of the Special Procedures staff which ultimately reviews your offer.

Moreover, you *do not want* the IRS officer to help you establish your offer. As mentioned in the prior chapter, the IRS officer will invariably urge you to offer more than you should. The chicken should not turn to the fox for comfort. All you want from the IRS officer is assistance in correctly completing the forms and a recommendation from the IRS officer to the Special Procedures staff that your OIC be accepted.

SEVEN STEPS FOR COMPLETING YOUR OFFER

There are seven key steps for completing the OIC documents:

1) Official Form 656, *Offer in Compromise,* or a verbatim duplicate, must be used to submit your offer. You may not alter any of the pre-printed terms of the offer. The form should be filed in the district office of the Internal Revenue Service in your area. If you have been working with a specific service employee on your case, file the offer with that employee.

2) Form 433-A, *Collection Information Statement for Individuals and/or Form 433-B, Collection Information Statement for Businesses,* must accompany Form 656, if the offer is being submitted on the basis of doubt as to collectibility. If you are an individual and you operate a business, you must submit both forms. These forms are *not* needed on "doubt as to liability" cases (for doubt as to liability, you need only to include a detailed explanation of the reasons you believe you do not owe the tax). For the offer to be considered, all blocks on Forms 433-A and/or 433-B must be completed. In those blocks that do not affect you indicate by writing

"N/A" (not applicable). With Form 433-A and/or 433-B, you will need to submit documentation to verify values of assets, encumbrances, and income and expense information listed on the collection statements when requested by the IRS.

3) Your full name, address, social security number and employer identification number must be entered at items 1 through 4 of Form 656. If this is a joint liability (husband and wife) and both wish to make an offer, both names must be shown. If you are singly liable for a tax liability (e.g. employment taxes) and, at the same time, jointly liable for another tax liability (e.g. income taxes) and only one person is submitting an offer, only one offer must be completed. If you are singly liable for one tax liability and jointly liable for another and both joint parties are submitting an offer, two Forms 656 must be submitted: one for the separate tax liability and one for the joint tax liability. If you want to compromise both your personal taxes and business (if a corporation or partnership), you must make separate offers for each.

4) You must identify all unpaid liabilities to be compromised in item 5 on Form 656. The type of tax and the period of the liability must be specifically identified. This includes:

  • 1040 / 1120 Income tax

  • 941 Employer's Quarterly Federal Tax Return

  • 940 Employer's Annual Federal Unemployment (FUTA) Tax Return

  • Trust Fund Recovery Penalty (formerly called the 100-percent penalty) assessment - incurred by responsible person of a business for failure to pay withholding and Federal Insurance Contributions Act Taxes (Social Security taxes)

  • Other Federal taxes (may include estate tax, road tax, excise tax, inheritance tax, or any other federal tax).

Be certain to include *every* tax you even possibly owe the IRS. If all taxes are not listed, your OIC will not be accepted or unlisted tax may not be discharged.

5) Mark the box in item 6 as to why the Service should accept your offer: "Doubt as to Liability ('I do not believe I owe this amount.')" *or* "Doubt as to Collectibility ('I have insufficient assets and income to pay the full amount.')" Where there is both doubt as to liability *and* collectibility, then mark both reasons.

6)   Enter the total amount you are offering the IRS to compromise your tax liability in item 7. The amount must not include any sums already paid or collected on the liability.

As discussed in the previous chapter, the amount you offer should be:

a)   the equity in your assets (the amount shown in item 30 titled "Equity in Asset" on Form 433-A or item 27 column (d) in Form 433-B), *plus*

b)   your average monthly income minus your necessary expenses (Form 433-A/B, page 4), multiplied by 60 months; but discounted to present value if payable within 90 days. In the Appendix, you will find detailed worksheets to help you calculate an acceptable offer amount using Forms 433-A and/or 433-B (see Appendix B - Offer in Compromise).

Along with the amount you are offering to pay, you must also include the following in item 7:

a)   Whether the amount you are offering is being paid in full with this offer.

b)   Whether you are making a deposit at the time of filing this offer; if so, the amount of the deposit. (Please note, you will not receive interest on this deposit payment whether the payment is applied to an accepted offer, applied to the liability with your permission, or returned to you upon withdrawal or rejection of the offer.)

c)   When the balance will be paid. The offer should be liquidated in the shortest time possible. The IRS suggests the balance to be paid in 10, 30, 60, or 90 days from notice of acceptance of the offer. If you are not paying balance in full, you must list the amount of any subsequent payment(s) and the specific date on which each payment is to be made.The IRS will add interest, which is compounded daily, from the date of acceptance to the date of full payment.

7)   You must sign and date the offer at item 9. If you and your spouse are submitting the offer on a joint liability both must sign. If the offer is to be signed by a person other than the taxpayer, a valid power of attorney must be submitted with the offer.

UNDERSTAND WHAT YOU ARE SIGNING

While Form 656 is easy to complete, it does create a legally binding contract between you and the IRS and obligates you to certain conditions even if your offer is *not* accepted. Be sure to carefully read the reverse side of the OIC (item 8) which states the terms and conditions (see Appendix).

In sum, it's key points provide as follows:

- You will comply with all provisions of the Internal Revenue Code regarding the filing of returns and the paying of required taxes for 5 years from the date the IRS accepts your offer. This condition does not apply to offers based only on doubt as to liability.

- If the IRS rejects your offer or you withdraw your offer, the IRS will return any deposits paid with the offer *unless* you agree, in writing, to have the amount applied to the amount you owe. If you have your deposit applied, the date the offer is withdrawn or rejected is considered the date of payment. The IRS will *not* pay interest on any deposit.

- You agree, in signing the offer, that the IRS can retain all payments, or credits previously paid on the taxes to be compromised. Keep in mind that you cannot apply these earlier payments to what you agree to pay under the OIC. For this reason, you should *never* pay anything toward delinquent taxes unless it is part of an OIC or an installment agreement with the IRS.

- Your offer automatically lets the IRS keep any refunds, including interest, because of overpayment of any tax or other liability, through the calendar year in which the IRS accepts the offer - not in excess of what you owe. You also agree that you will return any future refunds after submission of the offer. Also, you may not designate that a refund, to which the IRS is entitled, be applied to estimated tax payments for the following year. This condition does *not* apply if your OIC is based only on doubt as to liability.

- That you will not contest the amount of the tax liability in court once the IRS accepts your offer in writing.

- That you agree to extend the ten-year statute of limitations on collection for one additional year plus the period of time the IRS spent considering your offer, waiting for full payment of the amount offered, or waiting for other terms and conditions to be completed.

- That the IRS will keep all payments and credits made, received, or applied to the amount being compromised before you submitted your offer. The IRS will also keep proceeds from a levy served prior to your submitting the offer, regardless of the time proceeds are received. None of these such payments, credits, or proceeds will be applied against the amount offered.

- You must continue to pay on an installment agreement while an offer is pending. These payments will not be applied against the amount offered.

- If you fail to meet any of the terms and conditions of the offer, as stated on Form 656, your offer will be in default and the IRS can immediately file suit to collect:

  1) the entire unpaid balance of the offer,

  2) an amount equal to the original amount of the tax liability as liquidating damages, minus any payments received under the the offer,

  3) the original amount of the tax liability. If the IRS chooses *not* to file suit, they could still disregard the amount of the offer and apply any amounts paid under the offer to the original tax liability; they could also levy to collect the original amount of the tax liability.

Your offer documents, therefore, should initially include only:

- Form 656 *Offer in Compromise*
- Form 433-A *Collection Information Statement for Individuals* and/or Form 433-B *Collection Information Statement for Businesses*
- Your deposit, if any
- A cover letter explaining why the IRS should accept your offer, if desired. Provide the IRS with a reason as to why you can't afford to pay, explaining that you have insufficient assets or income to fully pay your tax liability. It's always persuasive to explain *why* the IRS cannot collect more through normal collection procedures. See sample cover letter at end of chapter.

SUBMITTING A DEPOSIT WITH YOUR OFFER

A small deposit with your offer shows good faith and is recommended. Your deposit is refundable, without interest, if your offer is withdrawn or rejected. The IRS may ask if they can apply your deposit to the delinquent tax liability - simply say "No, I would like my deposit returned" and the IRS is required to return your deposit.

What deposit is suggested? About five percent of your total offer. The larger the offer, the smaller the percentage. If money is scarce, make a smaller deposit. Keep in mind there is no *minimum* deposit. If you can afford only $500 or $1,000, then deposit that amount or whatever you can afford. Attach your deposit directly to Form 656.

HOW THE IRS PROCESSES YOUR OIC

If the offer is for "doubt as to collectability," you may submit it directly to the collection division of the IRS. This will probably be through the IRS officer assigned to collect your overdue taxes.

Offers for "doubt as to liability" are submitted to the examination division, not the collection division. You may, for instance, give the OIC to the tax auditor assigned to your case. It can be submitted any time during the audit period or anytime before a court determines it is duly owed.

Once the IRS receives your OIC, it will thoroughly search its computerized records to recap your tax history. What other taxes do you owe? What tax returns are still delinquent? Have you filed an OIC before? This review process takes about two or three months.

The IRS will simultaneously determine whether your offer is completed correctly and acceptable to process. What will the IRS look for?

- Does your OIC include your full name, address, social security or employer identification number?

- Is there a complete list of *all* outstanding taxes of *all* types? (Remember: it is your responsibility to determine your total unpaid tax obligation - you can request from the IRS a statement of your unpaid tax liability.)

- Have you stated why the IRS should accept your offer? ("Doubt as to Liability" or "Doubt as to Collectability")

- Is your offer specific as to the amount of your offer and how it will be paid?

- Have you submitted a detailed explanation of the reasons you believe you do not owe the tax, if your offer is submitted based on "doubt as to liability"?

- Have you submitted fully completed and signed collection information statements (Forms 433-A and/or 433-B), if your offer is submitted based on "doubt as to collectability"?

- Are there proper signatures by each party submitting the offer? If some one is signing for you, does a proper power of attorney accompany the OIC, or was one previously filed with the IRS?

HOW THE IRS CHECKS YOUR FINANCES

With your OIC accepted for processing, the IRS will next thoroughly verify and investigate your OIC *and* your finances. The IRS does not work on blind trust. It goes to great effort to make certain that your representations are true.

Unless they are already submitted, the IRS will ask for certain applicable documents and records:

- A record of current net earnings (pay stubs for the last month, earning statements)

- Bank statements and cancelled checks for the last 3 to 12 months on all personal and/or business accounts.

- Documents relating to all real estate interests (deeds, mortgages, contracts, leases, real estate tax bills). The IRS will be particularly interested in your property appraisals and how you appraised your real estate for purposes of formulating your offer.

- Bank books (Savings, CDs)

- Insurance policies

- Copies of tax returns for the three prior years. (The IRS can retrieve them if you don't have copies.)

- Titles and registrations for all vehicles (cars, trucks, boats, and planes).

- Stocks, bonds or other securities you own.

- Financial statements provided to any lending institution over the last 12 months.

- Documents showing your debts and other obligations (mortgages, notes, leases, bills, judgments, lawsuits, state or municipal tax claims). The IRS will specifically want to know their incurred dates, the original amount, present balance, how each debt is paid, and the security pledged to each creditor.

The IRS will next closely investigate whether any assets or funds are held for you by a "straw." The officer will want to know what unlisted assets you recently owned and how and when you disposed of or transferred them by asking you these questions:

- Have you sold or transferred any real estate, vehicles, stocks, bonds, or other assets within the past two years?

- Do you have access to a safe deposit box?

- Are you a grantor, trustee or beneficiary of a trust?

- Are you an officer, director or stockholder in a business or corporation?

- Are you a plaintiff in a lawsuit?

- Do you have any insurance claims pending?

- Do you own any paintings, jewelry, fur coats, heirlooms or similar valuables?

- Does anyone owe you money?

- Is anyone holding money or other property on your behalf?

- Do you anticipate receiving an inheritance within the next year?

These same questions are sometimes answered by having you complete an *IRS Data Sheet*. Although similar to *Collection Information Statement* Form 433-A or 433-B, the Data Sheet allows the IRS to more closely examine your finances from a slightly different perspective. By comparing answers, the IRS can better assess your truthfulness.

Finally, the IRS will verify all encumbrances against your property. To the extent an encumbrance decreases the equity available to the IRS, the IRS will question the validity of the debt. The IRS mostly inquires about recorded mortgages or security interests that have priority over their own lien. The IRS will also closely check the relationship between you and your creditor, the nature of the debt, and whether there was good consideration for the mortgage.

If the IRS determines a mortgage is not "arms-length" or that an asset was fraudulently transferred, then the IRS will require you to increase your offer by an amount equal to the mortgage or the equity in the fraudulently transferred asset.

Because OIC's are complex, expect more than one IRS officer to be involved in your case. For instance, the IRS Service Center will put together an *OIC Control Document* (Form 2515) containing your name, address, social security or EID number, the tax liabilities involved, terms of your offer, deposits received and a tax history transcript, which includes any prior offers. IRS investigators may also interview employees, friends, relatives and others who can verify the information the IRS relies upon to decide whether to accept your offer.

During this investigation period, the IRS District Office will check for outstanding or pending:

- Criminal investigations

- Tax appeals

- Bankruptcies

- Civil suits by or against you

- Federal and state tax liens

- Prior or pending IRS seizures or levies

Meanwhile, the IRS's vast computers will instantly verify your driver's license, social security, real property, corporation records, motor vehicles, professional licenses and virtually your entire financial, credit, civil and criminal background. There is little about you the IRS won't know!

The new IRS policy is to reduce paperwork and simplify the handling of OIC's, so the IRS now chiefly relies upon the data or information you furnish and will ask you only for such additional documentation as is reasonable.

OIC's based on inability to pay, or "doubt as to collectibility," are eventually sent to the IRS's Special Procedures Division for review by an Advisory Revenue Officer. If the Advisory Revenue Officer in Special Procedures concludes that your offer is unsatisfactory, the officer will recommend a summary rejection letter.

If the officer recommends accepting your offer, this will then be reported to a superior who, in turn, will transmit this recommendation to the District Director for final approval. However, any IRS employee in the chain of review may return the OIC to the Revenue Officer for further investigation or clarification.

Aside from the outright acceptance or rejection of your OIC is a third possibility: the Request for Amendment. This may occur when your offer is unacceptable, but you are reasonably close to what the IRS may accept. Here, the Revenue Officer may suggest an amended OIC and indicate what the IRS will accept. This will be discussed more fully in the next chapter.

It is important to remember that the entire IRS evaluation focuses on one issue: Does your offer represent your "maximum ability to pay," as discussed in the prior chapter. If they conclude it does, you are on your way to resolving your tax problems.

PROCESSING 'DOUBT AS TO LIABILITY' CASES

Offers in Compromise not based on collectability, but based on doubt as to liability, follow a slightly different procedure.

These cases are ordinarily assigned to the Examination Division of the IRS, but if it is a "Trust Fund Recovery Penalty" case (i.e. non-payment of withholding taxes), then the case is turned over to Collections.

The Revenue Officer handling the "Trust Fund Recovery Penalty" case will accumulate evidence concerning your responsibility for non-payment of withheld payroll taxes. At this point, you probably had an earlier hearing on your protest before an Appellate Hearing Officer, so it is up to you to provide additional information to justify reassessment of your liability. The Revenue Officer can completely overturn the assessment, declare it partially valid or decide that "a definite determination cannot be made".

When your liability is in doubt, the IRS will compromise based on the degree of doubt rather than your financial condition or the ability of the IRS to enforce collection.

The question of liability will most frequently arise from an audit when issues of what constitutes taxable income or a deductible expense become contested.

Considering the complexity of the tax code, it's remarkable that there are not many more OICs based on "doubt as to liability." Too many taxpayers simply pay the disputed tax, perhaps because they don't know about the OIC program or don't think an OIC is worth pursuing for the money involved.

When you want to show the IRS that there is a basis for mutual doubt on the liability, the burden is on *you* to provide such proof. Collecting applicable and persuasive case law to support your position, should you disagree with the legal interpretation or a question of law regarding your case, may very well mean the need for the assistance of a lawyer qualified to present a legal case.

More frequently, the IRS disputes factual issues, such as whether losses or expenses were actually incurred. The burden is still yours to provide tangible evidence (receipts, diaries, logs, pictures) that at least create a reasonable doubt about the claimed liability, with the evidence sufficiently significant to raise the level of doubt beyond a mere suspicion. Of course, the stronger the doubt as to liability, the less you need to offer the IRS, who will begin to appreciate the weakness of its position.

HOW TO STOP IRS COLLECTION DURING THE OIC

The OIC should not be used merely as a device to forestall collection. But the IRS usually will suspend collection efforts while your OIC is pending if they believe you submitted your OIC in good faith, it has a reasonable chance of acceptance, and that the IRS will not be prejudiced by delaying collection.

Generally, the Revenue Officer assigned to your case decides whether to suspend collection activity. The Revenue Officer will complete Form 657 which includes the Revenue Officer's evaluation of collectibility and his determination of whether to continue or suspend collection.

You should specifically request that collection activities against you be suspended and, to support your case, point out your cooperativeness and diligence in submitting the OIC.

The Revenue Officer will nevertheless file all notices of lien in all localities where you have assets. Filing tax liens while an OIC is pending is standard policy; however, the IRS may agree not to file a lien if you can show that your offer is made in good faith, that withholding a tax lien will not harm the IRS, and a tax lien will impair your ability to pay the IRS, such as when it prevents you from borrowing. While suspending collection is normal during an OIC, it is unusual for the IRS not to file a tax lien, as the IRS can always lift its lien to allow borrowing or a sale of assets that will pay the IRS.

EIGHT MORE TIPS FOR FILING YOUR OIC

1) Expect the IRS to take about a year to review your offer. You cannot prod the IRS to move faster. Remember, your OIC must undergo thorough investigation and work its way through many channels. Be patient. You will eventually receive an answer to your offer.

2) If your offer calls for installment payments, do not pay them *until* your offer has been formally accepted by the IRS. Do, meanwhile, file your tax returns on time or request an extension. If your current taxes are more than you can afford, you may want to include them in a new or amended OIC.

3) The IRS works slowly but expects taxpayers to react quickly to its demands. If the IRS asks you for additional documents or information, then submit it promptly or at least explain the reasons for any delay.

4) The IRS loves documentation. You can never give them too much paper to support your case. Do you claim poor health and poor earning capacity? Then submit ample medical reports to substantiate it. You need not wait to be asked for this documentation. Put yourself in the IRS's position. What documents or evidence would you want to see before you accepted a taxpayer's statement or representation?

5) Avoid comments or gestures that can be misconstrued as a bribe. Slang such as "I'll make you an offer you can't refuse," can get you into trouble. Put as much as possible into writing and work only through official channels so there are no misunderstandings.

6) Alert those who can corroborate your financial circumstances that they may be contacted by the IRS. It's probably smart to tell them about your pending OIC so you dispel their concerns or suspicions that you may have more serious IRS problems.

7) Reconsider your offer if your financial circumstances change significantly while the OIC is pending. If your fortunes improve, you do not have to increase your offer – provided your financial information was accurate when disclosed. The IRS, of course, will reject your offer *if* it becomes aware of your improved financial condition. On the other hand, if your financial condition deteriorates, then amend your offer downward or withdraw your offer in favor of bankruptcy or a determination that you are "temporarily uncollectible."

8) Expect hassles. Working with the IRS is never easy and your OIC can be a long and tortuous process. It takes patience and tenacity to settle for pennies on the dollar.

Sample Cover Letter

ARNOLD S. GOLDSTEIN & ASSOCIATES, P.A.
A PROFESSIONAL LAW CORPORATION
384 S. MILITARY TRAIL
DEERFIELD BEACH, FLORIDA 33442-3007

TEL (954) 420-4990 • FAX (954) 698-0057

March 24, 1997

Internal Revenue Service
P.O. Box 17167
Ft. Lauderdale, FL 33318

RE: John and Mary Taxpayer
      Social Security Nos.: 111-22-3333 / 123-45-6789
      Offer in compromise of $10,000 (1994-1996)

Dear Sir/Madam:

Please be advised that we represent the above-referenced taxpayers. Enclosed you will find Form 656 *Offer in Compromise*, Form 433-A *Collection Information Statement for Individuals*, and Form 2848 *Power of Attorney*.

These taxpayers have outstanding income tax liabilities for the years 1994 through 1996. While they actively seek to settle these debts, their financial situation presently makes this impossible. The taxpayers have little equity in their assets. Their chief asset, their home, has little equity. They have less than $100 cash, no securities, and no available pensions or insurance funds. Moreover, their monthly cash flow is negative.

With much effort, Mr. and Mrs. Taxpayer have been able to secure a loan from a family member for the sole purpose of settling this tax situation. Because of this loan, they are able to offer $10,000 to settle their tax debts. We have included herewith $500 as a good faith deposit with the balance to be paid within 60 days of written acceptance of the offer.

After a review of the taxpayer's financial situation, the service will realize that this offer exceeds the taxpayers' net realizable equity in assets and present value of future income. Thus, the offer should be recommended for acceptance.

The foregoing offer in compromise was prepared by me for the taxpayers based on information submitted by the taxpayers. While I believe the statements herein to be true, I do not know personally that the statements of fact contained herein are true and accurate.

Sincerely,

Arnold S. Goldstein, LL.M., Ph.D.

INTERNATIONAL OFFICES: —————— • LONDON • ZURICH
BEVERLY HILLS
BOSTON • NEW YORK • CHICAGO •

IF THE IRS
REJECTS YOUR OIC

Before the IRS liberalized its OIC program in 1993, more OICs were rejected by the IRS than were accepted. Now that the IRS more strongly encourages OIC settlements to enforced collection, it is reasonable to assume that you have a far greater chance of reaching agreement on an OIC.

WHY THE IRS MAY REJECT YOUR OFFER IN COMPROMISE

Still, there are many reasons why the IRS may reject your offer. The seven most common?

1) The amount offered is less than what the IRS believes they can collect through enforced collection. Remember, the OIC program is not designed to let taxpayers escape taxes they can afford to pay. If the IRS rejects your OIC for this reason, it will usually suggest that you amend your offer. This is by far the most frequent reason for rejection and will be further discussed in the next section.

2) The IRS believes you cannot or will not comply with the terms of your offer. This may occur when you have a history of chronic delinquency or have repeatedly fallen behind on earlier arrangements agreed to by the IRS. This may also happen if the IRS thinks you can't possibly honor the terms of your offer because of inadequate assets, insufficient income or excess liabilities.

3) You are delinquent in your tax filings or in paying estimated tax payments and Federal tax deposits due as of the date you file the offer. It is important to keep in mind that the IRS will not consider an OIC unless you have filed *all* tax returns due.

4) The taxpayer died before the OIC is accepted. The IRS will automatically turn back an OIC under these circumstances. This does not mean, however, that the executor of the estate cannot resubmit the OIC or a new OIC. The executor's OIC may also include any estate taxes together with past due income taxes.

5) The IRS doesn't believe the taxpayer was honest in disclosing assets or income. Even suspicions of dishonesty can cause the IRS to reject your OIC. If you think that may be the reason for rejection (the IRS seldom volunteers their suspicions), then it is up to you to candidly review the situation with the IRS so you can explain matters of concern and restore their confidence in your honesty.

6) The taxpayer is not cooperative or proceeding with reasonable dilige collection), then they will reject your OIC. Proceed diligently. stay within IRS timetables for submitting follow-up documents. If you do need more time, then request an extension from the IRS and explain why additional time is needed.

7) Public policy considerations discourage acceptance by the IRS. This may occur, for instance, if the taxpayer has a recent or tax-related criminal record. The IRS will cut deals with honest, law-abiding taxpayers who for one of a variety of reasons fell behind on his or her taxes. The IRS does not want to portray the image of cooperating with less-than-honest taxpayers.

Sometimes the IRS will issue a "summary rejection." This is a denial without weighing the merits of your offer because your OIC is

1) considered frivolous,

2) your financial information is incomplete, or

3) you have outstanding tax returns.

How to Handle the Request For Amendment

The IRS rejection letter will state with some detail the reason the IRS refused your offer. Several reasons may be cited. Some factors may be easily remedied, such as a rejection because you incorrectly completed your OIC.

More commonly, the IRS will reject an OIC and thus prod the taxpayer to increase the offer. This is done through a request for amendment.

You are entitled to see the report that lists the factors behind the rejection. The Special Procedures Officer will give you a copy or you can obtain it by request under the Freedom of Information Act.

If your OIC was rejected because it was too low, the officer must also tell you what amount definitely would be accepted.

Here a seasoned professional is most helpful. With many OICs behind you, you develop an instinct for where to start – where you will probably end – and how you will get there. This usually means several amended OICs until one is finally accepted.

If you do submit a good faith offer but the offer was too low to be processed or accepted, you must be granted the continuing opportunity to resubmit amended offers.

The IRS cannot capriciously or arbitrarily refuse your offer. There must be some reasonable basis for denial, and this usually means that the IRS has some reasonable basis for believing it can collect more from you through its normal collection power.

You can simply amend your offer by letter if the new offer is not significantly different and there is no material, financial, or personal change. If your new offer is substantially different or if there are new financial or personal circumstances, then complete a new OIC Form 656 and financial statements (Form 433-A and 433-B).

Do not withdraw your OIC. Once you file your OIC, it is usually best to firmly wait for either an acceptance, rejection, or request for amendment. Do not withdraw your offer *unless* you do not plan to make another offer and you want to cease your waiver of the statute of limitation for collection.

IRS officers often encourage taxpayers to withdraw their OICs on the basis that the IRS will most likely turn it down and the taxpayer will have a greater chance of success with a new OIC if they were not turned down on an earlier offer.

There is no basis for this. You can be turned down any number of times and it does not adversely prejudice subsequent offers.

More importantly, by forcing the IRS to issue a written rejection, you learn why your OIC is being turned down and discover what the IRS will accept. Without this information, you are "shadow-boxing."

HOW TO APPEAL YOUR CASE

You always have the right to appeal a rejected offer. If you do receive a rejection letter, you should file a written appeal within 30 days, unless you plan to submit an amended or new OIC. Missing an appeal deadline is never fatal because you can always submit a new OIC – on slightly different terms – and file a timely appeal when that OIC is rejected. This procedure follows closely the procedure for appealing an audit.

Your rejection letter will include detailed instructions for filing an appeal. Follow these instructions carefully. If the amount owed is $2,500 or less, you should make a verbal request for an appeals conference by calling the phone number at the top of their letter.

If the taxes you owe exceed $2,500, but are not more than $10,000, your appeal must be in writing, but only a brief written statement of the issues you disagree with is required.

Your letter need only refer to the following:

1) your name, address, social security number, and a daytime phone number,

2) a statement that you want a conference,

3) the date and number of their rejection letter,

4) the tax periods or years involved, and

5) a list of the issues/findings you do not agree with.

If the taxes you owe exceed $10,000, you must submit a written protest which must include all of the above *plus:* 6) a statement of fact, signed under penalties of perjury, that explains why you don't agree with their decision, and 7) if you rely on a law or other authority to support your position, explain what it is and how it applies.

Keep the 30 day filing period in mind. This applies to *all* appeals, except that you are allowed an additional 15 days if the IRS rejected your OIC because of insufficient information. This effectively gives you 45 days to provide new information concerning your case.

If you do appeal, your appeal and the written statement or protest and evaluation of the IRS officer handling your case will be sent to the appeals officer. You may be represented by yourself at the appeals conference or you may be represented by an attorney, certified public accountant, or an individual enrolled to practice before the IRS.

The officer's report is a critical document to examine because it explains why the IRS officer did not accept your offer. More importantly, it may indicate what amount and terms would be accepted by the IRS. You do have the right to inspect the officer's report which can be insightful in preparing an amended OIC that the IRS will accept.

Many OIC cases are ultimately resolved upon appeal. The appeals officer frequently bridges the difference between taxpayer and officer and concludes an OIC on terms acceptable to both the taxpayer and the IRS. Still, you must not appeal with expectations of complete victory. Taxpayers seldom win OIC appeals. Nor can you be certain the appeals officer will suggest settlement terms. The IRS staff may simply affirm or overturn an officer's decision concerning an OIC. In these instances the decision almost always favors the IRS officer.

Unfortunately, once your appeal is decided at the appeals conference, you have no further right to appeal. Nor can you appeal to the tax court.

Even though your odds of winning an appeal are slight, you have nothing to lose by trying. At the least you will forestall collection until you put one of your other options into play.

GETTING YOUR DEPOSIT REFUNDED

If your offer is rejected or if you withdraw your offer, the IRS *must* return your deposit. In fact, the IRS must escrow your deposit in a special fund so it is available for immediate return. But you must still be careful. The IRS officer may try to get you to apply the deposit to your tax bill even though the IRS rejected your offer. Always refuse this request. Despite IRS bluffs to the contrary, the IRS *cannot* apply your deposit unless you agree to it in writing!

RECONSIDER YOUR OPTIONS

What do you do if you have gone as far as you reasonably can with your OIC and the IRS still turns you down on appeal?

One option is to carefully reconsider what *you* think is a reasonable offer. You may have approached the OIC expecting more leniency than the IRS was willing to extend.

Closely examine the IRS's reasons for rejecting your offer.

Has the IRS misinterpreted certain information? Does the IRS question the validity of some information and need more documentation? Does the IRS know things about you that you didn't think they knew?

Perhaps your professional advisor misled you and painted too optimistic a picture about what the IRS would accept. Have one or two other professionals review your file. Do they consider your OIC reasonable? Do they see another proposal that may satisfy you and the IRS? And, yes, you can run into an exceptionally unreasonable IRS officer, or one who gets along poorly with you or your advisor and becomes as tough as possible.

Once you have dismissed these possibilities and find the IRS still insists on more than you can afford to pay, you must again reconsider your options. These are the same options you should have considered *before* you submitted your OIC. And because a rejected OIC means the IRS will quickly resume collection, you must move swiftly to protect yourself before they seize or levy your assets.

If you have insignificant assets and only modest income, why not go for "uncollectible" status? If you do have assets, then talk to a good bankruptcy lawyer. A Chapter 11 or 13 bankruptcy (giving you several years to pay the taxes) or a Chapter 7 (to completely wipe out the taxes if they are more than 3 years old) may be the right remedy for you.

You may also play the game once again. For instance, you may relocate and submit a new OIC through a different IRS office. You may also hire a new tax pro who is situated nearer another IRS office. This may prompt transfer of the file and dealing with a new and hopefully more lenient officer. There are any number of reasons to justify transfer of your file to a new IRS office and when personalities and politics become a factor, it is a strategy to consider. The new IRS office will know about your prior OICs; however, you will be dealing with new IRS officers who may be more reasonable. Also, play for time. An OIC rejected today may be accepted tomorrow. Perhaps your financial situation changed for the worse so your new OIC is now more attractive to the IRS. You may even succeed with an OIC that gives the IRS less than you offered before.

Solving your tax problems frequently means shifting gears and parlaying several different strategies. A strategy that originally seemed correct may give way to another solution that, with time, appears more logical. You see, a rejected OIC does not mean you are necessarily without other solutions to your tax problem.

CHAPTER 8

WHEN THE IRS ACCEPTS YOUR OFFER

Congratulations! Your tax troubles may soon be behind you. Start by carefully reviewing the IRS's acceptance of your offer. Once the IRS officially accepts your OIC, it will issue an *Offer Acceptance Report* (IRS Form 7249). The acceptance should clearly set forth the taxes that are compromised and all terms of the settlement. Specifically review the acceptance for these three points:

1) Does the acceptance specify *all* the taxes you owe and that are subject to compromise?

2) Does the acceptance accurately summarize all major terms of your settlement?

3) Is the acceptance duly signed by a revenue official authorized to bind the IRS?

If you are represented by a professional, he or she will have the responsibility to review the acceptance. If you are not represented, then it may be wise to hire a professional for this one specific task. Remember: the acceptance is the legal document that binds the IRS to your OIC, and you're not fully safe until you have a legally binding acceptance that specifies the exact terms you bargained for.

IF YOU DEFAULT ON YOUR OIC

If your OIC calls for installment payments, you may eventually find yourself in default of your agreement and unable to make the payments as promised. After all, you too face the same financial problems we all encounter from time to time – unemployment, unexpected or unavoidable bills, divorce, illness or a host of other problems that may make payment difficult or impossible.

If you anticipate a default, then contact the IRS *beforehand.* Do not default and make the IRS come to you looking for your payment. You can expect little cooperation unless you accept your responsibility to notify the IRS of your problems. Only then will the IRS feel that you take your OIC obligations seriously.

Whenever possible, contact the officer who handled your case. State your problem in writing so there can be no question that you took the initiative in alerting the IRS to your default.

Start by detailing the circumstances for your non-payment. Show why these problems will leave you with too little money to pay the IRS, and why the debts you are paying demand priority over IRS payments.

Use common sense. The IRS will not be sympathetic that you lost your job if you are still making payments on your expensive sports car. However, the IRS will work with you *if* you alert them to your problem, have a good excuse for non-payment, and are completely truthful. This last point is most important. Never lie to the IRS. The IRS may check your story! To corroborate your excuse, supply documentation (such as a job termination notice or medical bills). Keep in mind, that like yourself, the IRS has also invested considerable time and effort to reach a settlement and they don't want to cancel your agreement any more than you do.

What options are available to you if you do foresee a default on your OIC? You may ask the IRS to:

- Temporarily reduce or abate your payments

- Extend the payment schedule

- Accept alternate forms of payment

If your default will be temporary (less than one or two months), then request a temporary abatement or a reduction in payment. The IRS is more cooperative if you offer small interim payments because this shows your good faith.

Clearly state what you are proposing to the IRS. Let them know what interim payments you can make, when you expect to resume full payment, and when the IRS will be updated on your financial circumstances if you don't know when you can get back on schedule.

In effect, you are compromising an already compromised debt by asking for a further extension of time to pay. It is even possible to offer to settle an already compromised tax liability for a fraction of what you originally agreed to pay under the OIC. For instance, your financial situation may have deteriorated since your OIC, so the IRS may now doubt whether it can collect even the compromised amount.

There is no required form to compromise the balance owed.
You can do this by a simple letter request. However, as with an orig.
must state why it is in the best interest of the IRS for them to cancel a.
what you owe under the OIC. Rather than completely cancel the re
obligation, it is more likely the IRS will simply determine you "tempo
uncollectible" and suspend further collection.

You will have a far easier task convincing the IRS to defer payments rather than cancel or further compromise what you owe.

If the IRS agrees to your request for an extension, modification, or further compromise, it will notify you by formal reply letter. Until you receive such a notification, you are bound by the agreed terms of your OIC.

If the IRS decides not to extend, modify, or further compromise your obligation, they can immediately file suit to collect:

1)   the entire unpaid balance of the offer;

2)   an amount equal to the original amount of the tax liability as liquidating damages, minus any payments received under the the offer; or

3)   the original amount of the tax liability.

If the IRS chooses *not* to file suit, they could still disregard the amount of the offer and apply any amounts paid under the offer to the original tax liability; they could also levy to collect the original amount of the tax liability.

Notice that your default under the OIC can reinstate your original tax liability (less payments made). This is because the IRS agreed to compromise your tax liability *conditional* upon your performing under the OIC. Your default allows them to rescind their end of the agreement.

If you do plan to file bankruptcy after a default, then let the IRS know of your plans. They will probably suspend collection until you have had a reasonable opportunity to file and this will save both you and the IRS wasted efforts and aggravation.

WHEN THE IRS CAN CANCEL THE AGREEMENT

The OIC is a binding agreement between you and the IRS, but, like all contracts, it can be rescinded if the agreement was based upon misrepresentation, fraud, or mutual mistake.

The IRS does encounter taxpayers who are dishonest and fail to disclose assets or income as required on their offer. Should the IRS later discover these misrepresentations, they can rescind the OIC and pursue the original tax liability. This generally occurs when the misrepresentation was intentional and significant and the misrepresentation wrongfully induced the IRS into a settlement they otherwise would not have agreed to.

This once again underscores the importance of accuracy and truthfulness when dealing with the IRS. Your agreement with the IRS is meaningless unless the IRS remains bound to it. That means you need an honest agreement.

That's why it's a good idea to have your accountant or someone else familiar with your financial affairs review the financial statements that accompany the OIC. It is easy to misinterpret a question or overlook an asset that must be disclosed. Even innocent errors can cause problems far greater than a cancelled OIC agreement.

KEEP RECORDS OF YOUR PAYMENTS

Hopefully, you will fulfill faithfully and punctually your agreement with the IRS. It will certainly benefit you if you should run into future tax troubles.

It is important to keep meticulous records of all payments under the OIC so you can prove to the IRS that you have made all the payments due under the OIC. The IRS sometimes misplaces payments or credits payments to incorrect accounts. So, keep a ledger that accurately documents each payment. Your checks should be clearly marked with your account (Social Security or EIN) and the installment the check represents.

If your agreement calls for protracted payments, then it is a good idea to periodically have the IRS confirm your current balance. If there are bookkeeping problems between yourself and the IRS, they can then be resolved more easily.

HOW TO GET YOUR TAX LIEN RELEASED

Once you have fully paid what was due under the OIC, the IRS must send to you a *Certificate of Release of Federal Tax Lien* Form (668Z). You must receive a certificate for each office that has a lien on file. This may include the clerk of your city, town or county, the Federal District Court nearest where you reside and wherever real estate transactions for your locale are recorded. If you have moved, there may be liens filed where you originally lived. There may also be several liens for the same tax liability filed in the same place. This commonly occurs if your tax problems have extended for a number of years. To ensure that you obtain a Certificate of Release of Federal Tax Lien for *each* lien filed, you must conduct a complete lien search. This can be done in several ways:

- *Ask the IRS officer for copies of every lien the IRS filed against you.*

- *Have a commercial lien search service comb the public records.* These firms know how and where to look for liens, but do be certain they know everywhere you lived or worked from the very beginning of your tax troubles. Also, let them know of any change of name. I recommend Docu-Search. Their toll-free number is (800) 332-3034. They give good reliable nationwide service at a reasonable cost; however, there are many other excellent firms who provide the same service.

- *Review your credit report.* This may disclose outstanding tax liens, but don't rely upon your credit report alone. A credit report may easily overlook some tax liens. You'll see in the next section how to get your credit report.

- *Conduct your own lien search.* It's not as difficult as you may think. The clerk at the public recording office is usually cooperative and will assist you in your search.

Once you're satisfied you identified all the recorded liens, then make certain the IRS does file a Certificate of Release for each lien. Don't assume the IRS will do this on their own. Frequently they don't. You must be diligent in following up on this or you'll have outstanding tax liens that will haunt you for years. Remember: Even one outstanding tax lien can ruin your chances for credit.

Don't, however, expect the IRS to release its lien until *all* conditions of your OIC have been satisfied. This includes all initial and installment payments as well as transfer or assignment to the IRS of any other properties or rights due the IRS under the agreement.

The IRS *will* discharge its lien *before* the collateral agreement is fully satisfied if a lien may hamper your earning power, especially if the IRS is counting on sharing any increase in your future income.

HOW TO CLEAR YOUR CREDIT

As underscored before, a tax lien on your credit report will definitely hurt your chances for significant credit, such as a loan to buy a home, business, car, boat or any other major purchase. It may also prevent you from obtaining credit cards.

Unfortunately, the fact that you *had* tax liens may not be erased from your credit report for several years. However, a *past* lien isn't nearly as damaging as a current tax lien. That's why you must be certain *every* credit bureau updates your credit history to show that your outstanding tax liens have been fully paid and discharged.

Start by requesting a copy of your credit report from the three major credit reporting agencies:

TRW / Experian	**TRANS UNION**	**EQUIFAX**
P.O. Box 8030	P.O. Box 390	P.O. Box 740256
Lawton, UT 84041-8030	Springfield, PA 19064-0390	Atlanta, GA 30374-0256
(800) 682-7654	(513) 771-3090	(800) 685-1111
		(404) 885-8000

These bureaus will send you a copy of your credit report for free (if you were denied credit based upon their report) or for a nominal amount, usually $8. Once a year, upon request, TRW will send you a free copy of your credit report.

To obtain your credit report, write to one of the above address and include:

- your full name (if applicable, include middle initial and Jr., Sr., III, etc.)

- your complete address, include any prior addresses for a five year period

- your social security number

- your spouse's full name, if married

- your year of birth

- your signature

TRW also requires a copy of your driver's license, current billing statement, or other document that lists your name and address.

Review your credit reports. For each recorded lien (not noted as discharged) you must insist that the reporting agency contact the IRS or check the public records to confirm that the lien(s) have been released. You may also send the credit bureaus copies of the Certificate of Release of Federal Tax Lien. Follow up to make sure your credit report reflects the discharge of all tax liens against you.

Credit bureaus can be slow to update your credit report. You can easily be penalized with poor credit for many years only because the credit bureaus stubbornly show outstanding liens. So it is up to you to clear your credit profile and again rebuild your credit. One way to do it quickly and conveniently is with *Guaranteed Credit,* available from Garrett Publishing.

You can also help your credit picture if you are only in the process of resolving your tax problems. For example, if you are mailing your payments in installments then at least have your credit report reflect the fact that an agreement has been reached with the IRS and discharge of your lien is anticipated. You can submit up to a 100-word statement to that effect to the credit bureau and insist that it accompany your credit report.

STAY OUT OF TROUBLE WITH THE IRS

Once your tax problems are behind you, your goal should be to steer clear of future tax troubles. Here are five tips for avoiding surefire IRS problems:

1)   *Don't try to beat the system.* We must all file tax returns and failure to file will eventually catch up to you and cause you even bigger tax problems.

2)   *Hire a good accountant to stay on top of your taxes.* If you lack the discipline to comply with your tax obligations, hire an accountant who will prod you into compliance.

3)   *Keep good records.* Many taxpayers get into deep trouble with the IRS only because they failed to keep adequate records. If you are audited, you'll need good records or you may be hit with a larger tax bill than you can afford to pay.

4.   *Don't play games with Uncle Sam.* We all want to save on our taxes, but the IRS can severely penalize you if they find you are less than honest.

5)   *Stay abreast of the tax laws.* Yes, our tax laws can be complicated, but by understanding the laws, you can frequently alter your financial strategies to significantly lower your taxes. Perhaps you will find that you have overpaid your taxes and that the IRS now owes you money!

CHAPTER 9

How To Get The Professional Help You Need

At this point, you may feel that handling your own OIC is too complicated a task and that you need professional assistance. Let's see whether this is your best option and, if so, how to find and use the right professional.

SHOULD YOU HANDLE YOUR OWN CASE?

Let's start with the disadvantages of representing yourself because they are far more numerous than are the advantages:

- *You lack the professional's expertise on how to get your very best deal.* Odds are that on your own you will offer the IRS far too much to settle. You may also overlook alternatives to the OIC that would be more sensible in your situation. I have reviewed many taxpayer-negotiated OICs and found that these taxpayers consistently offered the IRS much more than was necessary to settle – sometimes two or three times more. It's false economy to save a few dollars on professional fees only to needlessly pay the IRS many times that amount in an overly generous settlement.

- *You may be too frightened, frustrated or intimidated by the IRS to effectively or comfortably handle your OIC.* Most taxpayers are far happier to keep their distance from the IRS and prefer to leave the sparring to their advisors. If you're uncomfortable with an IRS confrontation, then hiring a professional beats tranquilizers! Still, dealing with the IRS is not always as painful as you may imagine. In fact, most IRS officers are reasonable and helpful, particularly when they see you are making an honest effort to resolve your tax problems.

- *You may slip up and make statements that can get you into even more trouble – perhaps an audit or even criminal prosecution.* You must always be careful about what you say to the IRS. Professionals know where to draw the line. You may, for instance, volunteer incriminating information involving undeclared income. You may inadvertently reveal assets or sources of income that can sabotage a favorable settlement. You may make statements that can create tax liability for your spouse or business associate. One careless comment can get you into even bigger trouble! Yes, you should be honest with the IRS. But it's difficult to know precisely how candid you can be unless you are that seasoned tax professional.

- *You take valuable time away from your work or other more pleasant pursuits when you must wrestle with your own case.* This is probably the least important reason for handling your own OIC. After all, it's unlikely you will earn as much from your other pursuits as you will need to pay a professional. But, for a good many taxpayers, that statement is untrue. Physicians, dentists, lawyers, executives, successful business owners, and other high-income taxpayers will do appreciably better paying a tax professional while they more profitably ply their own occupations.

HOW TO SAVE ON PROFESSIONAL FEES

The one big advantage of representing yourself, of course, is that you will save big fees. And for most taxpayers this is no small matter.

Tax professionals can be costly. Their fees range from $25 per hour for an enrolled agent or new accountant in a rural area, to $300 or more per hour for a seasoned tax lawyer in a major city. And most tax consultants won't agree to a fixed fee to handle your OIC. They can't possibly anticipate how many hours will be required because they can't foresee the numerous contingencies or IRS stubbornness in negotiating a final agreement.

But do ask for a rough estimate or a fee range. Unless you have an exceptionally large tax liability or a very hostile officer, your fee should be under $5,000 and is more often about $2,000 to $3,000 for a simpler OIC. Any OIC involves too much paperwork to expect substantially lower fees.

Some tax professionals will agree to a contingent fee or a fee that's a percentage of the savings. This makes sense because it gives the professional a strong incentive to cut the very best deal. A contingent fee, while it may be reasonable in relation to the savings, may be excessive compared to an hourly fee. Consider this proposition very carefully. Your best alternative may combine a nominal hourly fee with a bonus based on results.

Don't hesitate to negotiate fees. Tax professionals seek new clients and do negotiate lower fees or at least additional time to pay the fees. Also, avoid large retainers. You won't know if you're satisfied with your advisor at first, so reserve the flexibility to change advisors without having to chase down the return of a hefty retainer.

Regardless of your fee arrangement, there's much you can do to keep your fees to a minimum:

- Request monthly statements. This will alert you to overcharges or extensive fees you cannot afford before they accumulate.

- See if a lower-priced associate in the professional's firm can handle the more routine aspects of your OIC. Also, do handle yourself whatever you can. Delegate only the critical parts of the case that you cannot handle yourself.

- Cooperate. Get your financial information together quickly and orderly. Don't make your professional chase you for information. That's a wasted expense.

- Keep communication with your professional to the essential minimum. Phone calls add up. Call sparingly, get to the point and hang up!

Most importantly: *Shop fees!* Yes, you need a competent professional, but you will find fees range widely amongst professionals of equal competence and background.

Here's another fee-saving option: Why not hire a tax professional to serve only as your consultant? The professional need not officially represent you before the IRS, but would answer your specific questions and guide you generally through the OIC process. If you don't mind facing the IRS and have the patience to handle the paperwork, this option will save you most of the fee and still keep you fully guided on the important points.

TAX PROFESSIONALS TO CONSIDER

You can choose among three types of tax professionals to represent you on your OIC:

1) Attorneys

2) Certified Public Accountants

3) Enrolled agents

Attorneys

An attorney in good standing in a state bar may represent taxpayers on IRS matters. This doesn't mean all lawyers are qualified to handle an OIC. Obviously, you need one with experience. A lawyer inexperienced with OICs has little value because they have yet to develop the "feel" of what the IRS will accept and are unfamiliar with the OIC procedure.

Your best bet is to call a tax lawyer. They are easily found by contacting your local or state bar association, or your family lawyer may refer you to one. Some states offer special certification to tax specialists which attests to their competence. Tax attorneys frequently have the LL.M. degree (master of laws), which is a post-graduate degree in taxation.

If you owe substantial taxes, or have significant assets, then strongly consider a tax lawyer. You will certainly want a tax lawyer if the IRS suspects fraud or is threatening criminal prosecution or if an appeal to tax court is likely.

Certified Public Accountants

As with attorneys, any CPA is permitted to handle OIC cases; however, this is no assurance of their competence. Call your state association of Certified Public Accountants. They can tell you how to find accountants in your area who are experienced with OIC cases. Your best choice may be your regular accountant – if he or she has solid OIC experience. After all, your accountant is already familiar with your finances and can more quickly and easily put together the information than can another professional unfamiliar with your finances. Contrary to popular belief, the majority of CPAs have little direct involvement with the IRS. Even those who routinely prepare tax returns may have had little exposure to OICs. If that is your accountant, then move on.

Enrolled Agents

Enrolled agents are neither attorneys nor accountants. They are usually former IRS officers or examiners who are now in practice for themselves and are permitted to represent taxpayers before the IRS. EAs earn their designation by having a minimum of five years experience practicing before the IRS or by passing a rigid qualifying exam administered by the IRS. EAs must also participate in annual continuing education. There are about 24,000 active EAs, 6,000 of whom belong to the National Association of Enrolled Agents.

To find enrolled agents in your area call the National Association of Enrolled Agents at (800) 424-4339.

How do you decide which type professional is best for you?

There is no easy answer because there are good and bad practitioners within each group. Still, there are some factors to consider.

A tax attorney is likely to be more expensive than either a CPA or EA. On the other hand, you enjoy confidentiality with an attorney as all written and verbal communication between you and your attorney is privileged. This means you can freely disclose your deepest secrets to your attorney in complete confidence. Moreover, if you must go to court with the IRS, only an attorney can represent you. Start with an attorney and you will not have to change advisors.

The one big advantage of an accountant? He or she is already familiar with your finances and tax history. But don't let your accountant handle your OIC for this reason alone. You need an accountant with a good track record with OICs. You will find CPAs are usually mid-priced between lawyers and enrolled agents.

Enrolled agents are sometimes your best candidate because they frequently worked for the IRS (sometimes handling OIC cases exclusively) and best know the inner workings of the IRS and how to strike your most favorable deal. An EA is also likely to be less expensive than an attorney or accountant. While these may appear to be compelling reasons to hire an EA, remember that some EAs cannot completely shed their IRS past and don't fight as hard as they could for their taxpayer-clients.

FULL SERVICE SPECIALISTS

There are also several firms that specialize in OICs. These firms either employ attorneys, accountants or EAs or refer their cases to qualified specialists. Due to their high volume of cases, these firms are oftentimes more economical, and because they handle only OICs and related cases, they offer considerable expertise. My own firm handles OIC cases nationwide. Arnold S. Goldstein & Associates, P.A. lists their services in the back of this book.

HOW TO FIND A TAX PRO

It is not difficult to find the tax pro who is right for you:

* *Ask your professional advisors.* Your accountant or attorney may not excel in OICs, but may refer you to another professional who does.

* *Personal referrals.* Do you have a friend or acquaintance who has gone through an OIC with good results? Perhaps their advisor will do equally well for you.

- *Professional associations.* Your local bar or accounting association may have a referral panel, but their referral does not necessarily insure competence as they may loosely categorize their specialists, such as under "taxation."

- Advertising. Yellow pages and newspapers feature tax professionals, however few advertise as OIC specialists. You have to screen these specialists to see if they have the requisite experience with OICs.

HOW TO SELECT AND WORK WITH YOUR PROFESSIONAL

Don't hire too quickly. Your *right* advisor must convince you that he or she has strong experience with OIC cases. This means at least 10-15 prior cases.

How aggressive is your candidate? Does he or she discuss or recommend other options to the OIC such as abatements or bankruptcy? What approximate outcome does he or she foresee? Does the result seem reasonable and realistic or only puffery to get you as a client?

Does the prospect give you confidence? Is it someone who appears sufficiently aggressive to stand up to the IRS? You don't need a timid tax pro on your side, or one who is intimidated by the IRS.

Shop around. You may have to talk to several prospects before you decide. Only by talking with several candidates can you assess each.

Can your prospect give your case the needed time? This is one chronic problem with accountants. They are so busy during tax season that they have little time for OIC cases. Delays in following through on a case do not sit well with IRS officers always anxious to resolve cases. But this may be an advantage if you need time to rearrange your financial affairs, although it's usually best to work promptly with the IRS and not stall.

Finally, consider the "chemistry" between you and your prospect. You need a pro who can offer more than technical capability. You may also need empathy and emotional support from your advisor. When you battle the IRS, you need a strong ally in every sense of the word!

CHAPTER 10

STRAIGHT ANSWERS TO THE 50 MOST-ASKED QUESTIONS ABOUT THE OFFER IN COMPROMISE PROGRAM

Q: How likely is it that the IRS will accept an Offer in Compromise?

A: In the past, the chances of acceptance were poor – only about one in four. The odds of settling with the IRS are now far better because the IRS has liberalized its OIC policies. Taxpayers and their advisors, in turn, have also become more realistic in their offers to the IRS. The IRS now approves about one out of two OICs.

Your chances will greatly depend upon your IRS District. Some district offices accept many more OICs than do others. This is a reflection of the attitude of district office supervisors toward OICs. However, if you closely follow the instructions in this book, you stand an excellent chance of reaching a fair and workable settlement with the IRS.

Q: How difficult is it to get the IRS to classify me as "temporarily uncollectible?"

A: The IRS must determine that you have no assets worth chasing and your present and foreseeable income does not exceed what you need to sustain a basic lifestyle. If the IRS decides, however, that you have even $50 in surplus income each month, it will expect that $50 to be applied to your tax liability. There are many more "53" or "temporarily uncollectible" determinations made each year than there are approved OICs. But keep in mind that "uncollectible" is only temporary. The IRS can always resume collection. So why not file an OIC while you are registered "temporarily uncollectible." With an accepted OIC, your tax problems are forever behind you, provided you comply with its terms.

Q: When should an Offer in Compromise be considered?

A: When your taxes are:

1) more than you can pay either through selling or borrowing against your assets or from income above what you need to support yourself and your family; and

2) you have too many assets and/or income to be classified as temporarily uncollectible, and

3) you have no other debts or your taxes are not dischargeable in bankruptcy thus disqualifying you as a bankruptcy candidate. Stated differently, you are a good OIC candidate when your assets are less than the taxes you owe and taxes are your primary financial problem.

Q: Can property and wages of a spouse *without* a tax liability be factored in by the IRS to determine the "ability to pay" of the tax-liable spouse?

A: While the IRS cannot legally claim a non-liable spouse's assets or income, the IRS when, negotiating settlements, nevertheless considers spousal assets and will make every effort to have you *borrow* from your spouse so you can increase your offer. Your spouse has no obligation to disclose *his* or *her* separate finances on matters involving *your* taxes. Most spouses cooperate, whether from misunderstanding their rights or hoping their cooperation will facilitate settlement with the IRS.

Q: Can penalties be compromised under an OIC?

A: Penalties and interest can both be compromised in the same way as the underlying tax liability. However, if penalties are your major concern, then consider an abatement, particularly if you have reasonable grounds for the IRS to waive the penalty. The abatement process is far simpler than an OIC, and it is your proper remedy when you can pay the tax, but believe you have justification for being excused from the penalties.

Q: Can the IRS refuse to consider an OIC?

A: No. It is your right as a taxpayer to submit an OIC, and the IRS cannot stop you.

Many IRS officials remain opposed to the OIC program and discourage OICs or refuse to consider them in good faith as is required. However, the IRS cannot reject your offer capriciously or in bad faith. If you believe this is happening in your case, you can appeal to a supervisor and demand an explanation as to why your offer has been rejected.

The IRS can summarily reject OICs that they believe are filed frivolously or submitted solely for purposes of forestalling collection.

Q: What should a business owner do who owes delinquent payroll taxes?

A: The first step is to stay current from this point forward. The IRS will close your business immediately rather than let you fall further behind.

If you are still in business, the IRS officer's actions will depend on:

1) whether you pay your current taxes,

2) your prospects for paying the tax arrears,

3) the difficulty and time involved in liquidating your business and

4) the money the IRS would get from a liquidation. That's why a heavily encumbered business can more confidently deal with the IRS than can a business with a large equity exposed to the IRS.

As a business owner, you have the same rights as an individual taxpayer to negotiate an installment agreement. Twelve-month agreements are routine and longer installment plans are possible. A Chapter 11 bankruptcy can also stop IRS seizure and automatically give you six years from the date of assessment to pay the back taxes.

Finally, you can submit an OIC to settle the back taxes. Business OICs are far less common than personal OICs, but when your business has fewer assets than tax liabilities, it can be a viable alternative.

Q: Can I settle state taxes as I do federal taxes?

A: Taxpayers commonly owe both IRS and state taxes and do negotiate simultaneous settlements. Most states have tax compromise programs similar to the IRS's. Other states compromise with delinquent taxpayers as a matter of practice if not official policy.

You should pro-rate your offers to the IRS and the state, paying each their proportionate share. Parity is important. Payment dates and other terms of your offer should also coincide, as should your financial disclosures. Finally, make certain each agency knows you owe the other and that settlement with each is conditional upon settlement with both.

Q: Are offers in compromise open to public inspection?

A: Yes, accepted OICs are public record for one year. And it's wise to inspect OICs that have been approved in your district within the past year for an idea of what the IRS may accept in your case.

Q: Can you file an OIC if your bankruptcy does not discharge your taxes?

A: Bankruptcy does not always discharge your taxes. Payroll taxes and income taxes less than three years old are two taxes not dischargeable in bankruptcy. You can file an OIC to compromise these or any other taxes not dischargeable in bankruptcy.

The time you were in bankruptcy plus six months is added to the IRS's statute of limitations to collect from you. Taxpayers emerging from bankruptcy with undischarged taxes should try to be classified "temporarily uncollectible" because the bankruptcy should convince the IRS that the taxpayer presently has no assets.

Q: What types of payment plans can you offer the IRS in a Chapter 13 bankruptcy?

A: There are four possible plans that usually extend payments over three to five years:

1) You can offer a *standard or uniform installment plan* that calls for constant payments over the term of the plan.

2) A *step-up plan* increases your payments as your income increases.

3) *Variable* or *seasonal plans* vary your payments to coincide with cash flow or cyclical income.

4) *Balloon plans* obligate you to pay any remaining tax balance with your final payment and may be used with any of the other plans.

Q: Is bankruptcy an option if I owe both old and current taxes?

A: According to a recent Supreme Court case, you can file Chapter 7 bankruptcy to fully discharge all taxes over three years old, and *then* file a Chapter 13 bankruptcy to discharge your current taxes under a plan. This is referred to as "Chapter 20" because it combines the double benefit of a Chapter 7 and Chapter 13! Discuss this with an experienced bankruptcy lawyer.

Q: What should I do if I discover an error in the information I provided the IRS as part of my OIC?

A: For material errors, amend your Form 433-A or explain the error in a letter to the IRS. Always put it in writing. Ignore small, immaterial inaccuracies. Notifying the IRS will needlessly delay the process and prompt the IRS to reconsider your application. If you are uncertain whether the error is significant, then correct the information.

Q: What can you do if a tax lien was erroneously filed against you?

A: You may appeal an erroneous tax lien by filing an administrative appeal, although you cannot use an administrative appeal to decide the underlying tax liability.

Erroneous tax liens commonly occur when:

1) a tax lien is filed after the tax liability was paid,

2) the taxpayer was in bankruptcy,

3) an examination assessment was improperly made, or

4) the statute of limitations for IRS collections has expired.

Q: Can the IRS seize or levy a taxpayer's property *without* advance notice?

A: Yes, but it is unusual. For it to occur the IRS must believe it would be in jeopardy if it did not act quickly and without notice. A jeopardy assessment would occur, for instance, if the IRS suspects you of transferring assets or planning to take your money out of the country. Jeopardy assessment taxpayers automatically have the right to IRS administrative review and judicial appeal; however, the lien or levy will remain in force pending its outcome.

Q: When will the IRS release a levy?

A:
1) When the tax, penalties, and interest are fully paid.
2) When the statute of limitations has expired.
3) When you reach an installment agreement or OIC with the IRS.
4) When the release will facilitate collection.
5) When the levy is causing extreme hardship.
6) When the taxpayer has other assets to satisfy the tax.

Q: What is the IRS's Problem Resolution Program (PRP)?

A: PRP assists taxpayers who are unable to resolve their tax problems on their own through ordinary procedures. Contact PRP only *after* you exhaust all resolution possibilities with IRS collection employees and their supervisors.

PRP also offers a convenient avenue of appeal when you disagree with the tax assessed or a collection procedure, or believe some other taxpayer right has been abridged.

Use Form 911, *Application for Assistance to Relieve Hardship* in the Appendix. A PRP representative will review your application and may issue a Taxpayers Assistance Order (TAO) directing the IRS-involved employees to correct their actions. IRS employees are available to help you complete the application. A word of caution: Don't be optimistic. Few TAOs are actually issued so PRP has not been particularly helpful to taxpayers.

Filing Form 911 will extend the statute of limitations by the amount of time the IRS spends considering the taxpayer's application.

Q: How do I know if I am legally obliged to give information to the IRS?

A: The Privacy Act of 1974 and Paperwork Reduction Act of 1980 requires that the IRS tell you, when you're asked a question, whether your response is voluntary, required to obtain a benefit, or mandatory. As a strict legal matter, you can always refuse to answer IRS questions or refuse to turn over documents.

Under these laws, the IRS must also tell you:

1) why it wants the information,

2) its legal authority in asking for it, and

3) what could happen if the IRS does not receive it.

Of course, without full disclosure of information and an attitude of complete cooperation, you have virtually no chance of having your OIC accepted. However, if you believe the IRS is asking improper questions, then decline to answer until you seek professional advice.

Q: Can politicians influence the IRS?

A: Many politicians intercede on behalf of their taxpayer constituents, particularly when they believe their constituents have been unfairly treated by the IRS. Contact your congressman only after you have tried and failed to get satisfaction through normal IRS channels.

Your congressman will need your complete file, a letter stating your grievance and how you tried to resolve it, and the results you want. Your congressman will also need a signed *Power of Attorney* (Form 2848) or *Tax Information Authorization and Declaration of Representative* (Form 2848D), both available at your local IRS office.

Q: What is the difference between a revenue officer and a special agent?

A: A revenue officer is a regular IRS employee responsible for the collection of taxes through standard procedures.

A special agent investigates possible *criminal* violations of the IRS code. If you are contacted by a special agent (who must disclose his or her status), then immediately terminate the interview and hire a lawyer.

Q: What will happen if I fail to file a delinquent tax return after repeated demands to do so by the IRS?

A: One possibility is that you will receive a federal summons compelling you to bring either the completed tax return or your books and records to the IRS office. This summons is backed by the power of the federal courts which can hold you in contempt if you fail to do so.

Another possibility is that the IRS will prepare your tax return for you. This is guaranteed to result in a much greater tax than had you prepared your own return.

Q: What if my tax return is due but I don't have the money to pay the tax?

A: Submit your tax return on the date due (or extension date), even if you can't pay the tax. You will be charged interest on your late payment but avoid a hefty late-filing penalty. Most taxpayers in this situation delay filing because they don't want the IRS dunning them. That's understandable. Nevertheless, whether or not you expect to eventually pay the tax, do file on time.

It is also important to file on time because the IRS has only ten years from the date of assessment to collect your delinquent taxes, and taxes are not assessed until after you file or after the IRS files for you.

Q: Does the IRS share tax information with state taxing agencies?

A: Yes. In fact, this is standard practice but it must follow strict guidelines. The IRS also shares information with the Department of Justice, other federal agencies and even certain foreign jurisdictions.

Q: Will banking in offshore havens save me taxes?

A: It's a myth that you can avoid U.S. taxes through foreign banking. American citizens must declare income earned anywhere in the world. Foreign banks do not issue Form 1099s on interest income, so the IRS must necessarily rely more on your honesty.

Offshore havens can effectively protect your money from IRS seizure. The Isle of Man, Cayman Islands and Gibralter are best for this purpose. Switzerland offers significantly less protection. Want more information? Read *Asset Protection Secrets* and *Offshore Havens,* both available from Garrett Publishing.

Q: Is conversation with my accountant privileged?

A: No. The IRS, the courts and others can compel your accountant to testify about your conversations and turn over letters and other correspondence between you. Only communication with your lawyer is privileged and protected. That's one advantage to having a lawyer represent you rather than an accountant. A solution is to have your attorney hire your accountant to handle your tax matters. Your accountant, working for your lawyer, would then come under the attorney-client privilege. Since confidential documents with your accountant can be subpoenaed, you should have these copies and all copies immediately returned to you.

Q: Can I deduct from my current tax bill the IRS refunds that are due me from prior years?

A: Yes. If you owe the IRS $5,000 this year and the IRS owes you a $1,500 refund from last year, you can pay only the $3,500 difference. Explain the reason for the reduced payment. The IRS discourages this because it prefers to close its files promptly, which only happens when you make full payment.

Q: What is meant by an "innocent spouse"?

A: When you and your spouse file a joint tax return, both you and your spouse are "jointly and severally" liable for any taxes due.

If it is later shown, for example, that one spouse had unreported income, the other spouse may try to escape civil and/or criminal liability for the tax on that unreported income under the "innocent spouse" rule (IRS 6013(e)). To claim this protection, the innocent spouse must neither have known about the understated income (or other tax) nor could have reasonably known about it. The "innocent" spouse not only avoids tax liability but also provides a safe harbor for the family assets.

Q: When a bank account is levied by the IRS, when must the bank turn over the money to the IRS?

A: Since June 30, 1989, banks have 21 days from date of levy to turn over funds to the IRS. This gives the taxpayer time to resolve the tax problem or settle disputes concerning ownership of funds in these accounts. The "21 day rule" applies only to banks. Other parties holding your funds must turn them over within the time provided for in the levy. Accounts receivable are paid to the IRS in accordance with their original credit terms.

Q: What steps are routinely taken by the IRS to collect delinquent taxes?

A: The standard collection process includes:

- First notice and demand for payment on the unpaid tax.

- Three more payment due notices sent about a month apart.

- 10-day notice of intent to lien.

- 30-day notice of intent to levy (final notice) by certified mail.

- Enforcement action (seizure or levy).

Q: How can I check on a tax refund that is due me?

A: Call *Tele-tax* (listed in the Appendix). *Tele-tax* is also a convenient way to get information on about 150 different tax topics. These topics answer many Federal tax questions. Up to three topics can be accessed with each phone call. The OIC Program is Tele-Tax topic number 204.

Q: Does the IRS offer free forms and publications?

A: Yes. And most of their publications are worth reading. Many are listed in the Appendix and are available from the IRS at (800) 829-3676 or by fax at (703) 487-4163. Web sites are also listed in the Appendix. And for those of you who prefer to use your mailbox, an order form is also included in the Appendix.

Q: What is an "Automated Collection System"?

A: Several years ago, the IRS set up an automated collection system (ACS) to improve efficiency. This systematized process helps IRS collectors contact delinquent taxpayers by mail and phone. It has enormously increased IRS productivity.

Q: How can taxpayers claim a tax refund?

A: Taxpayers who believe they overpaid their taxes may file a claim for refund directly with the IRS. If the claim is denied, the taxpayer can file a lawsuit for the refund in either the U.S. Court of Claims or Federal District Court.

Q: Can a taxpayer demand to see his or her tax files?

A: Yes. In most instances the IRS will show you your own file. If it refuses, the taxpayer can demand access to his or her files under the Freedom of Information Act.

Q: How does the IRS keep track of each taxpayer?

A: The IRS maintains a taxpayer account for each taxpayer. This IRS computer record contains your tax history, tax assessments, penalties, interest and credits for payment.

To help manage the system, the IRS also issues to each taxpayer a taxpayer identification number (TIN). This is usually the taxpayer's Social Security Number, but for corporations and trusts, it is a separate 13-digit number.

Q: What is the most common reason for the large tax liabilities that force taxpayers to file Offers in Compromise?

A: Large tax liabilities are generally caused by unpaid withholding taxes. Owners and other responsible parties within a business are personally assessed the unpaid trust portion, or taxes actually deducted from the employees. This is called the 100 percent penalty assessment.

If business owners cannot pay the full withholding tax, they should at least pay the trust portion – that amount withheld from the employees – and designate that the payment be applied *only* to the trust portion liability. The business will owe its share of the payroll taxes due, but its officers and other responsible parties will have no personal liability.

Other reasons include extensive audits, not filing for a number of years or tax shelter investments that are disallowed.

Q: Who can file an Offer in Compromise?

A: Any "taxpayer" may file:

- Individuals

- Married couples

- Trusts

- Corporations

- Limited partnerships
- Limited liability companies
- Foundations, associations and other non-profit organizations
- Estates

In each instance, the OIC must be signed by a duly authorized individual.

Q: **How does the IRS determine the "minimum bid price," or what the IRS will sell seized property for at public auction or private bid?**

A: The IRS starts with an estimated fair market value. This is then reduced by 25-percent. The minimum bid price is 80-percent of that amount. Of course, the IRS must pay all prior encumbrances and expenses of the sale from the sale proceeds received.

Taxpayers can object to the minimum price bid on their property and request a new professional appraisal be obtained by the IRS.

Q: **What can the IRS do if I fraudulently transfer my assets?**

A: The IRS may:

1) sue in Federal District Court to set aside the transfer.

2) sue the transferee for the value of the transferred property.

3) file an administrative claim against the transferee for the value of the transferred asset.

Because of their limited staff, the IRS seldom pursues fraudulent transfers.

Q: **What can a business owner do to protect business assets from IRS seizure?**

A: The business, to the extent practical, should be divided into separate corporations so if one corporation has a tax problem, the IRS has no recourse to the remaining corporations.

The business should also be heavily mortgaged or encumbered, leaving little or no equity for the IRS to seize.

Q: Do incorporated businesses commonly file Offers in Compromise?

A: Few businesses file OICs. Most OICs are filed by individuals. Businesses with severe tax troubles usually also owe other creditors and file Chapter 11 so they can compromise all their liabilities under one comprehensive reorganization plan.

Q: Do all IRS offices welcome OICs?

A: No. There is a difference in attitude and policy toward OICs between IRS offices and personnel. Although most offices now encourage taxpayers to file OICs when there appears to be no real ability to pay, some district offices still reject many OICs even when the taxpayer has clearly shown no such ability to pay.

If your district office is hostile toward OICs, then write your congressman, or hire a tax representative outside your district and attempt to transfer your OIC case to your representative's district.

IRS attitudes toward OICs have improved significantly since the program started and have become more widely used and encouraged by top IRS officials.

Q: How does the IRS value property held between husband and wife as tenants by the entirety?

A: This type of tenancy presents complex legal problems to the IRS, so it evaluates the interest of each spouse to be less than half the total value of the property. Twenty percent of the total value is generally considered each spouse's net worth in the property.

Property held as tenants in common or joint tenancy are fully valued based upon the taxpayer's percentage of interest.

Q: Can a revenue officer demand to inspect my house?

A: Yes. Under an OIC, this is an absolute IRS right and inspection of the taxpayer's personal goods and household effects is usually a condition for accepting the OIC. Works of art, jewelry, coins, stamp collections, silverware, china, antiques and other collectibles of value will be of particular interest. However, when the IRS visits your home, they do not arbitrarily go through your drawers and closets. Typically, the officer will just want to take a general "walk-through" of your house, much like in a real estate open-house. If you think an officer is going beyond the bounds of good taste during this inspection, stop the inspection and contact that officer's supervisor.

This right to inspect applies only to an OIC. If you do not allow the inspection of your home, your offer will be rejected. Without your permission, the IRS cannot enter your home unless they show you a warrant.

Q: How does the IRS compute the value of a taxpayer's ownership in a family business?

A: It is always difficult to appraise a small business, however, the IRS will attempt to value it as a "going concern" rather than as assets to be liquidated. If the IRS and the taxpayer cannot agree on this value, the IRS and taxpayer each can have the business professionally appraised.

Q: Can a taxpayer compromise some taxes and not others?

A: Your Offer in Compromise must include *all* owed taxes, plus penalties and interest. It must also include potential or contingent taxes and *every* type of tax, e.g., income taxes, highway taxes, employment taxes, and interest and penalties for each.

Q: Can you delete or modify preprinted provisions on Form 656 *Offer in Compromise?*

A: No. Deletions or revisions on the preprinted sections of Form 656 are not allowed. You may, however, attach items that modify or clarify your offer.

Q: Will the IRS accept an OIC from a taxpayer with a recent criminal record?

A: That depends on the crime, its notoriety, the taxpayer's reputation in the community and the taxpayer's compliance with the tax laws before and since the crime. If the IRS suspects that the crimes are ongoing, it will obviously deny the OIC for public policy reasons.

Q: Will the IRS inspect a taxpayer's safe deposit box before accepting an OIC?

A: Usually. Refusal to allow inspection will cause summary rejection of the offer.

Q: **How does the IRS determine whether a "collateral agreement" to share in the taxpayer's future income is needed?**

A: The IRS considers the taxpayer's:

- age
- earning capacity
- education
- health
- profession
- experience

Taxpayers should underplay these factors when presenting an offer. However, these agreements are rarely requested by the IRS as newer provisions in the Internal Revenue Manual seem to discourage collateral agreements.

Q: **When can a taxpayer sue the IRS for damages and what can a taxpayer receive in damages?**

A: It's difficult, but not impossible to sue the IRS. The taxpayer must show the IRS action to have been frivolous, malicious or wantonly groundless. This means something more than that the IRS "guessed wrong" in determining the correct action.

However, now that the *Taxpayer Bill of Rights 2* has been enacted into law, the IRS may be more willing to settle cases for the following reasons:

1) the cap on damages for "reckless" collections has been raised from $100,000 to $1 million;

2) to collect legal fees from the IRS, the taxpayer no longer needs to show that the IRS's position wasn't "substantially justified," but now the burden is on the IRS to show that it's position was substantially justified; and

3) the hourly rate for fee awards for recoverable actions has been increased from $75 to $110. The law also contains many other provisions benefiting the taxpayer.

Taxpayers who encounter IRS abuse should contact the National Coalition of IRS Whistleblowers, 6255 Sunset Blvd., Suite 2020, Los Angeles CA 90028, or P.O. Box 65471, Washington DC 20035. This group includes numerous present and past IRS employees as well as concerned citizens and politicians working to expose IRS abuses and pave the way for reform.

IRS TERMS

This glossary includes those terms most commonly used in the Offer in Compromise program. There are many other tax terms this glossary does not include.

A

Abatement - A partial or complete cancellation of taxes, penalties or interest owed by a taxpayer.

ACS - See Automated Collection System.

Adjustment - Changes to your tax bill.

Amended Tax Return - A tax return filed to make changes to a previously filed tax return. A taxpayer has three years to file an amended tax return.

Appeal - The IRS administrative process for taxpayers to contest decisions within the IRS.

Assessment - The recording of a tax liability against a taxpayer. Generally, the amount of any tax imposed shall be assessed within 3 years after the return was filed. (26 USCA 6501)

Asset - Any owned property.

Audit - An IRS review of the accuracy of a tax return. The IRS term for an audit is "examination".

Auditor - An IRS Examination Division employee who audits tax returns.

Automated Collection System (ACS) - A computerized collection process for IRS collectors to contact delinquent taxpayers by telephone and mail.

B

Bankruptcy - A legal process under federal law to help a debtor by enabling the debtor to start anew through the discharge of certain debts or through the repayment of the debts over time, during which time, the creditors cannot bother the debtor.

Basis (Tax Basis) - The cost of an asset, which may be adjusted downward by depreciation or upward by improvements.

C

Collateral Agreement - An agreement sometimes secured by the IRS prior to acceptance of an Offer in Compromise when the IRS wants to cover a future, reasonably possible event, such as a significant increase in income.

Collection Division - Tax collectors who work out of the IRS Service Center, Automated Collection or District Office.

Collection Information Statement (IRS Forms 433-A, 433-B, and 433-F) - IRS financial statements which require disclosure of personal information, particularly assets, income and expenses.

Commissioner of Internal Revenue - The head of the IRS.

Criminal Investigation Division (CID) - The branch of the IRS that investigates tax crimes.

Current Market Value - The amount you could reasonably expect to be paid for the asset if you sold it. Do not guess at the value of an asset. Find out the value from realtors, used car dealers, publications, furniture dealers, or other experts on specific types of assets. If you get a written estimate, please include a copy with your financial statement.

Delinquent Return - A tax return not filed by the due date (April 15) or by the dates allowed through the IRS extension periods (August 15 and October 15).

Depreciation - A tax deduction allowed for the wear-and-tear on an income-producing asset, such as rental real estate or business equipment.

District Office - Local IRS offices that includes auditors, collectors, criminal investigators and Problem Resolution Officers.

Documentation - Written proof.

Enrolled Agent (EA) - An EA is a tax accountant or tax preparer allowed to practice before the IRS.

Examination - Official IRS term for an audit. See Audit.

Exemption - An exemption may refer to a deduction allowed to a taxpayer because of his or her status, such as having certain dependents, being over 65, or being blind. It may also refer to assets that the IRS cannot take if it levies on your property to satisfy your tax debt.

Extension - An extension to file gives a taxpayer more time to file a return, but not to pay the taxes owed. A taxpayer can obtain an automatic extension until August 15 and can request a second extension until October 15 by filing with the IRS. The second extension is discretionary. A taxpayer can also request an extension to pay taxes, but they are rarely granted.

Failure To File Tax Return - The most common tax crime. Intentionally failing to file a return when you were obligated to do so is a misdemeanor. The maximum prison sentence is one year in jail and $25,000 for each year not filed.

Fair Market Value - The price a willing buyer and seller of property would agree on as fair; neither being under any compulsion to buy or sell and both having reasonable knowledge of relevant facts.

Fifth Amendment - A right guaranteed by the U.S. Constitution that protects people from being forced by the government to incriminate themselves. You can assert your Fifth Amendment right against the IRS by refusing to answer questions or provide them documents.

Freedom Of Information Act - A federal law giving citizens the right to see governmental documents, including their IRS files.

G

Gift - Transfers of property without any payment.

Group Manager - The immediate superior of a tax collector at a District Office.

I

Income - All monies and other valuables received, except items specifically exempted by the tax code.

Information Return - A report filed with the IRS showing income paid to a taxpayer. From W-2 (wages) and Form 1099 (other income, such as interest paid by a bank, stock dividends or royalties) are examples.

Installment Agreement (IA) - An IRS monthly payment plan for past due taxes.

Internal Revenue Code - The official tax laws of the U.S. as enacted by Congress. Also called the "tax code."

Internal Revenue Manual - The IRS handbook which sets forth the internal operating guidelines for IRS personnel.

Internal Revenue Service - The tax law administration branch of the U.S. Treasury.

J

Jeopardy Assessment - an expedited procedure by which the IRS imposes a tax liability without notifying you first. A jeopardy assessment is rare and used when the IRS believes the taxpayer is about to leave the country or hide assets.

Joint Tax Return - An income tax return filed by a married couple.

L

Levy - An IRS seizure of property or wages to satisfy a delinquent tax debt.

Lien - See Tax Lien.

Limitation on Assessment and Collection - See Statute of Limitation.

Liquidation Value - The amount the IRS can get from a distress sale of a taxpayer's assets, usually a public auction (typically 70% of fair market value).

M

Market Value - See Fair Market Value.

Non-Filer - A person or entity who does not file a tax return when required to do so.

Notice of Deficiency - An IRS notice informing a taxpayer that he or she owes the IRS the amount listed, which is the excess of the taxpayer's correct tax liability for the taxable year over the amount of taxes already paid for such year.

Notice of Tax Lien - See Tax Lien.

O

Offer in Compromise - A formal written offer to the IRS to settle your tax for less than the amount you owe or for less than the amount the IRS says you owe.

Ombudsman - An IRS troubleshooter who acts on the behalf of taxpayers with problems not solved through normal IRS channels. Ombudsman's are Problem Resolution Officers who work in Problem Resolution Programs located in District Offices and Service Centers. See also Problem Resolution Program.

100-percent Penalty - See Trust Fund Recovery Penalty.

P

Payroll Taxes - Federal income tax and FICA contributions including both Social Security and Medicare. These are also called Trust Fund Taxes. See also Trust Fund Recovery Penalty.

Penalties - Civil fines imposed on taxpayers who violate tax laws.

Pending, offer - An offer is pending starting with the date an authorized IRS official signs Form 656 and accepts your waiver of the statutory period of limitation, and remains pending until an authorized IRS official accepts, rejects or acknowledges withdrawal of the offer in writing.

Personal Property - All property other than real estate - such as cash, stock, cars.

Petition - A form filed with the U.S. Tax Court requesting a hearing to contest a proposed IRS tax assessment.

Power of Attorney (IRS Form 2848) - A form appointing a tax representative to deal with the IRS on your behalf.

Problem Resolution Program - An IRS program to assist taxpayers with problems not solved in normal IRS channels. The program is administrated by Problem Resolution Officers. See also Ombudsman.

Protest - A written or oral request to appeal a decision within the IRS.

Q

Quick Sale Value - The amount that can be realized from the sale of a taxpayer's assets when financial and other pressures force the taxpayer to sell quickly (typically 80% of fair market value).

Real Property - Land that is considered "Real Estate", including improvements made to that land.

Refund - An amount a taxpayer is entitled to be returned from the IRS on account of the overpayment of tax liability.

Regulations - IRS additions to the Internal Revenue Code.

Representative - See Tax Representative.

Return - See Tax Return.

Revenue Officer - An IRS tax collector.

Revenue Procedure - An administrative statement by the IRS regarding a matter of procedure affecting a taxpayer's rights or duties under the IRS Code.

Revenue Ruling - An official interpretation by the IRS of the proper application of the tax law.

Seizure - See Levy.

Service Centers - Ten regional IRS facilities where tax returns are filed and processed.

Special Agent - An IRS officer who investigates suspected tax crimes. See also Criminal Investigation Division (CID).

Statute of Limitation - Legal limits imposed on the IRS for assessing and collecting taxes, and on the Justice Department for charging taxpayers with tax crimes. The current statute of limitation for collection is 10 years from the date of assessment; however, the statute can be extended by certain actions of the taxpayer.

Summons - A legal order issued by the IRS or a court to compel a taxpayer or other person to appear and provide financial information to the IRS.

Tax Attorney - A lawyer who does tax-related work including IRS dispute resolution and tax return.

Tax Code - See Internal Revenue Code.

Tax Court - The only federal court where a taxpayer can contest an IRS tax assessment without first paying the taxes.

Tax Law - The Internal Revenue Code, written by Congress. Internal Revenue Code.

Tax Liability - The amount a taxpayer owes under the tax law, based on gross income and deductions.

Tax Lien - If you owe money to the IRS, the IRS has a claim against your property by "operation of law". This is done by recording a Notice of Federal Tax Lien at the county recorder's office or Notice to the public with your Secretary of State's office. The lien is used as security for a tax debt.

Tax Representative - A tax professional qualified to represent you before the IRS. See also Enrolled Agent, Tax Attorney.

Tax Return - A form on which individuals, partnerships and corporations report information to the IRS regarding their activities during a taxable year.

Taxpayer - A person subject to any internal revenue tax, regardless of whether he or she actually pays or is required to pay tax.

Taxpayer Account - An IRS computer record containing your tax history, and including all tax assessments, penalties and interest, and credits for payments.

Taxpayer Assistance Order - An order that a Problem Resolution Officer can issue to override an action taken by another division of the IRS. See also Ombudsman, Problem Resolution Officer, Problem Resolution Program.

Taxpayer Bill of Rights - Adopted by the IRS in 1988 and enacted into law on July 30, 1996. The purpose of this law is to educate taxpayers and to let them know in plain English what the IRS can and cannot do when dealing with taxpayers. It provides for increased protection of taxpayer rights in complying with the tax laws and in dealing with the IRS.

Taxpayer Identification Number (TIN) An IRS assigned number used for computer tracking of tax accounts. For individuals, it is their Social Security Number. For other entities, such as corporations, it is a separate 13-digit number.

Tele-Tax - IRS pre-recorded tax topic information, available by telephone.

Trust Fund Recovery Penalty (formerly called 100-percent Penalty) - A penalty incurred by the responsible person(s) of a business for failure to pay Withholding and Federal Insurance Contributions Act Taxes (social security taxes)

Trust Fund Taxes - See Payroll taxes.

Uncollectible (Form 53) - A temporary designation by the IRS meaning a taxpayer does not have significant assets or available income, at the present time, from which to satisfy an IRS debt in part or in full. This designation takes a case out of collection, until a taxpayer has an ability to pay.

Waiver - Voluntarily surrendering a legal right, such as the right to have the IRS collection period on a delinquent tax debt expire at the end of the statutory time period. The IRS may require waivers in exchange for granting installment agreements.

APPENDICES

APPENDIX A

- IRS OFFER IN COMPROMISE PROGRAM
- IRS COLLECTION MANUAL
- UNDERSTANDING THE COLLECTION PROCESS
- QUICK AND EASY ACCESS TO TAX HELP AND FORMS
- YOUR RIGHTS AS A TAXPAYER

APPENDIX B

- IRS FORMS
- DO YOU NEED HELP SOLVING YOUR TAX TROUBLES?
- GREAT BOOKS TO FURTHER ASSIST YOU

INTERNAL REVENUE SERVICE OFFER IN COMPROMISE PROGRAM

The following are excerpts from the Internal Revenue Service Manual (IRM) Section 5700 (Special Procedures) concerning IRS policies on Offers in Compromise. This manual is used by all IRS employees in the administration of the Offer in Compromise Program.

Read this material carefully. It will help clarify the chapter information.

57(10)0

OFFERS IN COMPROMISE

57(10)1
INTRODUCTION

The Service, like any other business, will encounter situations where an account receivable cannot be collected in full or there is a dispute as to what is owed. It is an accepted business practice to resolve these collection and liability issues through a compromise. Additionally, the compromise process is available to provide delinquent taxpayers with a fresh start toward future compliance with the tax laws.

57(10)1.1
OFFER POLICY

Policy Statement P-5-100 sets forth the Service's position on using compromises.

"The Service will accept an Offer in Compromise when it is unlikely that the tax liability can be collected in full and the amount offered reasonably reflects collection potential. An Offer in Compromise is a legitimate alternative to declaring a case as currently not collectible or to a protracted installment agreement. The goal is to achieve collection of what is potentially collectible at the earliest possible time and at the least cost to the government."

"In cases where an Offer in Compromise appears to be a viable solution to a tax delinquency, the Service employee assigned the case will discuss the compromise alternative with the taxpayer and, when necessary, assist in preparing the required forms. The taxpayer will be responsible for initiating the first specific proposal for compromise."

"The success of the compromise program will be assured only if taxpayers make adequate compromise proposals consistent with their ability to pay and the Service makes prompt and reasonable decisions. Taxpayers are expected to provide reasonable documentation to verify their ability to pay. The ultimate goal is a compromise which is in the best interest of both the taxpayer and the Service. Acceptance of an adequate offer will result in creating, for the taxpayer, an expectation of a fresh start toward compliance with all future filing and payment requirements."

57(10)1.2
COMPROMISE OBJECTIVES

1) To resolve accounts receivable which cannot be collected in full or on which there is a legitimate dispute as to what is owed.

2) To effect collection of what could reasonably be collected at the earliest time possible and at the least cost to the government.

3) To give taxpayers a fresh start to enable them to voluntarily comply with the tax laws.

57(10)1.3
PUBLIC POLICY

1) There are rare circumstances where acceptances of an offer may not be in the best interests of the government. Consequently, an offer may be rejected even though it can be shown conclusively that the amount offered is greater than what could be collected in any other manner. This will generally be limited to situations where public knowledge of the accepted offer would be seriously detrimental to voluntary compliance. A decision to reject an offer for public policy considerations should be rare and should be made only where a clear and convincing case can be made for the detrimental effects of acceptance. The authority is (to) reject Offers in Compromise for public policy reasons is restricted to District Directors.

2) If an offer is to be rejected for public policy reasons, the specific reasons should be fully documented in the case file.

57(0)1.4
TAXES, PENALTIES AND INTEREST CONSTITUTE ONE LIABILITY

A compromise is effective for the entire liability for taxes, penalty, and interest for the years or periods covered by the offer. All questions of tax liability for the year(s) or period(s) covered by such Offer in Compromise are conclusively settled. Neither the taxpayer nor the government can reopen the case unless there was falsification or concealment of assets, or a mutual mistake of a material fact was made which would be sufficient to set aside or reform a contract.

57(10)1.5
COMPROMISE OF EXPIRED TAX LIABILITY

The Service will not accept an Offer in Compromise of a tax which has become unenforceable by reason of lapse of time unless the taxpayer is fully aware of the fact that the collection of the tax is barred. Where such a situation exists, the offer itself (or a separate letter over the signature of the taxpayer) should show that he/she has been advised of the expiration of the statutory period for collection, but, notwithstanding such fact, still desires to have the offer accepted. In this type of case, no collateral agreement is necessary.

57(10)1.6
COMMISSIONER'S DELEGATION OF AUTHORITY TO ACCEPT OFFERS IN COMPROMISE

Delegation Order No. 11 redelegates the compromise authority vested in the Commissioner.

Regional Commissioners, Regional Counsel, District Directors, Assistant District Directors, Service Center Directors, Assistant Service Center Directors, Division Chiefs, Regional Directors of Appeals, Chiefs and Associate Chiefs, Appeals Offices have all been delegated Offer in Compromise acceptance and rejection authority. The authority delegated to Division Chief may not be redelegated. Service Center Directors and Assistant Service Center Directors may redelegate their authority but not lower than to Chief, Compliance Division and Chief, Collection Division (Austin Compliance Center). Chiefs, Field Branch and Chiefs, Special Procedures are delegated authority to accept Offers in Compromise in cases in which the unpaid liability (including any interest, penalty, additional amount or addition to tax) is $100,000 or less and to reject Offers in Compromise regardless of the amount of the liability sought to be compromised. The authority to reject Offers in Compromise for public policy reasons is restricted to District Directors.

57(10)1.62
WITHDRAWAL AUTHORITY

District Directors, Assistant District Directors, Regional Counsel, Regional Directors of Appeals, Chiefs and Associate Chiefs, Appeals Offices are delegated authority to reject and are authorized to acknowledge withdrawal of any offer regardless of the amount of the liability sought to be compromised. The Chief, Field Branch and Chief, Special Procedures are delegated authority to acknowledge withdrawal of any offer regardless of the amount of the liability sought to be compromised. The authority delegated to Chief, Field Branch and Chief, Special Procedures may not be redelegated.

57(10)1.7

JURISDICTIONAL RESPONSIBILITY

57(10)1.71
DISTRICT COLLECTION FUNCTION

1)   District Collection functions have jurisdictional responsibility for the following:

   a)   Consideration of all Offers in Compromise based on doubt as to collectibility as well as preparation of the necessary documents and letters. This includes offers to compromise proposed liabilities which are still the subject of settlement negotiations in the district Examination function or Appeals Office.

   b)   Consideration of penalty only offers. The service center will normally handle these except, in cases where service center management believes they should be considered in the district. The district also has jurisdiction on penalty offers where the issue is in doubt as to collectibility.

   c)   Consideration of all offers to compromise 100-percent penalty assessments based either on doubt as to liability or doubt as to collectibility.

d) Consideration of all offers in default, regardless of whether the basic offer was based on doubt as to liability or doubt as to collectibility.

e) Offers in Compromise based on both doubts as to liability and doubt as to collectibility will be assigned initially to the Collection function for a collectibility determination. If it is determined that the taxpayer may be able to pay an amount in excess of the amount offered, processing of the offer should be discontinued. The offer and copies of related documents should be forwarded through district channels to the service center and/or transferred to the Examination function as a doubt as to liability case. In either case the service center will be notified of the change in jurisdiction and the Form 2515 so notated.

57(10)1.72
DISTRICT EXAMINATION FUNCTION

1) The district Examination function has jurisdictional responsibility for investigation and processing of tax offers based solely on doubt as to liability, including preparation of the necessary documents and letters to effect their disposition.

2) Offers in Compromise received in the district Examination function will be processed in accordance with established Examination procedures. Any requests for information from Collection records should be coordinated through the appropriate Collection function. This may include information on liens, suits, judgments, bankruptcy or decedent estates.

57(10)1.8
DETERMINATION OF LIABILITY

1) Liability Less than Offer – If during the investigation of an offer, the liability is found to be equal to or less than the offer, the amount of the assessment in excess of the liability should be abated, and the taxpayer should be request to withdraw the offer, or the offer should be rejected. The taxpayer will be advised to pay the correct liability.

2) Liability Greater than Offer – If during the investigation of an offer, liability is found to be greater than the offer, but less than the amount assessed, the excess amount of the assessment should be abated. The taxpayer will be informed of the redetermined liability and be advised to pay the correct liability.

3) Definite Determination Cannot be Made – If a definite determination of the liability cannot be made, but there is doubt about the liability, the degree of doubt may be measured and the case closed by compromise. The amount acceptable will depend upon the degree of doubt found in the particular case.

4) The Examination function will dispose of completed offer investigations in essentially the same manner as the Collection function, except that:

a) The processing performed in the Collection function will be performed by the Quality Review Staff in accordance with existing Examination procedures.

b) Cases shall be referred to the Criminal Investigation function for concurrence if the following conditions exist:

1. The merits of the ad valorem fraud or negligence penalty are involved;

2. The case if one in which the Special Agent had recommended assertion of such a penalty in the final report in the case and;

3. The district Examination function is recommending acceptance of the offer.

c) If the Criminal Investigation function concurs in the recommended disposition of the case, concurrence should be made and by memorandum the entire file returned to the district Examination function for processing. If the Criminal Investigation function does not concur and no agreement can be reached with the Examination function as to the disposition of the offer, the entire file shall be forwarded to the district director for resolution. Thereafter, the case will be processed in accordance with established procedures. This is applicable only to cases in which no prosecution has been recommended or the question of prosecution has been settled and the criminal case closed.

d) In those offers accepted by the Examination function, the appropriate Form 7249, Offer Acceptance Report, should be forwarded to Collection for inclusion in the public inspection file.

e) If the offer was rejected or withdrawn, Form 1271, Rejection and Withdrawal Memorandum, and accompanying memorandum should be forwarded to Collection.

57(10)1.9
CASES PENDING IN DISTRICT EXAMINATION FUNCTION

When an offer to compromise a proposed liability is submitted on the basis of inability to pay during the examination process, the offer should be considered by the district office in the same manner as any other inability to pay case. If it appears to be an acceptable amount based on a preliminary analysis of the taxpayer's financial statement, the Examination function will secure from the taxpayer conditional agreement on a definite liability. The agreement form should be held in escrow pending final action on the offer. If the offer is accepted by a delegated official, action will then be taken to have the tax assessed. The acceptance letter should not be mailed to the taxpayer until the assessment has been made. It should be noted that if a statutory notice of deficiency has been sent, the period for filing a petition with the Tax Court is not suspended.

57(10)1.(10)
JURISDICTION OF THE APPEALS OFFICES

1) When an offer is based in whole or in part on doubt as to liability and the Appeals Office has determined the liability or the case is pending before the Appeals Office, the district director will forward the offer to Appeals for consideration.

2) If an Offer in Compromise based on doubt as to liability is pending in the Appeals Office, the Appeals Office may call upon the district director to conduct any investigation deemed necessary to reach a conclusion on the merits of the case. These investigations should be conducted as expeditiously as possible.

3) If any offer is submitted only on doubt as to collectibility and the liability was previously determined by Appeals, the acceptability of the offer will be determined by Appeals, the acceptability of the offer will be determined by the district office.

4) If an offer is submitted only on doubt as to collectibility and the liability is pending in Appeals, the Appeals Office will be notified and asked whether there is any objection to consideration. The Appeals Office will respond within 30 days. The actual investigation of the offer will be deferred during that period pending the response of the Appeals Office. The Appeals Office will inform the district director of any objection by memorandum.

5) If there are no objections and the offer is to be investigated, the Appeals Office will normally secure the taxpayer's conditional agreement to the liability or to the revised amount determined to be due. If the offer is accepted, the Appeals Office will be notified and it will arrange to have the liability assessed. The acceptance letter should not be mailed until the assessment has been made.

6) If the offer is rejected, Appeals will be notified so that they can again consider the merits of the liability.

7) It should be noted that the filing of an offer does not stay the running of the 90-day period set forth in a deficiency notice.

57(10)1.(11)
TAX COURT CASES

1) If an offer is submitted on a Tax Court case and it is based on doubt as to liability, the offer will be forwarded to the appropriate Appeals Office for consideration. It will be Appeals responsibility to work that offer.

2) If an offer is based solely on doubt as to collectibility, the procedures for handling Appeals cases will be followed.

3) When an offer is to be investigated, Appeals will normally secure a stipulation agreement to the proposed liability. This will normally be held in escrow.

4) If the offer is recommended for rejection, Appeals will be notified. Appeals will have 10 days to provide the district office with any information that should be weighed in making the final decision. However, the district office will decide whether to reject the offer and provide the taxpayer with the necessary appeal rights.

5) If the offer is accepted by the district office, Appeals will take the necessary action to get the stipulation filed with the Tax Court. The Appeals Office will then take steps to have the tax assessed. The acceptance letter should not be issued until the tax is assessed.

57(10)1.(12)
APPEAL OF REJECTED OFFERS

1) When Appeals decides that an offer is to be accepted, Appeals will take all the appropriate acceptance procedures. After the required reports have been signed by the delegated official, the case will be returned to the district office for processing.

2) When Appeals sustains the proposed rejection of the offer, Appeals will notify the taxpayer and the offer file will be returned to the district office for processing.

57(10)1.(13)
CASES UNDER JURISDICTION OF DEPARTMENT OF JUSTICE

1) The Service does not have the authority to accept an Offer in Compromise in the following types of cases:

   a) An offer covering a liability "in suit."

   b) Cases where the liability has been reduced to judgment.

   c) Cases in which recommendation for prosecution is pending in the Department of Justice or United States Attorney's Offices including cases in which criminal proceedings have been instituted but not disposed of.

   d) Cases in which a recommendation for prosecution is pending in the Office of the Chief Counsel, and in related cases in which Offers in Compromise have been submitted.

   e) Cases in which the acceptance of an offer by the Service is dependent upon the acceptance of a related offer or upon a settlement under the jurisdiction of the Department of Justice.

   f) The Chief Counsel will ordinarily be called upon for views and a recommendation on the acceptability of an offer on a liability under the jurisdiction of the Department of Justice. The district director will usually be requested to conduct an investigation of the taxpayer's financial condition and to make a recommendation regarding acceptance. Any amounts received by the district in payment of an offer or related collateral agreement accepted by the Department of Justice should be forwarded directly to the appropriate service center for posting.

57(10)2

MANAGEMENT OF THE OFFER PROGRAM

57(10)2.1
GENERAL

1) Management has the following responsibilities under the offer program:

    a) To ensure that the spirit and intent of Policy Statement P-5-100 are adhered to.

    b) To establish a procedural plan for reviewing Forms 656, Offer in Compromise, received directly from taxpayers to determine whether they are processable before sending them to the service center for processing. This could be accomplished either by each revenue officer doing the review or having the review centralized.

    c) To establish a procedural plan most appropriate for the district for handling the investigation, review and approval of offers. The issues to be covered include the following:

        1. *Receipt of Form 2515, Form 656 and Form 433A/B from the service center.*

        2. *Receipt and distribution of transcripts.*

        3. *Research of Special Procedures files.*

        4. *The assignment of offer investigations.*

        5. *Review and processing of completed investigation.*

        6. *Maintenance of information necessary to complete Form 4196, Collection Quarterly Report of Offer in Compromise Activity.*

        7. *Input of status 71 and storage of TDAs when collection is being withheld.*

        8. *Prompt resumption of collection action when an offer is rejected using information developed during offer investigation.*

        9. *Reversal of all status 71.*

d) The procedural plan should be designed to ensure the following:

1. *Timely processing, to ensure offers are competed within a reasonable time frame. Absent unusual circumstances it is the expectation that offer investigations be completed within six months.*

2. *Quality investigation limited to what is actually necessary.*

3. *Limited review.*

There is no requirement that the Special Procedures function be involved in this process.

e) The Service Center Collection Branch should be advised by each district of the organizational unit to receive all offer referrals and questions for that particular district.

57(10)2.2
FOLLOW-UP PENDING OFFER

No later than February 1st of each year, the service center will prepare and forward to the office having jurisdiction, a list of all pending Offers in Compromise more than six months old. The receiving office will report whether the case is opened or closed, returning a copy of the list to the service center within 30 days of its receipt.

57(10)3
POST REVIEW OF OFFERS IN COMPROMISE

57(10)3.1
REGIONAL REVIEW OF COLLECTION ACTIVITY ACCEPTANCES, REJECTIONS AND WITHDRAWALS

1) The Assistant Regional Commissioner (Collection) will establish a system of regional post reviews annually to sample a cross section of all types of offer cases. The sample size, mix of open and closed cases and methodology will be determined based on regional needs.

2) *In those cases where regional post review discloses a substantial error in fact or judgment on the part of a Collection employee, the region will prepare an advisory memorandum to the appropriate office. A periodic digest or compendium of review findings may also be prepared by the region and sent to district offices and/or service centers in the region.*

A copy of the digest, when prepared, should also be sent to the National Office, Assistant Commissioner (Collection), Attention: CO:O. All memoranda and digests should be edited to comply with disclosure regulations. See IRM 1272, Disclosure of Official Information Handbook, texts (12)70 through (12)75.

3) During the post review of completed offers, the regional reviewer also may identify unique cases and prepare an abstract of each such case. These abstracts together with recent IRM changes should be included in the digest of findings, if one is prepared.

4) The review should also look for uniform application of Policy Statement P-5-100.

57(10)3.2
NATIONAL OFFICE REVIEW OF OFFERS

The National Office will conduct periodic reviews as they relate to performance under the Annual Business Plan.

57(10)3.3
REGIONAL REVIEW OF EXAMINATION ACTIVITY ACCEPTANCES, REJECTIONS AND WITHDRAWALS

1) The Assistant Regional Commissioner (Examination) will establish a system of regional post review of all offers (acceptances, rejections and withdrawal) with liabilities of $5,000 or more (Chief Counsel cases are excluded from all post reviews). In this post review, documents for cases requiring review will be screened and, if required, the files on the cases may be requisitioned. This activity should be combined with the regular Examination post review program. Technical, accounting and procedural phases should be emphasized during the post review of all cases.

2) In those instances where regional review discloses a substantial error in fact or in judgment, the Regional reviewer will prepare an advisory memorandum to the office concerned. A copy or a digest may be sent to all other district offices in the region. All memoranda and digests should be edited to comply with disclosure regulations. See IRM 1272, Disclosure of Official Information Handbook, texts (12)70 through (12)75.

57(10)4
COLLECTION ACTIVITY REPORTING INSTRUCTIONS OF OFFER IN COMPROMISE ACTIVITY

In order to evaluate the Offer in Compromise program and disposition of cases, the National Office requires quarterly reporting on Form 4196, Collection Quarterly Report of Offer in Compromise Activity (report Symbol NO-5000-108). Instructions for the preparation and submission of the form are contained in IRM 5872.5.

57(10)5

ADVISING TAXPAYERS OF OFFER PROVISIONS

57(10)5.1
GENERAL

1) When criminal proceedings are not contemplated and an analysis of the taxpayer's assets, liabilities, income and expenses show that a tax liability cannot be realistically collected in full, the possibility of an Offer in Compromise will be discussed with the taxpayer (see 7(10)1 of LEM V).

2) The taxpayer will be advised what an offer is, what the Service procedures and policies are with respect to offers, what forms must be completed, and what benefits the taxpayer will receive from an offer acceptance. The taxpayer should be instructed to read the entire Form 656 including the instructions carefully. When necessary, the Service employee will assist the taxpayer in preparing the required forms.

3) Taxpayers will also be advised that collection will normally be withheld unless it is determined that the offer is delaying tactic and collection is in jeopardy. However, if the taxpayer is making payments under an installment payment agreement, the taxpayer should be told to continue the payments.

4) Before an offer is submitted, the taxpayer will not be told what specifically to offer. The taxpayer will be responsible for initiating the first specific proposal for compromise. However, the taxpayer should be advised that the proposal should not be a "fishing expedition" but a legitimate compromise proposal based on the ability to pay. The taxpayer should be advised that the service does not operate on the theory that "something is better than nothing."

5)   The taxpayer should be encouraged to submit a deposit as a sign of good faith. The taxpayer should be advised that if the offer is rejected, the service will return the deposit unless the taxpayer authorizes in writing that the deposit may be applied to the liability.

6)   The Revenue Officer should determine what information (e.g. evaluation, bank statements) is still needed to verify the ability to pay. The taxpayer should be encouraged to submit the information with the offer since the sooner this information is available the sooner the Service can make a decision.

7)   The taxpayer should be advised that submission of an offer does not constitute acceptance. No offer is accepted until the appropriate delegated official approves acceptance and the taxpayer is notified by letter that the offer has been accepted.

8)   The taxpayer will be advised that no abatement will be made or tax liens released until the total amount offered, including interest on any deferred payments, has been paid in full.

9)   The taxpayer will be advised that acceptance will require the taxpayer to comply fully with all filing and paying requirements of the law for five years. The taxpayer will also be advised that default of the condition shall be treated the same as default in payment under paragraph (7) on Form 656.

10) The taxpayer will be advised that they waive certain refunds or credits they may otherwise be entitled to receive.

11) The taxpayer will be advised that after the offer amount is paid the accrued interest must also be paid. Interest is due from the date of acceptance until the amount offered is paid in full. The interest provision of deferred payment offers should be explained and that Letter 277(C) will be sent reflecting the amount of interest due and a request for payment.

57(10)5.2
SOURCES OF OFFER FUNDS

1)   When discussing offer possibilities with the taxpayer, sources of potential funds should be discussed. Some potential sources could be:

a)   A non-liable spouse who has property which he/she may be interested in utilizing to secure a compromise of a spouse's tax debt.

b)   Relatives or friends

c)   Lending institutions

d)   Employers

e) Suppliers

f) Customers

57(10)5.3
LIENS ON PENDING ASSESSMENTS

If the offer is to provide for deferred payments and no lien has been filed, it is advisable to inform the taxpayer that to protect the government's interest, a lien will be filed after a proposed liability is assessed. This will avoid any misunderstanding. However, care should be taken to ensure that the lien will not adversely impact the taxpayer's ability to raise the funds necessary to satisfy the offer. See Policy Statement P-5-47.

57(10)6
PREPARATION OF THE OFFER (FORM 656)

57(10)6.1
NAME AND ADDRESS OF TAXPAYER

The full name, address, Social Security Number, and/or Employer Identification Number of the taxpayer must be entered on Form 656. If the liability is joint and both parties wish to make the offer, both names must be shown. If the taxpayer is singly liable for a liability (e.g., employment taxes) and jointly liable for a liability (e.g., income taxes) and only one person is submitting the offer, only one offer must be submitted. If the taxpayer is singly liable for one liability and jointly liable for another and both joint parties are submitting the offer, two offers must be submitted, one for the separate liability and one for the joint liability.

57(10)6.2
TOTAL LIABILITY ON FORM 656, OFFER IN COMPROMISE

1) A taxpayer must list all unpaid tax liabilities sought to be compromised in item (1) on Form 656. The type of tax and the period of the liability must be specifically identified. Examples of the most common liabilities involved and the proper identification are as follows:

a) Income tax for the year(s) 19XX...

b) Withholding and Federal Insurance Contributions Act taxes for the period(s) ended 9/30/XX, 12/31/XX...

c) Federal Unemployment Tax Act taxes for year(s) 19XX...

d) 100-percent penalty assessment incurred as a responsible person of Y Corporation for failure to pay withholding and Federal Insurance Contributions Act Taxes for the periods ended 9/30/XX, 12/31/XX...

e) Penalty for failure to file income tax return(s) for the year(s) 19XX.

57(10)6.3
AMOUNT OF OFFER

1) The total amount offered should be shown. If any amount is to be paid on notice of acceptance of the offer or at any later date, the taxpayer must include in item (2) as follows:

a) The amount, if any, deposited at the time of filing the offer.

b) Any amount deposited on a prior offer which is to be applied on the offer. (This does not include any amount the taxpayer previously authorized the Service to apply directly to the tax liability.)

c) The amount of any subsequent payment and the date on which each payment is to be made.

57(10)6.4
TERM OF PAYMENT

1) *A cash offer is one where the total amount offered is paid with the offer.*

2) *A deferred payment offer is one where any part of the amount offered is to be paid at any date(s) after submission of the offer.*

3) *The terms of a deferred payment offer should be precisely stated so there can be no doubt as to the taxpayer's intent if the offer is accepted. The due date of each payment should be specified, as in the following examples:*

a) $5,000.00 deposited with the offer and the balance of $25,000.00 to be paid within 30 days after the date of notice of the offer's acceptance.

b) $3,000.00 deposited with the offer and the balance of $25,000.00 to be paid at the rate of $1,000.00 per month, beginning on the 15th day of the month after the date of notice of the offer's acceptance and on the 15th day of each month thereafter.

4) In cases where deferred payment offers are submitted, the payments may begin immediately upon the submission of the offer especially if they come from current income, or upon notice of acceptance. Payments should be monthly on a deferred payment offer. The offer should be liquidated in the shortest time possible. If the balance of the offer is to be paid in one sum or in a series of installments which involve borrowing or liquidating certain assets, deferred payments should begin at or within a specified time after notice of acceptance. It is not practical to have a taxpayer liquidate assets where values may fluctuate, without knowing that the offer is accepted.

5) The Designated Payment Code 09 will be used for payments made on an Offer in Compromise.

57(10)6.5
GROUNDS FOR OFFER

1) Item 9 of Form 656 is to be used for giving the facts and reasons why the Offer in Compromise should be accepted. If the offer is based only on doubt as to collectibility, the taxpayer must submit a detailed statement which describes why the Service cannot collect more than offered from his/her assets and present and future income, taking into consideration that the Service has ten years to collect liability.

2) If the taxpayer has assets or income that are available to him/her but no available to the Service for collection action, the taxpayer must also explain why the Service should not expect some portion of these assets or income to be paid to the Service if the Service is to compromise the tax liability for less than is owed.

3) If the offer is based on doubt as to liability, the taxpayer must submit a detailed statement as to why the liability is not owed.

57(10)6.6
SIGNING THE OFFER

1) Where a husband and wife seek to compromise a joint liability, both must sign to ensure that the waiver and other provisions bind both parties. In the case of a corporation, the corporate name must be entered on the first line and the signature of the president or other authorized officer on the second line.

2) An offer submitted by a qualified fiduciary of the estate of a deceased taxpayer will be binding on the taxpayer's estate to the extent that it would be binding on a taxpayer who submits an offer on his/her own behalf. The fiduciary should submit evidence of his/her qualifications.

3) A Form 2848 is sufficient to allow complete representation for an Offer in Compromise with the exception of Appeals. (See Circular 230 for complete representation requirements of Appeals.) Form 2848 does not have to specifically grant the authority to execute Form 656.

57(10)6.7
OVERPAYMENTS

1) The taxpayer waives certain refunds or credits he or she may otherwise be entitled to receive. These overpayments of any tax or other liability, including interest and penalties, cover periods that end before, within, or as of the end of the calendar year in which the offer is accepted. Offset of any overpayment would be limited to the difference between the tax liability, including statutory additions, and the amount paid on the offer.

2) The overpayment of one spouse may not be applied against the separate liability of the other spouse unless a written consent to credit is obtained. Often consents to credit or the waiver of refunds are executed by related taxpayers with the express condition that they be made only if the offer is accepted.

3) Under no circumstances will this waiver provision be deleted in the case of a taxpayer who seeks a compromise on grounds of doubt as to collectibility.

4) When a tax offer is based solely upon doubt as to liability, and if the amount of the offer reflects such doubt and equals the apparently correct liability, including penalty and interest to date, then the waiver of refunds, included in subdivision (b), Item 4 of Form 656, should be eliminated. Otherwise the waiver of refunds would compel the taxpayer to pay an excessive amount should any refunds covered by the waiver provisions arise. If this waiver provision has not been deleted rom the offer before it reaches the reviewing officials, the deletion should be made before the acceptance recommendation is approved.

57(10)7
STATUTORY WAIVER

57(10)7.1
SUSPENSION OF STATUTE OF LIMITATIONS

1) The compromise agreement on Form 656, Offer in Compromise, provides that the taxpayer agrees to the suspension of the running of the statutory period of limitations on both assessment and collection for the period that the offer is pending, or the period that any installment remains unpaid, and for one year thereafter. This includes the period of time in which the offer is being considered by Appeals. For the suspension provisions to be effective, both the taxpayer and the authorized Service employee must sign the data before the expiration of the statutory period, and the date the employee signs the waiver must be filled in.

2) Where multiple offers are filed by one taxpayer, the effect of the waivers on the offers is cumulative. It should be noted however, that when an offer is filed within one year after rejection or withdrawal of a pervious offer, the overlapping period should not be counted once in determining the suspension of the statutory period of limitations. While there are various methods to determine the new expiration date, only the method shown in Exhibits 5700-21 will be used for uniformity in these calculations.

3) Where an offer is submitted by a proponent other than the taxpayer, who is not authorized to act for the taxpayer, the statutory period for assessment and collection are not suspended unless the taxpayer's signature is secured. The service center or district office, whichever discovers this fact first, will flag the offer in order to alert the examining officer of the possible need to protect both statutory periods.

4) Unless a significant error or omission exists which requires return of the offer to the proponent, to ensure that the waiver provisions are effective, the waiver acceptance in the lower left corner of Form 656 will be signed at the earliest possible time after receipt. If possible, waiver acceptance will be signed on the date a processable offer is received by a delegated employee (in accordance with Delegation Order 42) in the district office or at the service center. The offer is considered pending from the date the delegated Service employee signs and dates the acceptance of the waiver of the statutory period of limitations on Form 656, until it is accepted, rejected or withdrawn. The same procedure will be followed for collateral agreements. (See IRC 6501 and 6502.) The

Service employee authorized to sign the receipt of the waiver in IMF cases only will place the appropriate alpha collection statute expiration code "P" (primary), "S" (secondary) or "B" (both) in red in the far right of the date box at the bottom of Form 656 to identify which taxpayer the extension applies to.

57(10)7.2
COLLECTION WAIVERS–FORM 656, OFFER IN COMPROMISE VIS-A-VIS FORM 900, TAX COLLECTION WAIVER

1) The service takes the position that in any case where the taxpayer and the Service have agreed, by the execution of Form 900, Tax Collection Waiver, to extend the collection statute to a specific date, the acceptance of the waiver of the statute of limitations by an authorized Service employee when an offer is submitted will sus

pend the running of the statute of limitations. This will effectively extend the date specified on Form 900 by the number of days that the offer and any related collateral agreements are pending or by the number of days that any installments under the offer remain unpaid or that any other provisions of the offer are not carried out and for one year thereafter.

2) This position is not governing in the Fifth Circuit (covering Texas, Louisiana and Mississippi) or the Eleventh Circuit (covering Georgia, Florida and Alabama) where the decision in United States v. Newman, 405 F. 2d 189 (5th Cir. 1968), is controlling law. It should be noted that the rule established in United States v. Newman, 405 F.2d 189 (5th Cir. 1968) states that a Form 900 waiver replaces the statutory period of limitation with a date certain beyond which the Government's cause of action is barred. The Form 900 waiver now provides that the date certain specified therein is to be further extended by any Offer in Compromise.

57(10)8
PREPARING THE FINANCIAL STATEMENT

A taxpayer seeking to compromise a liability based on doubt as to collectibility must submit a Form 433-A, Financial Statement for Individuals, Form 433-B, Collection Information Statement for Business, and/or any other financial statement prepared by the taxpayer as long as it conforms with the information provided in the Form 433A/B and is signed under penalties of perjury. The taxpayer's financial statement must reflect "N/A" (not applicable) in those blocks that do not affect the taxpayer.

57(10)9

RECEIPT AND PROCESSING

57(10)9.1
GENERAL

1) When an Offer in Compromise is received from the taxpayer, a determination will be made whether the offer is processable. This determination should be made by the personnel designated under local procedures.

2) If an offer is not processable the waiver acceptance should not be executed and the Form 656 will be returned to the taxpayer within 14 days from receipt. The offer will be returned to the taxpayer specifying what must be corrected or added before offer processing can begin. The taxpayer may correct an unprocessable offer by either:

   1. Entering and initialling the change on the Form 656 submitted or

   2. Filing a new Form 656.

3) An offer is unprocessable if:

   a) *The taxpayer is not identified*

   b) *The liabilities to be compromised are not identified*

   c) *No amount is offered*

   d) *Appropriate signatures are not present*

   e) *Financial statement is not provided*

   f) The amount offered does not equal or exceed the amount shown in item 27 column (d) on Form 433-B or line 37 titled "equity in assets" on Form 433-A.

   g) An obsolete Form 656 has been used.

   h) Under no circumstances will an offer be returned solely on the basis that the cost of investigation does not justify consideration of the offer.

4) One copy of the offer will be retained in the district so that the assignment, initial processing, consideration and investigation of the offer is not delayed. The other two copies of the processable offer will be forwarded to the appropriate service center for processing.

5) The service center will return the processed offer to the appropriate function along with two copies of Form 2515 (Record of Offer in Compromise). One copy of Form 2515 will be used for control purposes.

57(10)9.2
WITHHOLDING COLLECTION ON ACCOUNTS SOUGHT TO BE COMPROMISED

1) Collection activity will be withheld on any open accounts if it is determined that the offer merits consideration and there is no reason to believe that collection of the tax liability will be jeopardized. If there is any indication that the filing of an Offer in Compromise was solely for the purpose of delaying collection of the liability or that the delay would jeopardize the government's interest, immediate steps should be taken to collect the unpaid liability. (See Treasury Regulation 301.7122-1(d)(2) and Policy Statement P-5-97.)

2) If the taxpayer is currently paying under the term of an installment agreement, the taxpayer should be told to continue those payments.

3) Where the grounds for the offer are strictly doubt as to liability and there is no evidence that filing the offer was solely for the purpose of delaying collection or that the delay would jeopardize the government's interest, collection will be withheld.

4) If the accounts are assigned to a revenue officer disposition of the accounts will be held in abeyance until notice of the TC 480 is received.

5) Accounts will be updated to status 71 upon receipt of notification of the TC 480 if a decision has been made to withhold collection.

6) A status 71 should not be input if one of the co-obligors has not submitted an offer on a joint liability.

7) Form 657 (Revenue Officer Report), which requires managerial approval, will be used by the revenue officer assigned the accounts to document the decision to continue or suspend collection activity.

8) When collection is to be withheld the TDAs covering accounts sought to be compromised will not be placed in the closed TDA files so that all case documentation will be available. Local management will determine where the TDA case file will be retained. The Form 657 will be completed and associated with the

revenue officer history documentation and the related TDAs. The Form 657 will include information on collection potential and all investigative steps that have already been taken and the dates of those actions. The Form 657 is to be used by the offer examiner to determine what investigative steps still need to be taken.

57(10)9.3
TAXPAYER CONTACT

1) Within 30 calendar days from receipt of the offer, the examining officer should contact the taxpayer. The taxpayer should be notified of any information that the examiner needs to make a decision. The request should be reasonable and the taxpayer should be given a reasonable time to comply. However, a specified date must be given. The taxpayer will be notified that the offer will be rejected if the information is not supplied.

2) If the taxpayer does not comply, the offer should be rejected absent unusual circumstances. As outlined in Policy Statement P-5-100, the offer process cannot work if the taxpayer does not cooperate.

3) If personal contact cannot be made, Letter 1027(DO) may be used, setting out in as much detail as possible the information needed. Again, the taxpayer will be given a specific deadline and advised of the consequences of noncompliance.

57(10)10

ADEQUATE OFFER

57(10)10.1
DETERMINATION OF ADEQUATE OFFER

1) An offer is adequate if it reasonably reflects collection potential. This will include amounts that can be collected from other parties through suit, assertion of transferee liability, 100 percent penalty and other actions. Additional consideration will be given to assets and income that are available to the taxpayer but beyond the reach of the government.

2) The starting point in the consideration of an offer submitted based on doubt as to collectibility is the value of the taxpayer's assets less encumbrances which have priority over the federal tax lien. Ordinarily, the liquidating or quick sale value of assets should be used. Quick sale or liquidating value is the amount which would be realized from the sale of an asset in a situation where financial pressures cause the taxpayer to sell in a short period of time. It should be recognized, however, that the acceptance of an offer serves the best interest of the government. Therefore, it would not be unreasonable in a given case to use forced sale value in determining collection potential. Additionally, since valuations of property, except cash or cash equivalents, are not scientifically exact, care should be exercised to avoid inflexible, non-negotiable values.

3) The Service also takes into consideration the amount that can be collected form the taxpayer's future income. In evaluating those future prospects, the taxpayer's education, profession or trade, age and experience, health, past and present income will be considered. In evaluating future income potential an evaluation must be made of the likelihood that any increase in real income will be available to pay the delinquent taxes. The Service needs to take into consideration the increasing cost of living as a factor in determining amounts potentially collectible form future incomes.

4) Rejection of an offer solely based on narrow asset and income evaluations should be avoided. The Service should attempt to negotiate offer agreements which are in the best interest of all parties. Included in determining the government's interests are the cost of collection. If an offer is rejected because more can be collected than is offered, it is generally expected that the amount determined to be collectible will actually be collected.

57(10)10.2
NEGOTIATING AN ACCEPTABLE OFFER

1) The examining officer should determine what would be an acceptable offer. The taxpayer will be given an opportunity to increase the offer. Because asset values are generally not carved in stone, offer examiners should remain flexible toward negotiating an offer that, considering all factors, would be in the Government's best interests.

a) If for any reason the offer cannot be given favorable consideration, the taxpayer should be provided the opportunity to withdraw the offer. If the taxpayer withdraws the offer, he/she should be informed that this action forfeits any appeal rights and also resumes the running of the statutory period for collection. Managers should ensure that the withdrawal is not utilized to eliminate the proper investigation of offers that have legitimate collection potential.

b) If the offer is to be rejected, the taxpayer should be advised of the available appeal procedures. If discussions with the taxpayer reflect an understanding of the basis for the planned rejection, the taxpayer should be provided an opportunity to withdraw the offer. Under these circumstances the withdrawal letter should contain the same information as if the offer were actually rejected. The information in these cases will be used to assist in further collection. These offers will be processed in the same manner as rejected.

c) In rejection or withdrawal situations where the taxpayer has made a deposit, the offer examiner should ask the taxpayer to compete Form 3040, Authorization to Apply Offer in Compromise Deposit to Liability, or include a similar authorization in withdrawal letter.

d) In situations where an offer is acceptable and a collateral agreement(s) is warranted, the taxpayer will be informed of such agreement as soon as possible in the negotiation period.

2) If after all attempts to negotiate have failed, the taxpayer should be advised that the offer will be rejected. Every effort should be made to issue the rejection memorandum as soon as possible after the decision to reject has been made.

57(10)10.3
AMDISA CHECK

Although no examination of open, unaudited returns is required when an offer is recommended for acceptance, AMDISA will be checked to determine if any tax years are being examined, such as TEFRA cases etc. If there is a return being examined, the Examination function will be contacted and advised that an offer has been submitted. Action deemed appropriate can then be coordinated between the functions.

57(10)11
AMENDED OFFERS

57(10)11.1
GENERAL

1) Changes in the amount or terms of the offer may be amended by

a) The taxpayer submitting a new Form 656, which is the preferred method;

b) The taxpayer making and initialing a change on the original offer.

2) In those rare instances where an amended offer reflects additional periods and/or class of tax, a new form must be secured.

57(10)11.2
RECEIPT OF AMENDED OFFERS IN THE DISTRICT

1) When an amended offer is received by an office within a district, a copy of the amendment and any payment received will be sent promptly to the Service Center Collection Branch (SCCB). SCCB will forward the amended Form 656 and the required copies of amended Form 2515 to the office of jurisdiction of the original offer. Field investigation should not be delayed during this process.

2) If the amendment is submitted on a new Form 656, the waiver acceptance on the face of the amended offer must be signed with the name and title by the delegated employee before sending a coy to the Service Center Collection Branch.

57(10)11.3
RECEIPT IN THE SERVICE CENTER

Amended offers received in the service center will be forwarded to the office of jurisdiction with a new form 2515, Record of Offer in Compromise, identified by the suffix "A" in the serial number block. The amount of payment received with the amended offer will be entered in item 5 of Form 2515.

57(10)12

OFFER INVESTIGATION

57(10)12.1
GENERAL

1) The purpose of the investigation is to determine whether the amount offered reasonably reflects collection potential. All available internal sources will be used to aid in making a determination regarding the offer. These would include, but are not limited to, the following: financial statements, previous records checks, currently not collectible accounts, 100 percent penalty files, open and closed bankruptcy files and contact with other collection personnel when prior activity is known. The expectation is that

collection issues previously addressed by field personnel will not be reexamined. Reinvestigation of issues already investigated will not be done unless there is convincing evidence that such reinvestigation is absolutely necessary. Offer examiners are not expected to conduct independent investigations. It is expected that the results of previous investigations will be used and only supplemented when necessary. For example, if a Revenue Officer has completed all the investigative requirements as outlined in IRM 5375, Currently Not Collectible Conditions, an offer submitted by the taxpayer can be considered without further investigation. Additionally, investigative actions less than 12 months may be used by the offer examiner.

2) The extent of the investigation should be practically governed by such issues as the amount of the liability, the amount of investigation previously completed and the information included on the taxpayer's financial statement. The amount of investigation will be limited to the amount normally required in a TDA case. Unless unusual circumstances exist, the examination should not extend beyond that required to report a TDA as currently not collectible. Management should take steps to ensure that investigations are not excessive. The fact that an offer has been submitted does not require extraordinary investigative actions. Additionally, officials delegated acceptance authority should not expect the investigative efforts to be beyond what is normally required in a TDA case. Extraordinary actions should not be taken solely because of the existence of an offer. The acceptance, rejection and withdrawal memorandums will include the reasons why personal inspection of assets was warranted.

3) The IDRS Command Code RTVUE will be requested for the taxpayer's last filed return to review for any assets or sources of income not listed on the financial statement. The taxpayer return only need be secured when RTVUE indicates a need.

57(10)12.2
DISTRICT OFFICE TRANSFER OF OFFERS

1) When an offer is received in a district office and the taxpayer is not located within the receiving district, region or service center area, the offer will forwarded through normal channels to the service center serving the district where the taxpayer resides. The appropriate function will prepare a memorandum specifying assignment to the correct district.

2) In situations where the taxpayer's authorized representative is located in a district other than where the taxpayer resides, the offer should normally be assigned to the district where the taxpayer is located.

57(10)12.3
COURTESY INVESTIGATION

If the taxpayer moves or relocates during the course of the offer investigation, the examining officer may decide to request a courtesy investigation rather than transferring the offer. However, if the investigation would be time consuming or complex, the offer and related accounts should be transferred.

57(10)12.4
INDICATIONS OF FRAUD

1) If the examining officer discovers indications of fraud in connection with an Offer in Compromise, the case should be referred to the Criminal Investigation function, in the same manner as any other fraud referral.

2) Action on the offer and contact with the taxpayer should be held in abeyance until the Criminal Investigation function determines a course of action. If the referral is rejected, investigation of the offer can resume. If the case is accepted, the examining officer will not contact the taxpayer regarding the status of the offer until after Criminal Investigation has informed the taxpayer of the fraud investigation. After this has been done, the taxpayer should be informed.

57(10)13

EVALUATION OF SPECIFIC ASSETS

57(10)13.1
CASH

1) The amount of cash on hand, as well as that in savings accounts and on deposit with the offer, should be considered. In analyzing a taxpayer's checking accounts and fluctuating savings accounts, the average balance over a reasonable period (generally 3 months) should be used rather than the amount on hand at a specific date in order to avoid a distorted picture of the taxpayer's cash position. Deposits in escrow accounts should not be overlooked and all special and trust accounts should be fully explored.

2)   Cash deposited with the offer is an asset. However, if any portion of the deposit is borrowed with the provision that the sum must be repaid if the offer is unsuccessful, this amount should be treated as an encumbrance and the balance as the taxpayer's equity. If any portion of the amount borrowed has been repaid during consideration of the offer, this amount should be treated as the taxpayer's equity in deposit. Avoid allowing double exemptions for encumbrances. This most often occurs when the taxpayer borrows money to deposit on the offer and pledges some asset, such as a bank passbook, as collateral. When that happens, the bank deposit is encumbered, but the offer deposit is not.

3)   The Examining officer should determine the taxpayer's interest in the bank accounts by ascertaining the manner in which they are held and by applying the legal principles in the legal Reference Guide for Revenue Officers.

4)   The Examining officer should exercise judgment in determining whether the contents of the taxpayer's safe deposit box warrants personal inspection.

5)   Some term accounts at banks or savings and loan associations may be subject to a penalty for early withdrawal. If it is anticipated that the taxpayer will incur such a penalty by withdrawing funds for payment of the amount offered, the amount of the penalty should be considered an encumbrance.

57(10)13.2
SECURITIES

1)   Listed Stocks – The current value of stocks listed on an exchange or traded daily over the counter can usually be determined by reviewing stock quotations in the daily newspaper. The quick sale value is normally the same as the market value less the cost of sale.

2)   Unlisted Stocks – This type of security is traded by not listed on an exchange or quoted over the counter. Valuation should be determined by taking an average of "bona fide" bid and asking prices over a reasonable period, again allowing for the costs of sale.

3)   Closely Held Stock – A closely held corporation may be defined as one in which the shares of stock are owned by a relatively limited number of stockholders. Frequently, the entire stock is held by members of one family. As a result, little or no trading is found in the stock and there is no established market for the shares. In such circumstances, it will be necessary to rely upon any financial data and relevant information that is available. The sources of such information may include:

a) The taxpayer or his/her designated representative.

b) *Financial publications and periodicals.*

c) *Corporate income tax returns.*

d) *Appraisals prepared by qualified, impartial experts.*

e) *Credit reports.*

4) The value of such stock, for compromise purposes, should reflect the net worth of the assets of the closely held corporation, its earnings record, dividend policy, current financial condition, anticipated future prospects, and its value as a going concern. However, when the taxpayer holds a minimal interest in a closely held corporation, has no control over its affairs, and his/her interest cannot be liquidated, such interest will be considered to have no value for compromise purposes.

57(10)13.3
LIFE INSURANCE

1) Where the insured has reserved the right to change the beneficiary or to borrow against the policy without the beneficiary's consent, the unsecured interest in the policy, including the cash surrender value, is property within the meaning of IRC 6321.

2) The cash loan value, plus all accumulated dividends and interest left with the company, is an asset to considered.

3) For purposes of the offer, cash loan value is the amount the taxpayer can borrow on the policy from the insurance company, minus any automatic premium loans required to keep the contract in force.

4) Information needed to value a taxpayer's cash loan value should include the dates and amounts of any policy loans or automatic premium payments.

57(10)13.4
PENSION AND PROFIT SHARING PLANS

1) *If a taxpayer is required, under terms of employment, to contribute a percentage of his/her gross earnings to a retirement plan and the amount contributed, plus any increments, cannot be withdrawn until separation, retirement, demise, etc., this asset will be considered as having no equity.*

2) *Where the taxpayer is not required as a condition of employment to participate in a pension plan, but voluntarily elects to do so, the equity for compromise purposes shall be the gross amount in the taxpayer's plan reduced by the employer's contributions.*

3) *If the taxpayer is permitted to borrow up to the full amount of his/her equity in a plan, this should be taken into consideration in determining the taxpayer's collection potential.*

4) The current value of property deposited in an Individual Retirement Account (IRA), 401(k), or Keogh Act Plan Account should be considered in determining collection potential. Cash deposits should be included at full value. If assets other than cash are invested (e.g., stock, mutual funds), the current value of the investment should be used to determine collection potential. The penalty for early withdrawal and the additional tax that must be paid should be subtracted to determine this value.

57(10)13.5
FURNITURE, FIXTURES, AND PERSONAL EFFECTS

1) In determining the adequacy of an offer, the taxpayer's valuation of furniture, fixtures, and personal effects listed on the financial statement is generally sufficient. The examining officer should exercise judgment in determining whether the taxpayer's assets warrant personal inspection. It is important to note that assets of substantial artistic or intrinsic value, such as jewelry, paintings or etchings, silverware, oriental rugs, antique furniture, coin, stamp, or gun collections, statuary and the like, should not be overlooked.

2) If the assets consist of business property, the examining officer should take into account any value of the fixtures the taxpayer owns.

3) The statutory exemption from levy applies to the taxpayer's furniture and personal effects and should be taken into consideration in the value of the taxpayer's interest in the property. (See IRC 6334.)

4) In any case where the taxpayer has evidence which proves that the furniture, fixtures and personal effects in his/her house are jointly owned and the assessment is made against only one of the owners the taxpayer proportionate share of the equity should be determined. This should not be less than 50% in the case of husband and wife. The value of the asset after this determination has been made should then be reduced by the statutory exemption.

57(10)13.6
MACHINERY AND EQUIPMENT

1) The value of machinery and equipment is to be determined on the basis of all relevant facts and evidence. Some assets may have value only to the taxpayer or someone in the same business as the taxpayer, while other assets will have a ready market and value easily determined from guides prepared by the industry. The value of some unusual assets, such as farm machinery and specialized equipment, can be ascertained by contacting dealers, or manufacturers of these assets.

2) Factors which should be considered in arriving at quick sale value include the difficulty of dismantling and removing machinery and equipment, the availability and size of the market for such assets, and the adaptability of such assets to other uses.

3) The examining officer may wish to request appraisals or use the services of a valuation engineer where a difficult valuation problem is involved.

4) Generally, the examining officer will use the same techniques as would be used to determine equity in potential seizure situations.

57(10)13.7
TRUCKS, AUTOMOBILES, AND DELIVERY EQUIPMENT

Assets such as trucks, delivery equipment, and automobiles usually have a ready market value which is easily determined from guides prepared by national associations and from information secured from dealers and agencies. The examining officer should exercise judgement in determining whether the taxpayer's vehicle(s) warrant personal inspection. Inspection is generally not necessary.

57(10)13.8
RECEIVABLES

1) Accounts should generally be grouped according to age such as under 90 days old and 90 days and over. However, aging of receivables should be determined on an individual case basis. In addition, a reserve for bad debts should be considered when determining net accounts receivable. Substantial accounts receivable either not pressed for payment or where the debtor is a relative, officer, or stockholder of the taxpayer should be closely examined.

2) In determining the value of the receivables where they have been discounted or pledged, the provisions of IRC 6323(c), dealing with certain commercial transactions and financing agreements, should be reviewed.

3) Notes receivable are acknowledged debts and generally not discounted as drastically as accounts receivable. Each should be examined carefully for underlying collateral and for the ability of the maker to satisfy the debt.

4) Consideration should also be given to what action would be taken on the receivable if the offer was rejected and what the potential recovery would be if levy action was taken.

57(10)13.9
REAL ESTATE

57(10)13.91
GENERAL

1) In determining the value of real estate, the highest and best use of the property must be considered. If the property being evaluated represents a recent purchase by the taxpayer, or if similar property in the vicinity has changed hands recently, such sales are relevant evidence of the value of the property in question. The fluctuation of property values in the area should be considered in determining how current an existing appraisal needs to be.

2) If the taxpayer's valuation was based on an appraisal by a qualified and disinterested appraiser, the taxpayer should provide a copy of each appraisal.

3) Where the property being evaluated was not purchased recently or there have been no recent sales of similar property in the area, the taxpayer may be requested to engage the services of a disinterested, qualified appraiser to appraise the property. However, such a request should be limited to situations where the value cannot be determined through some less costly methods. Normally the same methods used to determine the taxpayer's equity before seizure will be used. (See IRM 56(12)2.1.)

4) The value of any leasehold interest should be ascertained. In many cases, a property interest is retained through the lease contract (see Chapter 300 of IRM 57(16)0, Legal Reference Guide for Revenue Officers.)

5) The assessed valuation of real estate may be taken into consideration in determining the value of real estate when it reasonably reflects the quick or forced sale value or when it can be adjusted by a generally accepted percentage to achieve those values.

57(10)13.92
JOINTLY OWNED REAL PROPERTY

1) When real property is held jointly with another person, or another has some interest in the property, state law determines the extent of the taxpayer's ownership or interest therein. The legal distinction applicable to the terms "tenancy by the entirety," "joint tenancy" and "tenancy in common" will not be discussed here. (See Chapter 300 of IRM 57(16)0, Legal Reference Guide for Revenue Officers.) This subsection deals with Service practice as it relates to the adequacy of an offer where assets are jointly owned. It is reasonable to expect that if a taxpayer wishes to compromise a tax liability, the taxpayer should be asked to include in the amount offered at least a portion of the amount accessible to the taxpayer but unavailable to the Service for collection action.

2) In the consideration of real estate and other related property held by tenancy by the entirety, where the assessment for the liability is made against only one spouse, not less than 20 percent of the net equity in the property based on its quick sale value, should generally be included in the total assets available in arriving at an acceptable Offer in Compromise. (See (4) below.)

3) In the consideration of real estate and other property held by tenancy in common, or joint tenants, where the assessment is made against only one of the owners, the taxpayer's proportionate share of the quick sale value should be included in the total assets. Normally, if husband and wife own real estate as tenants in common, each is deemed to have a 50 percent share in the property. (See (4) below.)

4) These practices are considered equitable, but they are flexible and may be adjusted up or down as circumstances warrant, especially in cases where the other party has made little, if any contribution to the property. There is always the possibility that the character of the property may be changed by death, abandonment or alienation. The overall goal is to determine whether the amount offered reasonably reflects what can be collected in any other manner and is in the overall best interest of the government. Therefore, the criteria in (2) and (3) above may be ignored in appropriate cases.

5)   If the liability is due from both taxpayers jointly, the total quick sale value of the property should be reflected in their offer. If an offer covers the joint liability of husband and wife, as well as the husband's or wife's individual liability, the suggested method of determining the realizable equity would be to apply it first to the joint liability, and if any equity remains, the 20% or 50% computation may be applied to the remainder. (See (2) and (3) above.)

57(10)13.10
USE OF VALUATION ENGINEERS

If dissatisfied with the taxpayer's appraisal or, where necessary, to complete the investigation, the examining officer may require the services of a valuation engineer. The valuation engineer's services should be requested by memorandum to the Examination function, according to regional and district instructions. Recommendations of the engineer will be adopted as the position of the Service unless there are clear and compelling reasons for not doing so. Use of valuation engineers should be limited to cases where no other reasonable alternatives are available.

57(10)13.11
EVALUATION OF INCOME

1)   There is no fixed percentage of a taxpayer's present or future earned and unearned income that must be accounted for in deciding the acceptability of an offer. The issue is how much of the taxpayer's income is or will be realistically available to pay the delinquent taxes. In evaluating future prospects the taxpayer's education, profession or trade, age and experience, health, past and present income will be considered. An evaluation must be made of the likelihood that any increase in real income will be available to pay the delinquent taxes. Consideration should not be given to increases in income solely based on an increase in the cost of living. In cases where it is determined that the taxpayer can make installment payments, the Service normally considers that any agreement that requires more than five years to complete has a high probability of not being completed. The Service must then decide the "present value" of those five years of payment. To determine the present value of those payments use chart in Exhibit 5700-19.

2) Generally, if the taxpayer can now pay us "present value," we will give serious consideration to accepting the offer. The present value may also be a considering factor when less than five years remain on the collection statute in determining the acceptability of an offer.

57(10)13.12
POTENTIAL VALUE OF ASSETS AND EARNING POWER

The likelihood of an increase in the value of assets in the near future and any data that might affect the taxpayer's future income and earning power should be considered. An analysis of current income, profit and loss statements, sales records, and orders n hand should be made.

57(10)13.13
BANKRUPTCY, RECEIVERSHIP AND ESTATE CASES

1) *In compromise cases of decedents, estates in process of administration and in bankruptcy and receivership cases, offers must show that the executor, administrator, receiver, trustee or other person making the offer is property authorized to do so. A copy of the order of the court, or other evidence of authorization, should accompany Form 656.*

2) *A general statement of the circumstances which resulted in the bankruptcy or receivership, and the purpose of the receivership; that is, whether the object is liquidation of assets, conservation of assets, foreclosure of a mortgage, reorganization, etc. A copy of the petition in bankruptcy or for the appointment of a receiver, and a copy of the court order appointing the receiver or trustee can be used in lieu of a general statement. Copies of all pertinent schedules field with the court should be furnished.*

3) *Generally it is not the practice of the Service to consider acceptance of an offer submitted by a taxpayer in a Chapter 11, Chapter 12, or Chapter 13 proceeding, since the reorganization plan must provide for the payment of the liability in full.*

4) *In investigating an offer from a decedent's estate, consideration must be given to the amount which may be collectible from the enforcement of any liability for the tax by a beneficiary or transferee.*

57(10)13.14
LIABILITY OF HUSBAND AND WIFE

1) An "innocent spouse" may be relieved of liability in certain cases under IRC 6013(e) and IRC 6653(b). In the event that one of the jointly liable taxpayers claims to be an "innocent spouse," the questions should be referred to the district Examination function for determination.

   a) *Should the offer be acceptable, the report should not be prepared until after the district Examination function has made its determination.*

   b) *If the offer is to be recommended for rejection or withdrawal, the report should be prepared without delay. The report should briefly state that the question was raised and referred to the district Examination function.*

57(10)13.15
EFFECT OF TRANSFEREE LIABILITY ON ADEQUACY OF OFFER

1) If transferee liability exists, an acceptable Offer in Compromise of the transferor's liability would necessarily include a sum substantially equal to the amount the Government might reasonably expect to collect from the transferee. In concluding what amount should be due, consideration must be given to all of the evidence available. One important element is the fact that the burden of proof of transferee liability rests with the government.

2) In borderline cases where there is serious question whether transferee liability may be established an sustained, it has occasionally been possible to compromise by accepting offers which include additional sums in consideration of the transferred assets(s). In other words, the amount acceptable should be based in part on the degree of doubt regarding the sustaining of any transferee liability. The offer examiner and/or the revenue officer who is considering the viability of an offer should obtain as much information as possible about the circumstances surrounding the transfer.

3) In those compromise cases in which the examining officer believes that a transferee assessment should be made, he/she should prepare, in addition to the rejection memorandum, a separate report recommending assertion of the transferee liability. See Chapter 800 of IRM 57(16)0, Legal Reference Guide for Revenue Officers, for a detailed discussion of transferee liability.

57(10)14

COMPROMISE OF EMPLOYMENT AND COLLECTED EXCISE TAX LIABILITIES

57(10)14.1
GENERAL

1) When the same business is operating, we would normally not accept an offer for an amount less than the tax, exclusive of penalties and interest. However, if considering all factors, including the taxpayer's demonstrated ability to stay current, it is obvious that accepting an offer would be in the total best interest of all parties, an offer can be accepted for an amount less than the tax as long as the amount offered reasonably reflects collection potential.

2) Where taxpayers are no longer in the same business as when the liability was incurred, the amount of the offer should reasonably reflect collection potential.

57(10)14.2

COMPROMISING CORPORATE EMPLOYMENT TAX

57(10)14.21
WITHHOLDING AND EMPLOYMENT TAXES

1) When an offer is submitted by a corporation to compromise outstanding employment taxes and such offer does not equal the trust fund portion of the tax, the assertion of the 100 percent penalty need not be held in abeyance pending final disposition of the Offer in Compromise.

2) The statutory waiver on an offer submitted by or on behalf of a corporation to compromise its tax liability will not extend the time for assessing the 100 percent penalty against a responsible person. It has been held that a 100 percent penalty provided by IRC 6672 is a liability separate and distinct from the corporate tax. In view of the distinct and separate character of the two liabilities, action extending the period of limitations as to one liable party does not automatically have a like effect on the other party.

3) An acceptable offer would be one which represents an amount which could reasonably be collected in any other manner either from the corporation or the responsible persons.

57(10)14.22
100 PERCENT PENALTY CONSIDERATIONS

1) In order to protect the interest of the government when the 100 percent penalty can be asserted, one of the three alternatives below should be used whenever an offer has been submitted by or on behalf of a corporation to compromise a "trust fund" liability.

   a) Assess the 100 percent penalty against the responsible persons.

   b) Secure Form 2750, Waiver Extending Statutory Period for Assessment of 100 Percent Penalty, from each responsible person. Other protective measures can also be taken; e.g., securing a collateral agreement, a mortgage, an escrow arrangement, or a bond from the corporation's principal officer or stockholder.

   c) Require the corporation and its responsible persons to make a joint offer covering the taxes assessed against the corporation and the 100 percent penalty not yet assessed. Secure appropriate waivers, etc., from responsible parties (See IRM 5633.21). If the joint offer is accepted, it is not necessary to assess the 100 percent penalty, since payment(s) on the offer will be credited to the corporate liability. Should the offer be defaulted and thereafter terminated, the 100 percent penalty can then be assessed, since the responsible parties will have executed the appropriate waiver(s).

2) The method selected will be governed by the specific facts of each case. Should the joint offer in (1)(c) above be used, it must be clearly stated on the offer that it has been submitted to compromise the individual's liability for the 100 percent penalty as well as the total liability of the corporation.

3) None of these protective steps need be taken if:

   a) The corporation files a cash offer equaling the proposed trust fund portion of its liability; and

   b) There is enough time left, before the statutory period expires for assessing the penalty, in which to complete action on the corporation's offer.

4) In 100 percent penalty Offer in Compromise cases, a determination will be made on whether the taxpayer was a stockholder in the company form which the liability arose, and whether the taxpayer has, or will have a capital loss on any stock. Consideration should be given to securing a collateral agreement on Form 2261-C waiving the loss.

57(10)15

COLLATERAL AGREEMENTS

57(10)15.1
PURPOSE AND DEFINITION OF COLLATERAL AGREEMENT

1) A collateral agreement enables the government to collect funds in addition to the amount actually secured via the offer; thereby recouping part or all of the difference between the amount of the offer and the liability compromised.

2) Collateral agreements are not used to enable a taxpayer to submit an offer in a lesser amount than his/her financial condition dictates. Neither should they be used to collect amounts which should have been included with the offer itself.

3) Collateral agreements should not be routinely secured but secured only when a significant recovery can reasonably be expected. For example, a future income collateral would be appropriate where it is reasonably expected that the taxpayer will be receiving a substantial increase in real income. A collateral agreement would not be entered merely on unfounded speculation about real increase in income. Additionally, a collateral agreement should not be secured to cover statistically improbable events such as lottery winnings. Securing of a collateral agreement should be the expectation is that all collateral agreements, except those designed solely to amend and clarify an offer, will be monitored for compliance. Therefore, agreements which require monitoring and which contain terms not in conformance with those outlined in the IRM will not be entered into unless approval is secured form the National Office. The request should be sent by memorandum to the Director of Operations in the office of the Assistant Commissioner (Collection).

4) A collateral agreement can also be used to amend and clarify and offer.

5) In cases where a taxpayer is compromising his/her portion of a joint assessment, a collateral agreement should be secured from the taxpayer submitting the offer as a means of protecting the government's right to collect the liability of the co-obligor.

57(10)15.2
GUIDELINES FOR SECURING COLLATERAL AGREEMENTS AS ADDITIONAL CONDITIONS

1) Future income collateral agreements for both individuals and corporations usually run for a period of five years. The beginning year of the collateral agreement should be the year following the year in which the offer is accepted.

2) *When a taxpayer submits more than one offer to compromise different tax liabilities, a separate agreement should not be secured for each offer. It is not necessary to reference the collateral agreement on the Form 656, but the collateral agreement should accurately describe the offer or offers to which it relates, describing the date and amount of each offer, the types of tax, and the periods covered. If an amended offer is filed after a collateral agreement has been secured, the agreement should be changed to conform with the amended offer.*

3) *When more than one agreement is required from a taxpayer, it is generally advisable to incorporated the terms of the agreements into one collateral agreement document. When one agreement is secured special care should be taken to ensure technical and legal accuracy and consistency of the terms, and to avoid any provisions which would nullify the government's chances of recoupment. When a future income agreement is one of the agreements secured, other provisions, such as those providing for adjustment in the basis of assets or waiver of net operating losses, frequently can be incorporated into paragraph 10 on Forms 2261 and 2261-A, as shown in the following examples:*

   a) *Where an agreement to adjust the basis of assets is incorporated in Form 2261 or 2261-A, item 10, "for the purpose of computing income taxes of taxpayer for all years beginning after 19XX, the basis for certain assets, under existing law for computing depreciation and the gain or loss upon sales, exchange or other disposition shall be as follows:*

   Name of assets_____$_____

   That in no event shall the basis set forth above be excess of the basis that would otherwise be allowable for tax purposes, except for this agreement. The limitations and provisions set forth in paragraphs numbered 5, 6, and 7 of this agreement are also applicable to this paragraph, together with those relating to the release of liens in paragraph numbered 9, subject to payment of any additional amounts of taxes which may become due and payable under the provisions of this paragraph."

b) Where an agreement waiving a net operating loss is incorporated in Form 2261 item 10, "any net operating loss deductions, under the provisions of Section 172 of the Internal Revenue Code."

4) Other agreements, such as a waiver of bad debt loss or other deductions, may also be incorporated as an additional paragraph on the future income agreement, Form 2261 and 2261-A. When another collateral agreement is incorporated in the Form 2261 or 2261-A, care should be taken to see that the provisions of the printed form relating to the amount which can be recouped, the waiver of the statue of limitations default, and release of liens are applicable to the added paragraph. Where there is insufficient space on the Form 2261 or 2261-A to insert such paragraph, simply type the paragraph numbers followed by "See Attached" and fasten a separate sheet containing the added provisions.

5) In lieu of submitting a future income collateral agreement, a taxpayer may increase the amount of his/her offer. The offer should be increased by at least an amount equivalent to what the Government could reasonably expect to recover via the future income agreement.

57(10)15.3
TERMS AND CONDITIONS

1) Under the terms of a future income agreement, each year the agreement is in force, the taxpayer is required to submit Form 3439, Statement of Annual Income (Individual), or Form 3439-A statement of Annual Income (Corporation), and a copy of his/her Federal Income Tax Return, with the payment computed to be due. Individual taxpayer's agreement generally provide for payments ranging from 20 to 50 percent of "annual income" (less Federal Income Tax) in excess of an amount which represents the taxpayers's ordinary and necessary living expenses. "Annual income " as computed under the terms of the agreement is intended to represent all income available to the taxpayer for payment under the collateral agreement in any given year. A figure is excluded for ordinary and necessary living expenses and the payment required represents only graduated percentages of income available to the taxpayer which exceeds ordinary and necessary expenses.

2) In arriving at the amount of annual income to be excluded for ordinary and necessary living expenses, each individual taxpayer's case is unique. The terms should be the result of negotiations between the taxpayer and the Service. The government cannot tell the taxpayer what his/her cost living should be. On the other

hand, the Government is not required to consider every expenditure claimed by the taxpayer as being ordinary and necessary. In working out a mutually acceptable exclusion figure, many factors must be weighed. The Government should consider the anticipated rate of inflation, excepted changes in the size of the family, state and local taxes, FICA taxes withheld and unusual expenses such as alimony, child support and high medical and dental costs. This should be projected over the life of the agreement.

3) The memorandum recommending acceptance should explain the basis for the agreement. Form 433-A and 433-B (if applicable) or Form 4822, Statement of Annual Estimated Personal and Family Expenses, (Examination form), may be used to determine the taxpayer's living expenses. The figures shown thereon should be as accurate as possible.

4) In corporate cases, a similar analysis should be made.

57(10)15.4
DEFINITION OF "ANNUAL INCOME"

1) If the examining officer and the taxpayer decide that some of the deductions taken in arriving at the adjusted gross income of individuals or the taxable income of corporations should not be allowed in computing, "annual income", the standard definition on the forms 2261 and 2261-A should be changed before the agreement is signed. However, such changes should extremely rare because it will increase the cost on monitoring.

2) Both the individual and corporate taxpayer are permitted to exclude from "annual income" the Federal income tax paid for the year for which annual income is being computed, and a payment made under the terms of the Offer in Compromise itself (Form 656) for the year in which such payment is made. However, taxpayers may not exclude payments on future income agreements form "annual income." A provision limiting deductions for net operating losses is also included on the Forms 2261 and 2261-A. Waiver overpayments made under the terms of an Offer in Compromise do not constitute "payments made under the terms of an Offer in Compromise" which can be used as a deduction when computing annual income for the purpose of this section.

3) It is usually advisable to use the standard definition on the agreement forms. However, in certain cases, to assure maximum recoupment, it is sometimes essential to refine the definition of "annual income" and include features pertinent to a specific

situation. Changes should not be made which might nullify the government's chance of recoupment and thereby make the agreement ineffective, or give any taxpayer a special or added advantage. For example, the definition of "annual income" would not ordinary be changed to include a deduction for state income or sales taxes paid, which are includible under necessary living expenses.

4) In certain Offers in Compromise cases it is in the best interest of the government to include contributions made by the taxpayer to a Keogh plan or an Individual Retirement Account (IRA), in computing "annual income" under the terms of a Form 2261. Additional paragraph should be added to the form and numbered "10" or the next ascending number. The paragraph must specifically provide for the contributions to be added back to adjusted gross income, as defined in IRC 62, in computing "annual income."

a) The paragraph to be used to included contributions to a Koegh plan is as follows:

"That in computing annual income, the deductions allowed by Code Section 404 for contributions on behalf of self-employed individual will be added back adjusted gross income as defined in Code Section 62."

b) The paragraph to be used to include contributions to an individual Retirement Account as follows:

"That in computing annual income, the deduction allowed by Code Section 219 for contributions to an individual retirement account described in Code Section 408(a) or for an individual retirement annuity described in Code Section 408(b), will be added back to adjusted gross income as defined in Code Section 62."

57(10)15.5
COMPUTATION OF "ANNUAL INCOME"

1) The term, "annual income" must be interpreted strictly in accordance with the definition set forth in the collateral agreement accepted as a part of the taxpayer's offer. The definitions on Form 2261 and 2261-A pinpoint the deductions which must be added back to adjusted gross income (individuals) and taxable income

(corporations), the addition of nontaxable income and deduction permitted for income tax paid and the payments made on the Offer in Compromise in computing "annual income." Experience has shown, however, that misunderstanding arise over which deductions and additions are proper under the "annual income definition-particularly with regards to the definition of Form 2261.

2) To clarify the computations of "annual income" for individuals, the usual deductions and additions are outlined below. The starting point in arriving at the "annual income" figure is adjusted gross income as defined in IRC Section 62 with the following deductions and additions:

   a) Add to adjusted gross income:

      1. Losses from sale or exchange of property; these includes losses from sale or disposition of capital assets of the taxpayer, bad debt loss, worthless stock, etc., which were taken as a deduction in arriving at adjusted gross income on the taxpayer's return. "Sale or exchange" is intended to include dispositions through foreclosures repossession, etc.

      2. All nontaxable income and profits, or gains from any source whatsoever (including the fair market value of gifts, bequests, devises, or inheritances)-this is intended to be all-inclusive and covers all income, earning, gifts, etc., not includible on taxpayer's return but which were actually or constructively received. These include items such as sick pay, insurance proceeds, and nontaxable gains realized form a condemnation award or involuntary conversion under IRC Section 1033. As an example of what might be considered a gift, it was held that a taxpayer's interest in a home, which was purchased with the wife's funds after his offer was accepted and titled in the names of the taxpayer and wife, was considered a gift to the taxpayer and the fair market value of his interest included in "annual income."

3) Also IRC Section 86 provides that gross income will include a certain portion of Social Security and Railroad Retirement benefits over a base income amount. (It should be noted that in the case of a married taxpayer filing a separate return, the base amount is zero). Since the law now provides for inclusion of these benefits in gross income, they also comprise a portion of the taxpayer's annual income for purposes of computing the amount due on the collateral agreement.

b) Subtract from adjusted gross income:

1. Federal income tax actually paid for the year in question at the time the "annual income" statement is submitted. Appropriate adjustments may be in the Statement of Annual Income at a later date, it and when additional taxes are paid or refund is made, even though occurring in a subsequent year. Self- employment tax is considered a part of income tax and, therefore, deductible but Federal Insurance Contributions tax withheld from wages may not be deducted. When a joint return is filed and only one spouse is liable under the collateral agreement, it is reasonable to require the taxpayer to compute his/her deduction for current Federal income tax paid on the basis of the ratio of his/her adjusted gross income to the total joint adjusted gross income.

2. Payment made on the Offer in Compromise itself for the year in which such payment is made, 1.2 payment made on the principal amount of the offer, together with any interest paid. Amounts deposited with the offer is accepted, since prior to the date the offer is accepted, such deposits are funds of the taxpayer and maybe withdrawn at any time. Payment made under the collateral agreement may not included as a deduction under "payments made under the terms of an Offer in Compromise" which can be used as a deduction when computing annual income for the purpose of this section.

c) Taxpayer is a stockholder in closely held corporation in cases where there is a possibility that the taxpayer could incorporate his/her business, manipulate earning from a corporation in which he/she is stockholder, or in a similar manner attempt to defeat the purpose of the collateral agreement, the definition of "annual income" of Form 2261 embraces provisions which require the taxpayer to include his/her proportionate share of the :corporate annual income" in excess of $10,000 using a basis the corporate net income determined for federal income tax purposes subject to limitations set forth in the paragraph numbered 3 of Form 2261. If the corporation's taxable year does not coincide with the taxpayer's taxable year, the taxpayer should include his/her proportionate share of the net corporate income for the corporation year ended during the year for which the annual income is being computed.

57(10)15.6
ENFORCEABLE CONTRACT

The election by the taxpayer to be taxed as a corporation does not change status of the income from such business for the purpose of computing "annual income" as an individual under the collateral agreement. Nor does it affect the individual's basis for certain assets. The courts have not hesitated to penetrated the corporate veil and look beyond the juristic entity at the actual and substantial beneficiaries. Therefore, in computing the amount due and payable by the Individual under the collateral agreement, the income earned while electing to be taxed as a corporation under IRC 1361, and the pro rata share of the corporation's earning to be re-computed in accordance with the terms and conditions of the collateral agreement – should be included in the amount "annual income" figure. Failure to pay the amount due shall constitute a default within the meaning and intent of the default paragraph contained in the collateral agreement.

57(10)15.7
AGREEMENTS REDUCING THE BASIS OF ASSETS

1) In cases where the basis of assets owned by the taxpayer is substantial, a collateral agreement reducing the basis of assets may be considered. Negotiations with the taxpayer could result in an adjusted basis downward as low as zero. For 2261-B, collateral Agreement-Adjusted Basis of Specific Assets, is used to reduce the basis of assets. It should provide for the reduced basis as of the beginning of the taxpayer's tax year in the year offer is accepted or the following year.

2) Assets which are adaptable to reduced basis include land, buildings, expensive items of machinery and equipment, stocks, bonds, interest in a partnership, certain noted, accounts receivable, etc. Assets not adaptable to a reduced basis are those of negligible value, accounts and notes receivable if they consist of numerous small items, inventories and other items which are depleted rapidly or are difficult to trace.

3) It is obvious that an agreement reducing the basis of assets is not appropriate in every case. For example, where the difficulty of determining compliance and the creation of tax problems would offset or nullify the benefit of the reduction, or where the liability involved is small, an agreement of this type would be of no value.

57(10)15.8
AGREEMENTS WAIVING LOSSES

1) Where net operating losses and capital losses were incurred before, during or after the periods covered by the offer, particularly if such losses may be carried over two years ending after the date of acceptance, a collateral agreement waiving any carryback or carryover benefits may be considered, thus increasing the taxpayer's tax liabilities for the affected periods. Form 2261-C, Collateral Agreement—Waiver of Net Operating Losses and Capital Losses, is designed to cover all net operating losses, capital losses, and unused investment credits, sustained for the year indicated, subject to the limitation contained in the form. In corporation cases, if a future income collateral agreement has been secured on Form 2261-A, it is not necessary to secure a separate agreement waiving operating losses incurred prior to the calendar year in which the offer is accepted, since such a waiver is incorporated in Form 2261-A.

2) When an individual or other non-corporate taxpayer has a net capital loss carryover, consideration should be given to securing a collateral agreement waiving any carryover benefits. Under IRC 1212(b), individuals and other noncorporate taxpayers may carry over a net capital loss for an unlimited period until the loss is exhausted. Use Form 2261-C in this situation.

3) A collateral agreement waiving capital losses, is effective until the full amount of the liability which was compromised, plus interest and penalty that would have been due in the absence of the compromise, is recouped by payments on the offer and related collateral agreement. To arrive at the amount of the loss carryover which may be available after full payment of the liability, the original loss would be reduced by the amount of capital loss which would have been taken in the absence of compromise.

57(10)15.9
AGREEMENT FOR ONE OBLIGOR INVOLVED IN JOINT ASSESSMENT

1) An individual may submit an offer to compromise his/her portion of a joint liability. The situation may arise in the case of husband and wife, or any other individual jointly and severally liable for the tax. The question then is whether such a compromise would in effect compromise the liability of both and prevent the collection of any additional sum from the other party. Very little has been written on the subject in a tax situation except in the case of United States v. Wainer (C.A. 7th 1954) 211F.2d 669. In that case, the Court

reserved the government's right to collect the balance of the tax from the possessor of interest in the property, after crediting the assessment with the amount paid under the terms of the compromise made with the co-obligor. Chief Counsel's opinion regarding these situation is outlined as follows:

a) *In general under the provisions of the Code the liability for the tax on a joint return is expressly made "joint and several." These words have an established and definite common law meaning. Congress did not specifically provide that the release of one of the obligors should discharge the other. We must, therefore, look to the common law, or to the statues of the various states, to determine the effect of the release. The state statues on this subject are not uniform.*

b) Effect of State Legislation—Many States have enacted legislation d eclaring that a release of a joint or several obligor shall not effect the other obligors. An express reservation of the right to proceed against a co-obligor who is not a party to the release is held by many courts to prevent the release from discharging the other party. However, there is no uniformity as to the amount for which the other obligor may be held. In some States, the balance can be collected from the other obligor(s) whereas in others, only the proportionate share of the total liability can be collected from them. Other courts follow the common law rule which requires the execution of an agreement (between the Service and the taxpayer) known as a "covenant not to sue" the "released" obligor. In this type of case, the balance of the unpaid liability can be collected from the remaining obligor or obligors.

c) Conclusion in light of the case of United States vs. Wainer, it is reasonably clear that the same rule regarding the legal effect of the release of a co-obligor in cases involving contracts and judgements will be applied in cases involving Federal taxes. State statutes and decisions on the subject will be considered and followed, although no husband-wife joint tax assessment case involving the release or compromise of tax liability of one them appears as yet to have reached the courts. It would not seem to be safe to proceed on any other principle.

2) To protect the interest of the Government insofar as collection from the other parties to a joint assessment (husband and wife or other joint obligors) is concerned, a co-obligor agreement should be secured from the maker of the offer. If both parties have submitted separate offers which are going to be recommended for acceptance, co-obligor agreements will be secured from each taxpayer. Every attempt should be made to secure a joint offer thus, eliminating the

need for a co-obligor agreement. If this attempt is unsuccessful, the execution of a collateral agreement such as Pattern Letter P-229, exhibit 5700-24, reserves the right of the Government to proceed against joint obligors of the taxpayer. In common law jurisdiction where taxpayers are jointly liable for the payment of an assessed tax, the acceptance of an Offer in Compromise from one of the taxpayers will release not only that taxpayer from further liability for the remaining tax, but will also release the other taxpayer from liability as well, unless, the acceptance reserves the right to proceed against the other obligor. Pattern Letter P-229 is a collateral agreement secured from the taxpayer (or the maker of the offer) and used in common law jurisdictions as a means of reserving the government's right to proceed against co-obligors of the taxpayer. The agreement does not release the taxpayer from the liability for the difference between the amount of the Offer in Compromise and the total amount of the outstanding tax liability, but it does prohibit the government from taking any collection action (by suit, levy and seizure or any other means) against the taxpayer for recovery of that difference. By utilizing this agreement, the government has preserved its right to proceed against the co-obligors of the taxpayer for the remaining liability.

3) In states in which the statutes provide that the remaining obligor can be pursued for any unpaid balance of the tax liability, the agreement (Pattern Letter P-230, Exhibit 5700-25) should be used. It states that the offer is submitted to compromise the individual's liability only and shall not be constructed as proposing to release any co-obligors.

4) In the following instances, a co-obligor agreement would not be warranted.

   a) The offer is equal to or in excess of the taxpayer's proportionate share of the liability.

   b) No possibility exists for collecting any amount from the other joint obligor(s).

   c) The proportionate share of the liability which remain outstanding is in excess of the amount collectible from the other joint obligor(s).

      1. While the situations above outline practical considerations which could justify a deviation from the general rule, no action should be taken which would jeopardize the government's interest. The amount of the liability involved and other particulars have to be considered before deciding which procedure to use.

57(10)16

ACCEPTANCE RECOMMENDATION

57(10)16.1
GENERAL

1) When it is determined that the offer should be recommended for acceptance, the following documents will be prepared:

    a) Form 7249, Offer Acceptance Report (Exhibit 5700-20)

    b) A memorandum, which fully supports the acceptance recommendation.

    c) A supplemental information report, if required, and

    d) The acceptance letter P-673 (exhibit 5700-29), with all enclosures, (a copy of Form 656 and all collateral agreements).

2) The work papers and/or history sheets, maintained as part of the case file, should reflect the scope of the examination and contain all the documentation of facts and information which formed the basis for the recommendation.

57(10)16.2

PREPARATION OF FORM 7249, OFFER ACCEPTANCE REPORT

57(10)16.21
GENERAL

1) *All items of Form 7249 should be completed. The "date Assessed" column should reflect only the earliest unpaid assessment for each module. Compute accrued interest and penalties to a date approximating the date of actual acceptance, taking into consideration the time usually required to complete all processing actions on the case. Lien fees and other collection costs may be combined with "Assesses Penalties" and separate assessment dates need not be shown for them.*

2) *When the liability covered by the offer is spread over more years or periods that can be shown on the lines provided in the Schedule of Liability, the remaining years and/or periods will be carried over to a second sheet rather than crammed into one tabulation. For the sake of uniformity, the first page of the report showing the liability should be cut off along the line just below the word "Total." The statement "Unpaid liabilities continued on next page" should be inserted in the space provided for the totals.*

57(10)16.22
SEPARATE FORM 7249 FOR EACH OFFER

When one taxpayer, or related taxpayers, such as a husband and wife, partners, or a group of consolidated corporations, files several offers to compromise separate assessments, and the collectibility of the liabilities arises from the principal source, a separate Form 7249 should be prepared for each offer, with one memorandum, setting forth reasons for acceptance. When more than one offer is involved, acceptance authority will determined by the total of all unpaid liabilities and statutory additions.

57(10)16.23
SIGNATURE AND INITIALS OF FORM 7249

Form 7249 should be signed by the examining officer and by all reviewers. Management should ensure that reviews are kept to the absolute minimum. When the offer involves an unpaid liability, including interest, additions amount, addition to the tax, assessable penalty or $500 or more, Form 7249 must not be signed by the delegated official until the required legal opinion is obtained from the district counsel. In cases involving liabilities under $500, Form 7249 may be signed as soon as it is concluded that the offer is acceptable.

57(10)16.24
LEGAL OPINION OF COUNSEL

1) The primary role of Counsel in reviewing offers is to determine whether or not the offer is legally sufficient to meet the standard of doubt as to liability or doubt as to collectibility.

    a) Factual determinations by the Service will not be re-examined by counsel unless patently erroneous. Asset valuations are largely matters of administrative discretion and judgement and they should rarely be questioned by Counsel.

    b) When a file is lacking information sufficient for Counsel to render a reliable legal opinion, it should be brought informally to the attention of the forwarding office.

    c) When considering a case based on doubt as to collectibility, the amount should be considered legally sufficient if it is within a reasonable range of the predicted results in litigation.

    d) An offer based on doubt as to collectibility should be considered legally sufficient if it closely approximates the taxpayer's collection potential considering what would be legally and practically obtainable through available enforced collection procedures, either administrative or judicial. All sources subject to enforced collection should be considered, including fraudulently conveyed assets and other sources of collection form third parties. Forced sale values can be considered legally sufficient.

e) Counsel's signature on the Form 7249 constitutes the legal opinion required by I.R.C. 7122. If Counsel determines that the offer is not legally sufficient, the Form 7249 will not be signed and the offer may not be accepted by the authorized official. In such cases, a memorandum will be prepares explaining why the offer is not legally sufficient.

f) Occasionally, although an offer may be legally sufficient, Counsel may have reservations as to whether it should be accepted, based on policy or other non-legal concerns. Such concerns will be promptly discussed with the responsible Service officials. Is these reservations are not successfully resolved, Counsel will nevertheless issue the necessary legal opinion. Issues not related to the legal sufficiency of the offer are not grounds to decline to issue the opinion. If Counsel wishes to comment on its concerns or to recommend that the offer be rejected, this will be done in a separate memorandum.

57(10)16.3
ACCEPTANCE MEMORANDUM

The examining officer will prepare a memorandum which fully supports the acceptance recommendation. Management should ensure that this memorandum contains only the information needed to allow the delegated official to make a decision.

57(10)16.4
SUPPLEMENTAL INFORMATION REPORT

A supplemental information report should only be prepared when the examining officer wants to discuss issues about the taxpayer's private affairs which would be pertinent to the delegated official's overall understanding of the case. Information previously discussed in the acceptance memorandum need not be reiterated in the supplemental report.

57(10)16.5
ACCEPTANCE LETTER

Pattern Letter P-673 should be used when accepting the offer. Enclosed with this letter will be a copy of the Form 656 and all collateral agreements.

57(10)16.6

FINAL PROCESSING OF COMPLETED OFFER

57(10)16.61
ACCEPTANCES

1) After the delegated official, see Delegation Order No. 11, as revised, accepts an offer by signing the appropriate Form 7249 and acceptance letter and having his/her signature fixed to at least one copy of these documents, the case will be returned to the function designation responsibility to process offers and will complete the following:

   a) Date the signed original and all copies of the acceptance letter.

   b) *Make a sufficient number of photocopies of the letter as may be required and any documents outlining the terms and condition of the agreement.*

   c) *Mail the original acceptance letter to the taxpayer as of day the letter is dated. If the liability has not yet been assessed, the letter will not be sent before the tax is assessed.*

   d) *Make a sufficient number of photocopies of the Form 7249.*

   e) *Post Form 2515 in the compromise case file and a copy of Form 2515 offer control file with the date of acceptance.*

   f) *Place the signed original and one copy of the Form 7249 and a copy of the acceptance letter in the offer case file.*

   g) *Transmit the offer file to the Service Center Collection Branch.*

   h) *Place a copy of Form 7249 in the file designated by the district director for public inspection.*

   i) *If the amount of the offer is full paid at the time of acceptance of the offer, whether or not there is a collateral agreement involved:*

      1. *TDAs covering accounts compromised are to be place in the closed TDA file.*

      2. *Federal tax liens, covering only those accounts compromised, will be released, provided nothing is due at that time under a collateral agreement.*

   j) If the offer is a deferred payment offer, whether or not there is a collateral agreement involved:

1. TDAs covering accounts compromised are to be places in the closed files.

2. Federal tax liens covering the accounts compromised cannot be released until the amount of the offer, including accrued interest, has been paid in full, provided nothing is due at that time under collateral agreement.

2) Upon acceptance of an offer involving a co-obligor situation on a joint income tax liability, the service center will establish a NMF TDA against the co-obligor for the full amount of the remaining liability, unless otherwise directed.

57(10)16.7
IMPLEMENTATION OF OFFER AGREEMENT AFTER ACCEPTANCE

The district and service centers, each with certain fixed responsibilities, are jointly charged with coordination and follow-up on accepted Offers in Compromise. Enforcement safeguards are provided to ensure compliance with the terms of installment offers and collateral agreements.

57(10)16.8
RELEASE OF LIENS

57(10)16.81
DISTRICT OFFICE RESPONSIBILITIES

1) When all the terms and conditions of the offer have been met, the Federal Tax lien(s) relating to the liability will be released. Failure to issue a prompt release could have a serious adverse affect on the taxpayer who could seek redress from the Service. If a future income collateral agreement is involved, the taxpayer must be current with its terms and conditions:

    a) If it is not clear whether the taxpayer has complied with all the terms of the offer, the advice of District Counsel should be sought.

    b) The taxpayer who submitted the offer to compromise his/her liability only (and such offer having been accepted) is entitled to a release of the Government's lien unless the issuance of the release is prohibited by the lien provisions of any related collateral agreement. To protect the Government's rights under its lien against any remaining parties liable for the unpaid assessment, parts of Forms 668-Y, Certificate of Release of Federal Tax Lien, should be modified accordingly. (See Exhibit 5700-40).

57(10)16.9

PUBLIC INSPECTION OF ACCEPTED OFFERS IN COMPROMISE

57(10)16.91
AUTHORITY

Public inspection of certain information regarding all Offers in Compromise accepted under Section 7122 of the Code is authorized by Section 6103(k)(1) of the Internal Revenue Code.

57(10)16.92
PUBLIC INSPECTION PROCEDURES

For a period of one year, a copy of the appropriate Form 7249, Offer Acceptance Report, for each accepted offer (including those accepted by the service center director) will be made available for examination in the office of the district director, having jurisdiction of the taxpayer. The inspection file will be maintained so that it is readily available for examination by the public.

57(10)17

REJECTION AND WITHDRAWAL REPORT

57(10)17.1
GENERAL INFORMATION

1)   When an Offer in Compromise is not acceptable or has been withdrawn, the following documents will be prepared:

   a)   Form 1271, Rejection or Withdrawal Memorandum

   b)   Rejection or withdrawal letter to the taxpayer, and

   c)   A memorandum outlining the reasons for rejections.

57(10)17.2
PREPARATION OF FORM 1271 FOR REJECTION OFFERS

All items of Form 1271 should be completed by the examining officer except the sate of rejection letter. This block will be completed by the function designated to complete final processing of the offer and will reflect the date the rejection letter is mailed. The Description of Liability section will reflect the current balance tax, penalty and interest, for periods identified on Form 656. The figures should reflect the most recently identifiable balance due. The delegated official will sign all rejection reports. The person preparing Form 1271 as well as all reviewers should also sign.

57(10)17.3
REJECTION MEMORANDUM

A memorandum outlining the reasons for rejection must accompany Form 1271. The memorandum should be as brief as possible. If the offer was based on doubt as to collectibility, the fact as to collectibility must be set out in sufficient detail including the amounts and terms determined to be acceptable, so that the information can be used both for further collection action and as a basis for discussion of the case in the event the rejection is appealed. Additionally, if any account was currently not collectible or in installment status, the memorandum should contain a recommendation whether the account should be reactivated.

57(10)17.4
PREPARATION OF FORM 1271 FOR WITHDRAWN OFFERS

1)   All items of Form 1271 should be completed by the examining officer except for the date if the withdrawal letter. This block will be completed by the function designated to completed the final processing of the offer and will reflect the date withdrawal letter is mailed to the taxpayer.

2)   The delegated official will sign all withdrawal reports. The person preparing For 1271 and all reviewers should also sign.

57(10)17.5
WITHDRAWAL MEMORANDUM

Generally, the memorandum withdrawal accompanying Form 1271 will not require as much detail as a rejection case. However, any other information which the examining officer determined useful for further collection action or reference purposes should be included in the memorandum. If appropriate a recommendation as to whether accounts in currently not collectible status should be reactivated should be made.

57(10)17.6
REJECTION AND WITHDRAWAL LETTERS

1) When it is determined that the offer is unacceptable or has been withdrawn, a letter will be addressed to the taxpayer advising that the offer is rejected or that it is considered as withdrawn. The opening paragraph should show the nature of the offer (cash or deferred payment), the amount of the offer, the class of tax or penalty to be compromised, the years of periods covered by the offer, and the reason for the rejection of the offer. The amount of the liability should not be mentioned in this letter. In withdrawal cases where the offer is signed by the taxpayer, by specifically authorized representative or by an officer in corporation cases, the withdrawal letter should be addressed to the taxpayer. A copy of the letter will be sent to the authorized representative if requested in the power of attorney. The portion of the taxpayer's letter withdrawing the offer should be quoted and not paraphrased.

2) The following pattern letters are used to advised a taxpayer that the offer is rejected or considered withdrawn:

   a) Pattern Letter P-238 (Exhibit 5700-36)-Rejections letter for all classes of tax.

   b) Pattern Letter P-241 (Exhibit 5700-38)-Withdrawal letter.

3) These pattern letters are not intended to be all-inclusive, but will be applicable in most cases. When the reasons of rejection given in the pattern letter do not apply or when the quoting of the taxpayer's letter withdrawing the offer will confuse the issue, the pattern letters should be adjusted to suit the particular case involved.

4) The rejection letter will explain the written appeal procedure and give him/her 30 days in which to respond with an appeal. The rejection letter will contain the specific reasons for the rejection.

5) The delegated official will sign all rejection letters.

57(10)17.7
REJECTION BECAUSE OF THE DEATH OF THE TAXPAYER

1) The death of the taxpayer or other proponent while an offer is under consideration makes the offer legally unacceptable. To clear Service records a pro forma rejection letter will be issued. (Exhibit 5700-37)

2) In the case of an individual offer, the letter should be sent to "Estate of (taxpayer's name)." In the case of a joint, it should be sent to the surviving spouse, who should also be advised that the offer may be re-submitted showing one party as deceased.

57(10)17.8
TAXPAYER RESPONSE TO REJECTION LETTER

1) A taxpayer may appeal an examining officer's determination orally or in writing if the total liability does not exceed $2,500 for any taxable year or taxable period. In any such case the taxpayer may submit, if desired, a written statement outlining the facts, law or arguments on which the taxpayer relies. When any case is to be forwarded to Appeals based on an oral request, the Form 2873 should so state and name the Service employee to whom the request was made.

2) If the total liability exceeds $2,500 for any taxable year or period, the taxpayer must file a written protest to receive Appeals consideration.

3) If a taxpayer responds timely to an appeal, and the information in the protest letter is insufficient to adequately process the appeal, the taxpayer or proponent will be advised of the required information and provided 15 days to perfect the protest.

4) The taxpayer's protest will be evaluated. If new information is submitted, this should be evaluated. If the reevaluation leads to a different conclusion, the taxpayer will be notified and the case will not be forward to Appeals.

5) If it is determined that the case file should be forwarded on to Appeals office, the case file should contain the amount and terms determined to be acceptable or the reasons why the offer was inappropriate.

57(10)17.9
REJECTED AND WITHDRAWN OFFER PROCESSING

1) After the official delegated to reject offers or acknowledge withdrawal of offers has signed Form 1271 and the rejection or withdrawal letter, the case will be returned to the appropriate function which will:

   a) *Date the rejection or withdrawal letter,*

   b) *Make a sufficient number of photocopies of the letter as may be required,*

c) *Mail the original rejection or withdrawal letter to the taxpayer, including instructions for preparing a written appeal. See Exhibit 5700-36.*

d) *Make a sufficient number of copies of Form 1271, as many as be required,*

e) *Post the Forms 2515 in the compromise case file and in the offer control file with the date of rejection or withdrawal,*

f) *When a recommendation has been made on Form 1271 to reactivate accounts in currently not collectible status, note the copies of the rejection or withdrawal letter with instructions to SCCB (Service Center Collection Branch) as follows: "input TC 531 simultaneously with TC 481 or TC 482, as applicable."*

g) If there is no appeal or the offer is withdrawn, place the original and one copy of Form 1271 and two copies of the rejection or withdrawal letter in the Offer in Compromise case file. Transmit the Offer in Compromise case file to Service Center Collection Branch.

h) Any accounts in status 71 should be reversed by the district office and a determination made as to whether further collection action should be initiated or allowed the case to proceed through normal processing. Reversal of status 71 on accounts which were previously in status 26 will generate hard copy TDAs and go directly to the new T-sign. A copy of Form 1271, the memorandum outlining the basis for rejection and withdrawal, and other information that will aid collection of the liability will be forward to the revenue officer to be associated with the reissued TDAs. If the accounts were in a status other than 26, and the decision has been made to enforce collection input 22, "0 DOAO-6401 and send the file to the responsible unit. Hard copy TDAs will be generated.

i) If the offer is rejected or withdrawn, the amount deposited will be refunded unless the taxpayer authorizes that the payment be applied to the liability. If an executed Form 3040, Authorization to Apply Offer in Compromise Deposit to Liability, is not included in the case file of the rejected offer or if the taxpayer's withdrawal letter does not specify the disposition to be made of the offer deposit, issue a Form 2209, Courtesy Investigation, requesting that a Form 3040 be secured. The offer deposit will be applied to the liability as of the date of the offer is rejected or withdrawn.

57(10)18
OFFERS INVOLVING PROPOSALS TO DISCHARGE PROPERTY FROM THE EFFECT OF TAX LIENS

Whether a proposal for subordination or discharge of specific property from the effect of a Federal tax lien will be processed on its merits will depend upon the acceptability of the Offer in Compromise. If not acceptable, the offer should be rejected and the proposal for discharged should be processed to a conclusion. If acceptable, the offer should be processed, since the acceptance and payment of the offer full would permit the release of all property from the Federal tax lien, including the property covered by the application to discharge from the effects of Federal tax lien. After a deferred payment offer has been accepted, a proposal to discharge certain property may be considered and approved provided the proposal represents the full value of the taxpayer's interest in the property and the total proceeds (to the extent of the value of the government's interest in such property under its lien) are applied on the unpaid balance of the accepted offer.

57(10)19
CASES INVOLVING ASSIGNMENTS FOR THE BENEFITS OF CREDITORS

In these cases the consideration of an Offer in Compromise frequently presents questions concerning the right of the government to priority in the collection of the tax claims over the claims of other creditors of the taxpayer. The right of these other creditors are based on liens which may be recognized by state law, but because of the taxpayer's assignment his/her assets for the benefit of creditors, the provisions of 31 USC 3717 apply. In evaluating the rights of all creditors, all fact and circumstances relating to the carious claims must be made. This includes all pertinent dates, such as the origin and filing of all claims and liens and the steps which have been taken toward the enforcement of the claimants and liens and the steps which have been taken toward the enforcement of the claimant's alleged rights. An assignee for the benefit of creditors, as well as an executor or administrator of a decedent's estate, may become personally liable if the priority rights of the United States are disregarded when the funds of the estate are disbursed. In assignment cases, particularly those where a corporation is the assignor and the tax liability sought to be compromised consists of withholding of Federal Insurance Contributions taxes or any of the taxes which the assignor might be required to withhold or collect from others and pay over to the government, the possibility of enforcing the 100 percent penalty provisions of the code should be considered. For a discussion of the liability under 31 USC 3713 (formerly 31 USC 191), see the Legal Reference Guide for Revenue Officers.

57(10)20
RESCISSION OF ACCEPTED OFFERS

57(10)20.1
GENERAL

1) A compromise is a contract which is binding and conclusive on both the government and the proponent and precludes further inquiry into the matters to which it relates. In the absence of fraud or mutual mistake, the courts have consistently denied either party recovery of any part of the consideration given with a settlement when it was properly rendered under a compromise agreement. However, an Offer in Compromise, which has been accepted under a mutual mistake as to a material fact, or because of the false representations made by one party about a material fact, may be rescinded or set aside. The meaning, validity and consideration of such contract is subject to interpretation by a court.

2) If has been held that unconscious ignorance by both parties of a fact material to the contract, or belief by both parties in the present existence of something material to the contract, constitute a mutual mistake of fact. In certain court cases it has been decided that any compromise settlement entered into under a mutual mistake was in effect without consideration and therefore, was not a bar to the taxpayer's right to recover. Ordinarily, the fact that both parties have misconstrued the law does not rendered the compromise subject to rescission-a compromise is rescindable because of a mutual mistake of fact but not because of a mutual mistake of law.

3) To constitute fraud which will nullify a compromise, it must appear that the representations as to material facts were false; that the maker knew them to be false; that they were made for the purpose of including, and did induce the other party to make the contract; and that the latter had the right to rely on them and did rely of them thereby sustaining injury. When revoking such an accepted offer, the possibility of actually being able to collect an amount larger that realize under the accepted offer is an important factor.

57(10)20.2
RESCISSION PROCEDURE

1) An offer may be rescinded, if legally justifiable, in the following manner:

   a) The appropriate function will prepare a letter to the taxpayer identifying the Offer in Compromise and advising that the acceptance of the offer is rescinded and the acceptance letter revoked. The letter should state the grounds for rescission in general terms and contain a demand for payment of the unpaid tax liability. The letter will be signed by the appropriate approving official.

b) If the liability was $500 or more, the rescission letter must be approved by district counsel. If the liability was under $500, approval is not required.

c) If the offer had been accepted by an Appeals Office, the case should be sent to the appropriate Appeals office for final determination that offer be rescinded.

57(10)21

COMPROMISE OF AN ACCEPTED OFFER

57(10)21.1
GENERAL

There are cases in which the taxpayer is unable to pay the balance of an accepted offer and/or the balance of the contingent liability under the terms of collateral agreement. In this situation the Service has the option of temporarily adjusting the terms of the offer, formally compromising the existing compromise, or exercising the default provisions of the offer.

57(10)21.2
AUTHORITY TO COMPROMISE BALANCE DUE UNDER A COMPROMISE CONTRACT

1) IRC Section 7122 authorizes the Commissioner to accept an Offer in Compromise of an accepted Offer in Compromise.

2) A proposal to compromise the balance of an accepted offer must rest on doubt as to collectibility, or doubt as to liability and collectibility. doubt as to liability will arise only where there is doubt as to the meaning and interpretation of Form 656 and/or the collateral agreement.

57(10)21.3
RECEIPT AND PROCESSING

Proposals received in district offices will be immediately transmitted to SCCB for processing, together with any payment received. The office of jurisdiction which initially accepted the offer will consider that taxpayers proposal.

57(10)21.4
FORM AND AMOUNT OF OFFER

1) *No offer form (such as Form 656) is prescribed for use in submitting such a proposal. The proposal should be made in letter form, addressed to the Commissioner of Internal Revenue and mailed to the Service Center Collection branch monitoring the offer.*

2) The total amount offered to satisfy the balance due under a compromise contract must be paid in full on or before notice of acceptance of the proposal,

3) The proposal letter should contain the following information:

   a) The amount proposed and the terms of payment within limitations discussed in (2) above.

   b) The date of acceptance of the original offer.

   c) The waiver of any and all claims to amounts due from the United States up to the time of acceptance, to the extent of the difference between the amount offered and the amount of the c,aim covered by the offer. Pattern letters included as Exhibit 5700-42 to 5700-44 are furnished to cover the usual situations encountered.

4) When the proposal is based on doubt as to collectibility, the taxpayer must submit a financial statement. In addition, the following information should be obtained, where applicable:

   a) copy of taxpayer's most recent income tax returns

   b) latest profit and loss statement;

   c) appraisal of work in process at present time to determine its value;

   d) estimate of the remaining liability under the terms of the future income collateral agreement;

   e) reasons why request is being made to compromise the existing agreement.

57(10)21.41
CONSIDERATION OF PROPOSAL

1) The consideration of such a proposal will be made by the office of jurisdiction which originally accepted the taxpayer's offer. Acceptance of the taxpayer's proposal will depend on whether it is in the best interest of the Government. The factors to be considered

for accepting the proposal are the same utilized when considering the merits of an offer submitted on a form 656.

2) The information required to support the proposal should fit the case. The taxpayer's statement of his/her current financial condition should be accompanied by a description of future prospect and any other information which might have a bearing upon the acceptability of the offer, The taxpayer's income for the past three years should be ascertained, and when all information is available, the amount of his/her future income should be estimated and projected over the period covered by the remaining terms of the original Offer in Compromise agreement. Comparison should then be made between the amount of the taxpayer's offer and the amount which is anticipated to be recouped under the remaining terms of the original Offer in Compromise agreement.

57(10)21.42
PROCESSING COMPLETED INVESTIGATIONS

1) After the investigation, the examining officer will forward the proposal, investigative report, memorandum containing a complete statement of the facts in the case and his/her recommendation to the appropriate function for review. The appropriate function will prepared or review the acceptance or rejection letter. (See Pattern Letters included as Exhibit 5700-45, 5700-46 and 5700-48).

2) If the taxpayer's proposal is acceptable, the procedures for acceptance of original offers will be followed.

3) If the proposal is not acceptable, the examiner's memorandum and the rejection letter, together with the case file, will be forwarded to the official with delegated authority to reject offers, for approval and signature.

4) Final processing of accepted or rejected proposals will be conducted by the appropriate function, following the guidelines for acceptance or rejection of original offers.

57(10)21.5

COLLECTION FUNCTION PROCESSING OF POTENTIAL DEFAULTED CASES

57(10)21.51
GENERAL

1) Upon receipt in the district, the case will be assigned in a manner determined by district management.

2) An attempt will be made to secure compliance. Any remittance received will be attached to the case file and forwarded through the appropriate function to the service center for deposit. Cash remittances will be converted to bank draft or money orders.

3) If compliance is not immediately secured, the case will be evaluated in light of all the information submitted by the service center and a decision will be made whether to recommend termination of the offer or consider temporary adjustment of its terms. The offer should not be terminated unless the evidence indicates that termination is in government's best interest.

4) Before termination of an offer, the taxpayer may be allowed to reduce his/her payments temporarily, providing there is evidence that the taxpayer is acting in good faith and not attempting to place assets beyond the reach of the government. This does not require a formal revision of the terms of the conditionally accepted offer. The following courses of action should be considered before terminating an offer.

   a) Where a deferred payment offer has not been paid full and there is the possibility the taxpayer may be able to pay the balance within six months or less, the taxpayer can be granted an extension of time for payment. Taxpayers in default should be advised of the serious consequences of defaulting on an offer and the actions the Service can pursue. Any request for extension of time for payment by the taxpayer should be in writing.

   b) If a taxpayer requests an extension of time for payment exceeding six months, or permission to make payments different than those specified in the offer or the collateral agreement, the request will be analyzed and a decision will be made based on the taxpayer's financial condition. This decision cannot, however, result in the taxpayer paying less than the amount accepted. If the request is granted, a letter signed by an appropriate delegated official should be sent to the taxpayer. The letter should inform the taxpayer that action to terminate the offer will be held in abeyance. It should be specific to the temporary terms of repayment or *other provisions agreed upon. The letter should specify that this action is not to be construed as an amendment to the offer or as a waiver of the government's right under the default provisions. The case file and a copy of letter should be returned to the service center with memorandum summarizing the changes authorized.*

c) If a bond has been filed or other security obtained for payment of the offer, consideration should be given to collection from such source. It may be necessary to refer the case to the District Counsel for review and decision.

d) If the payment default has been caused by the death of the taxpayer, the examining officer should determine whether the estate of the taxpayer can and will pay the balance due on the offer. If it appears that sufficient funds are available but there will be a delay before funds are dispersed, a moratorium may be recommended. If authorized by the appropriate approving official, as described in (b) above, a letter as described in (c) above will be issued.

5) When the investigation is completed, all cases, along with reports and recommendations, will be returned to the appropriate function for final action. If the offer is to be terminated, a letter should be prepared for the signature of a delegated official, (See Delegation Order No. 11 as revised).

6) If the offer was originally accepted by the Appeals Office or by regional counsel, the termination recommendation will be referred to the appropriate office for preparation of the termination letter and signature by the appropriate delegated official, (See Delegation Order No. 11).

57(10)21.52
PROCESSING TERMINATION CASES

1) *When an Offer in Compromise is in default, the delegated official, (See Delegation Order No. 11, as revised), has the following options under the specific terms of the offer.*

a) Proceed immediately by suit to collect the entire unpaid balance of the offer; or

b) Proceed immediately by suit to collect as liquidated damage, an amount equal to the compromised liability, minus any deposits already received under the terms of the Offer in Compromise, with interest on the unpaid balance from the date of default at the annual rate as established by section 662 of the Code; or

c)   Disregard the amount of such offer and apply all amounts previously deposited thereunder against the amount of the compromised liability, and without further notice of any kind, asses and/or collect by levy or suit the balance of such liability. A recommendation for suit should be referred to Counsel for consideration and proper action.

2)   Except in cases coming within the jurisdiction of the Appeals Office, the appropriate Collection function will prepare the termination letter for the delegated official's signature, (See Delegation Order No. 11, as revised), and return the case file and a copy of the termination letter to the service center under a separate Form 3210, Document Transmittal, which should be highlighted as a "terminated offer." Where appropriate, SPF will follow normal procedures to revoke the lien release and reinstate the tax lien against the taxpayer.

3)   Pattern Letters P-242, P-243 and P-244 (Exhibits 5700-101 through 103) are used in cases where taxpayer has not complied with the terms of the offer and/or related collateral agreement. The termination letter should refer to the applicable terms of the offer and/or collateral agreement and to the taxpayer's failure to comply with these terms.

4)   The Service Center Examination function should be advised of the termination of all Offers in Compromise involving collateral agreements, other than those agreements pertaining only t future income and those Form, 2261-D.

57(10)22

PENALTY OFFERS

57(10)22.1
JURISDICTION OF PENALTY OFFERS

1)   The service center has authority to consider penalty offers based upon doubt as to liability. District office action or investigation is not necessary unless the offer is based upon doubt as to collectibility or there are unusual circumstances or complex questions involved. In the latter case, the Service Center Collection function will first consult the district office liaison in an effort to settle questions over the telephone rather than transferring the case. The necessity for an actual transfer will be jointly decided by the appropriate district manager and the manager of the Service Center Collection function.

2) Fraud, penalties, including interest, and negligence penalties, including interest, require district office consideration.

3) Penalties that are not subject to reasonable cause determination are not subject to compromise based on doubt as to liability. These offers can only be based on doubt as to collectibility and these offers will be assigned to the district office.

57(10)22.2
PRELIMINARY REQUIREMENTS

57(10)22.21
ADMINISTRATIVE APPEAL PROCEDURE

The Service has an administrative procedure whereby a taxpayer may appeal the validity of a penalty assessment either before or after paying it. In addition, the Appeals officer may be delegated authority to settle penalty assessments. Therefore, before informing the taxpayer about the option of submitting an offer to compromise a disputed penalty, the administrative appeal procedure should be explained and taxpayers should be encourages to use it.

57(10)22.3
PROCESSING OF PENALTY OFFERS

1) A penalty offer will not be favorably considered if the penalty itself is already paid. Since there is no outstanding liability subject to subject to compromise, the offer should be rejected immediately. Normal rejection procedures will be followed.

2) If a penalty is full paid in error (such as an offset from another module) the offer may still be considered. If the offer is accepted, the excess of payment over the amount of the offer would be refunded to the taxpayer.

57(10)22.4
TAX, INTEREST AND PENALTIES MUST BE PAID

1) A penalty cannot be compromised before the tax, if any, interest on the tax and any other penalties are paid. When an offer to compromise a penalty is filed and if these items have not been paid, action on the offer will generally be held in abeyance until payment is made. The taxpayer will be notified and given a reasonable time to pay the liability.

2) If the outstanding tax, interest on the tax and other penalties are not paid within a reasonable time, the offer should be rejected.

The Official
IRS
Collection
Manual

5223

Analysis of Taxpayer's Financial Condition

(1)   The analysis of the taxpayer's financial condition provides the interviewer with a basis to make one or more of the following decisions:

   (a)   require payment from available assets;

   (b)   secure a short-term agreement or a longer installment agreement;

   (c)   report the account currently not collectible;

   (d)   recommend or initiate enforcement action (this would also be based on the results of the interview);

   (e)   file a Notice of Federal Tax Lien; and/or

   (f)   explain the offer in compromise provisions of the Code to the taxpayer.

(2)   In all steps that follow, information on the financial statement will be compared with other financial information provided by the taxpayer, particularly the copy of the taxpayer's latest Form 1040. If there are significant discrepancies, they should be discussed with the taxpayer. In the event further documentation is needed, it will be the taxpayer's responsibility to provide it. Discrepancies and their resolution will be noted in the case file history.

(3)   Analyze assets to determine ways of liquidating the account:

   (a)   if the taxpayer has cash equal to the tax liability, demand immediate payment;

   (b)   otherwise, review other assets which may be pledged or readily converted to cash (such as stocks and bonds, loan value of life insurance policies, etc.);

   (c)   if necessary, review any unencumbered assets, equity in encumbered assets, interests in estates and trusts, lines of credit (including available credit on bank charge cards), etc., from which money may be secured to make payment. In addition, consider the taxpayer's ability to make an unsecured loan. If the taxpayer belongs to a credit union, the taxpayer will be asked to borrow from that source. Upon identification of potential sources of loans, establish a date that the taxpayer is expected to make payments; and

   (d)   if there appears to be no borrowing ability, attempt to get the taxpayer to defer payment of other debts in order to pay the tax first.

(4) When analysis of the taxpayer's assets has given no obvious solution for liquidating the liability, the income and expenses should be analyzed.

(a) When deciding what is an allowable expense item, the employee may allow:

1. expenses which are necessary for the taxpayer's production of income (for example, dues for a trade union or professional organization; child care payments which allow a taxpayer to work);

2. expenses which provide for the health and welfare of the taxpayer and family. The expense must be reasonable for the size of the family and the geographic location, as well as any unique individual circumstances. An expense will not be allowed if it serves to provide an elevated standard of living, as opposed to basic necessities. Also, an expense will not be allowed if the taxpayer has a proven record of not making the payment. Expenses allowable under this category are:

   a. rent or mortgage for place of residence;
   b. food;
   c. clothing;
   d. necessary transportation expense (auto insurance, car payment, bus fare, etc.);
   e. home maintenance expense (utilities, home-owner insurance, home-owner dues, etc.);
   f. medical expenses; health insurance;
   g. current tax payments (including federal, state and local);
   h. life insurance, but not if it is excessive to the point of being construed as an investment;
   i. alimony, child support or other court-ordered payment.

3. Minimum payments on secured or legally perfected debts (car payments, judgments, etc.) will normally be allowed. However, if the encumbered asset represents an item which would not be considered a necessary living expense (e.g., a boat, recreational vehicle, etc.), the taxpayer should be advised that the debt payment will not be included as an allowable expense.

4. Payments on unsecured debts (credit cards, personal loans, etc.) may not be allowed if omitting them would permit the taxpayer to pay in full within 90 days. However, if the taxpayer cannot fully pay within that time, minimum payments may be allowed if failure to make them would

ultimately impair the taxpayer's ability to pay the tax. The taxpayer should be advised that since all necessary living expenses have been allowed, no additional charge debts should be incurred. Generally, payments to friends or relatives will not be allowed. Dates for final payments on loans or installment purchases, as well as final payments on revolving credit arrangements after allowing minimum required payments, will be noted so the additional funds will be applied to the liability when they become available. If permitting the taxpayer to pay unsecured debts results in inability to pay or in only having a small amount left for payment of the tax, the taxpayer should be advised that a portion of the money available for payment of debts will be used for payment of the taxes and that arrangements must be made with other creditors accordingly.

(b) As a general rule, expenses not specified in (a) above will be disallowed. However, an otherwise disallowable expense may be included if the employee believes an exception should be made based on the circumstances of the individual case. For instance, if the taxpayer advises that an educational expense or church contribution is a necessity, the individual circumstances must be considered. If an exception is made, document the case history to explain the basis for the exception.

(c) The taxpayer will be required to verify and support any expense which appears excessive based on the income and circumstances of that taxpayer. However, proof of payment does not automatically make an item allowable. The criteria in (4)(a) apply.

(d) In some cases, expense items or payments will not be due in even monthly increments. For instance, personal property tax may be due once a year. Unless the taxpayer substantiates that money is being set aside on a monthly basis, the expense will be allowed in total in the month due and the payment agreement adjusted accordingly for that month. Expense items with varying monthly payments should be averaged over a twelve-month period unless the variation will be excessive. In such instances, exclude the irregular months from the average. For example, if a utility bill will be excessive during the three winter months, average the other nine months.

(e) In arriving at available net income, analyze the taxpayer's deductions to ensure that they are reasonable and allowable. The only automatically allowable deductions from gross pay or income are federal, state and local taxes (including FICA or other mandatory retirement program).

1. Other deductions from gross pay or income will be treated and listed as expenses, but only to the extent they meet the criteria in (4)(a) above.

2. To avoid affording the taxpayer a double deduction for one expense, ensure that such amounts remain in the total net pay figure and are also entered on the expense side of the income and expense analysis.

3. If the exemptions on the W-4 are going to be decreased, make the appropriate adjustments in the net income figures.

(f) To reach an average monthly take-home pay for taxpayers paid on a weekly basis, multiply the weekly pay times 52 weeks divided by 12 months (or multiply amount times 4.3 weeks). If the taxpayer is paid biweekly, multiply pay times 26 weeks divided by 12 months (or multiply amount times $2 \frac{1}{6}$). If the taxpayer is paid semimonthly, multiply pay times 2.

(g) The amount to be paid monthly on an installment agreement payment will be at least the difference between the taxpayer's net income and allowable expenses. If the taxpayer will not consent to the proposed installment agreement, he/she should be advised that enforced collection action may be taken. The taxpayer should also be advised that an appeal of the matter may be made to the immediate manager.

(5) When an analysis of the taxpayer's financial condition shows that liquidation of assets and payments from present and future income will not result in full payment, consider the collection potential of an offer in compromise.

5225

Verification of Taxpayer's Financial Condition

(1) In some cases it will be necessary or desirable to obtain additional information about the taxpayer's financial condition. The extent of the investigation will depend upon the circumstances in each case.

(2) If items appear to be over- or understated, or out of the ordinary, the taxpayer should be asked to explain and substantiate if necessary. The explanation will be documented in the case history. If the explanation is unsatisfactory or cannot be substantiated, the amount should be revised appropriate to the documentation available.

5231.1

General Installment Agreement Guidelines

(1) When taxpayers state inability to pay the full amount of their taxes, installment agreements are to be considered.

(2) Future compliance with the tax laws will be addressed and any returns and/or tax due within the period of the agreement must be filed and paid timely.

(3) Levy source information, including complete addresses and ZIP codes, will be secured.

(4) Equal monthly installment payments should be requested. Payment amounts may be increased or decreased as necessary.

(5) Once the determination is made that the taxpayer has the capability to make a regular installment payment, that agreement will be monitored through routine provisions unless the payment amount is less than $10 (in which case the account should be reported currently not collectible). The major benefits of this approach are issuance of reminder and default notices (if the account is system-monitored) and enforcement action if the agreement is not kept.

(6) The taxpayer should be allowed to select the payment due date(s). But if there is no preference, the date when the taxpayer would generally be in the best financial position to make the payment(s) should be chosen.

(7) If the interviewer and the taxpayer cannot agree on the amount of installments, the taxpayer should be advised that an appeal may be made to the immediate manager.

(8) An installment agreement which lasts more than two years must be reviewed at the mid-point of the agreement, but in no event less than every two years.

Levy and Sale

5311

Introduction and General Concepts

(1)   Under the Internal Revenue Code, levy is defined as the power to collect taxes by distraint or seizure of the taxpayer's assets. Through levy, we can attach property in the possession of third parties or the taxpayer. Generally, a notice of levy is used to attach funds due the taxpayer from third parties. Levy on property in possession of the taxpayer is accomplished by seizure and public sale of the property. There is no statutory requirement as to the sequence to be followed in levying, but it is generally less burdensome and time consuming to levy on funds in possession of third parties.

(2)   Levy authority is far reaching. It permits a continuous attachment of the non-exempt portion of the wage or salary payments due the taxpayer, and the seizure and sale of all the taxpayer's assets except certain property that is specifically exempt by law. Prior to levying on any property belonging to a taxpayer, the Service must notify the taxpayer in writing of the Service's intention to levy. The statute does not require a judgment or other court order before levy action is taken. The Supreme Court decision in the matter of *G.M. Leasing Corporation v. United States*, 429 U.S. 338 (1977), held that an entry without a warrant and search of private areas of both residential and business premises for the purpose of seizing and inventorying property pursuant to Internal Revenue Code section 6331 is in violation of the Fourth Amendment. Prior to seizure of property on private premises, a consent to enter for the purpose of seizing or writ of entry from the local courts must be secured.

(3)   Procedures are designed (except in jeopardy cases) to give taxpayers a reasonable chance to settle their tax liabilities voluntarily before the more drastic enforcement actions are started. At least one final notice must be issued before service of a notice of levy.

(4)   Under the self-assessment system, a taxpayer is entitled to a reasonable opportunity to voluntarily comply with the revenue laws. This concept should also be followed in connection with levy action. This does not mean that there should be a reluctance to levy if the circumstances justify that action. However, before levy or seizure is taken on an account, the taxpayer must be informed, except in jeopardy situations, that levy

or seizure will be the next action taken and given a reasonable opportunity to pay voluntarily. Once the taxpayer has been advised and neglects to make satisfactory arrangements, levy action should be taken expeditiously, but not less than 10 days after notice.

(5) Notification prior to levy must be given in accordance with (2) above. It should be specific that levy action will be the next action taken. In the event the service center has not sent the taxpayer the 4th notice which includes notice of intention to levy at least 10 days before the levy, the revenue officer must provide the notice to the taxpayer as indicated in (2) above.

(6) A notice of levy should be served only when there is evidence or reasonable expectation that the third party has property or rights to property of the taxpayer. This concept is of particular significance, since processing of notices of levy is time consuming and often becomes a sensitive matter if it appears the levy action was merely a "fishing expedition."

5312

Statutory Authority to Levy

(1) IRC 6331 provides that if any person liable to pay any tax neglects or refuses to pay the tax within 10 days after notice and demand, the tax may be collected by levy upon any property or rights to property belonging to the taxpayer or on which there is a lien.

(2) IRC 6331 also provides that if the Secretary determines that the collection of tax is in jeopardy, immediate notice and demand for payment may be made and, upon the taxpayer's failure to pay the tax, collection may be made by levy without regard to the 10-day period. However, if a sale is required, a public notice of sale may not be issued within the 10-day period unless IRC 6336 (relating to sale of perishable goods) is applicable.

(3) Under the IRC, the term "property" includes all property or rights to property, whether real or personal, tangible or intangible. The term "tax" includes any interest, additional amount, addition to tax, or assessable penalty, together with any cost that may accrue.

(4) Generally, property subject to a Federal tax lien which has been sold or otherwise transferred by the taxpayer, may be levied upon in the hands of the transferee or any subsequent transferee. However, there are exceptions for securities, motor vehicles and certain retail and casual sales.

(5) Levy may be made on any person in possession of, or obligated with respect to, property or rights to property subject to levy. These include, but are not necessarily limited to, receivables, bank accounts, evidences of debt, securities and accrued salaries, wages, commissions, and other compensation.

(6) The IRC does not require that property be seized in any particular sequence. Therefore, property may be levied upon regardless of whether it is real or personal, tangible or intangible, and regardless of which type of property is levied upon first.

(7) Whenever the proceeds from the levy on any property or rights to property are not sufficient to satisfy the tax liability, additional levies may be made upon the same property, or source of income or any other property or rights to property subject to levy, until the account is fully paid. However, further levies should be timed to avoid hardship to the taxpayer or his/her family.

5314.1

Property Exempt From Levy

(1) IRC 6334 enumerates the categories of property exempt from levy as follows.

   (a) *Wearing apparel and school books necessary for the taxpayer or for members of his family*—No specific value limitation is placed on these items since the intent is to prevent seizing the ordinary clothing of the taxpayer or members of the family. Expensive items of wearing apparel, such as furs, are luxuries and are not exempt from levy.

   (b) *Fuel, provisions and personal effects*—This exemption is applicable only in the case of the head of a family and applies only to so much of the fuel, provisions, furniture, and personal effects of the household and of arms for personal use, livestock, and poultry as does not exceed $1,500 in value.

   (c) *Books and tools of a trade, business or profession*—This exemption is for so many of the books and tools necessary for the trade, business, or profession of the taxpayer as do not exceed in the aggregate $1,000 in value.

(d) *Unemployment benefits*—This applies to any amount payable to an individual for unemployment (including any portion payable to dependents) under an unemployment compensation law of the United States, any state, the District of Columbia or the Commonwealth of Puerto Rico.

(e) *Undelivered mail*—Addressed mail which has not been delivered to the addressee.

(f) *Certain annuity and pension payments.*

(g) *Workmen's compensation*—Any amount payable to an individual as workmen's compensation (including any portion payable to dependents) under a workmen's compensation law of the United States, any state, the District of Columbia, or the Commonwealth of Puerto Rico.

(h) *Judgment for support of minor children*—If the taxpayer is required by judgment of a court of competent jurisdiction, entered prior to the date of levy, to contribute to the support of his/her minor children, so much of his/her salary, wages, or other income as is necessary to comply with such judgment.

(i) *Minimum Exemption from Levy on Wages, Salary and Other Income*—IRC 6334(a)(9) limits the effect of levy on wages, salary and other income, by an amount of $75 per week for the taxpayer and an additional $25 a week for the spouse and each dependent claimed by the taxpayer. Income not paid or received on a weekly basis will, for the purpose of computing exemptions, be apportioned as if received on a weekly basis.

(2) In addition, Public Law 89-538 exempts deposits to the special Treasury fund made by servicemen and servicewomen (including officers) and Public Health Service employees on permanent duty assignment outside the United States or its possessions.

(3) Except for the exemptions in (1) and (2) above, no other property or rights to property are exempt from levy. No provision of state law can exempt property or rights to property from levy for the collection of federal taxes. The fact that property is exempt from execution under state personal or homestead exemption laws does not exempt the property from federal levy.

(4) The revenue officer seizing property of the type described in (1)(a), (b), and (c) above should appraise and set aside to the owner the amount of property to be exempted.

538(10)

Records of Attorneys, Physicians, and Accountants

(1) Records maintained by attorneys, physicians, and accountants concerning professional services performed for clients are usually of little intrinsic value and possess minimum sale value. Questions of confidential or privileged information contained in these records may cause complications if the records are seized. Additionally, the case files of the professional person frequently either are, or contain, property of the client, and therefore to this extent are not subject to seizure. Accordingly, it is not believed desirable to seize case files or records for payment of the taxpayer's tax liabilities.

(2) When office facilities or office equipment of attorneys, physicians, or public accountants are seized for payment of taxes, case files and related files in seized office facilities or office equipment of such persons will not be personally examined by the revenue officer even though information concerning accounts receivable may be contained in the files. When storage facilities (filing cabinets, etc.) are seized, the taxpayer should be requested to remove all case files promptly.

583(11)

Safe Deposit Boxes

538(11).1

General

(1) The procedures outlined below should be followed in an attempt to secure the opening of a taxpayer's safe deposit box in instances in which the taxpayer's consent to or cooperation in opening the box cannot be obtained.

(2) Ordinarily two keys are used to open a safe deposit box: a master key held by the bank or trust company which owns the box and an individual key in the possession of the person who rents the box.

(3) Irrespective of the possession of the necessary equipment to do so, it is not to be expected that a bank or trust company will open a safe deposit box without the consent of the lessee of the box unless protected by a court order. Under these

circumstances the government must prevent the taxpayer from having access to the box, or obtain a court order directing that the box be opened, by force if necessary.

(4)   At the time that a safety deposit is secured, Publication 787, Seal for Securing Safety Deposit Boxes, will be signed by the revenue officer and affixed over the locks for security while the box remains under seizure. When the box is eventually opened, all residue from the seal should be removed by the revenue officer, or the bank official in the revenue officer's presence, with isopropyl alcohol or a similar solvent. To avoid damage to the safety deposit box, no sharp implement or abrasive substance should be used. The seal will dissolve when saturated with alcohol and rubbed with a cloth.

583(11).2

Preventing Access to Safe Deposit Box

(1)   A notice of lien should be filed prior to seizure since assets other than cash may be in the safe deposit box.

(2)   A notice of levy, Form 668-A, with a copy of the notice of lien attached, should be served on an officer of the bank or trust company and request made for surrender of the contents of the box.

(3)   The official may advise that the institution does not have the necessary key to open the safe deposit box or that the institution does not have the authority to open it. He/she may also suggest that the lessee's (taxpayer's) consent be secured, or that a court order be obtained to open the box.

(4)   Under these circumstances, the revenue officer should not insist that the box be opened and no attempt should be made to have the box opened by force. The box should be sealed by affixing a seizure notice, Publication 787, Seal for Securing Safety Deposit Boxes. It should be placed over the locks in such a manner so that the box cannot be opened without removing, tearing or destroying the affixed seal. The bank or trust company should then be advised not to permit the box to be opened except in the presence of a revenue officer.

(5)   Usually, taxpayers who have been reluctant to cooperate will eventually find it necessary to open their boxes, and will only be able to do so in the presence of a

revenue officer. At that time, the revenue officer, with Form 668-B in his/her possession, will be in a position to seize any property in the box.

(6) When the rental period of the safe deposit box expires and is not renewed, a bank or trust company usually has the right and power to open the box. The revenue officer should attempt to ascertain the true situation in any given case, and if the right and power exists, should try to take advantage of this opportunity to seize the contents of the box.

538(11).3

Obtaining Court Order To Open

(1) Occasionally, the procedure outlined in IRM 538(11).2 will not be satisfactory and immediate action may be desirable or necessary. For instance, the statute of limitations may be about to expire, the taxpayer may have disappeared or be in concealment, or the taxpayer or bank officials may refuse cooperation and deny access to a safe deposit box.

(2) Under these circumstances a Summons should be prepared and served on the taxpayer-boxholder in an attempt to secure information as to the contents of the box and to gain access. If this action does not accomplish the desired results, a writ of entry should be sought or a suit requested to open the safe deposit box.

Currently Not Collectible Accounts

5610

Determination of Currently Not Collectible Taxes

5611

General

(1) A Collection employee may determine that the accounts are currently not collectible.

(2) Reporting an account currently not collectible does not abate the assessment. It only stops current efforts to collect it. Collection can start again any time before the statutory period for collection expires.

5632

Unable-To-Pay Cases—Hardship

5632.1

General

(1) If collection of the liability would prevent the taxpayer from meeting necessary living expenses, it may be reported currently not collectible under a hardship closing code. Sometimes accounts should be reported currently not collectible even though the Collection Information Statement (CIS) shows assets or sources of income subject to levy.

    (a) [The Manual] provides guidelines for analyzing the taxpayer's financial condition.

    (b) Since each taxpayer's circumstances are unique, other factors such as age and health must be considered as appropriate.

    (c) Document and verify the taxpayer's financial condition.

    (d) Consider the collection potential of an offer in compromise.

(2) Consider an installment agreement before reporting an account currently not collectible as hardship.

5712

Grounds for Compromise

5712.1

General Guidelines

The compromise of a tax liability can only rest upon doubt as to liability, doubt as to collectibility, or doubt as to both liability and collectibility. IRC 7122 does not confer authority to compromise tax, interest, or penalty where the liability is clear and there is no doubt as to the ability of the Government to collect. To compromise there must be room for mutual concessions involving either or both doubt as to liability or doubt as to ability to pay. This rules out, as ground for compromise, equity or public policy considerations peculiar to a particular case, individual hardships, and similar matters which do not have a direct bearing on liability or ability to pay.

5713.2

Advising Taxpayers of Offer Provisions

(1) When criminal proceedings are not contemplated and an analysis of taxpayer's assets, liabilities, income and expenses shows that a liability cannot realistically be paid in full in the foreseeable future, the collection potential of an offer in compromise should be considered. While it is difficult to outline the exact circumstances when an offer would be the appropriate collection tool, the existence of any of the following should govern offer consideration.

   (a) Liquidation of assets and payments from present and future income will not result in full payment of tax liability.

   (b) A non-liable spouse has property which he/she may be interested in utilizing to secure a compromise of spouse's tax debt.

   (c) The taxpayer has an interest in assets against which collection action cannot be taken. For example, the taxpayer who owes a separate liability, has an interest in property held in "tenancy by the entirety" which cannot be reached or subjected to the Notice of Federal Tax Lien because of the provisions of state law. Under the compromise procedures, the taxpayer's interest is included in the total assets available in arriving at an acceptable offer in compromise.

(d) The taxpayer has relatives or friends who may be willing to lend or give the taxpayer funds for the sole purpose of reaching a compromise with the Service.

5721

General

The offer in compromise is the taxpayer's written proposal to the Government and, if accepted, is an agreement enforceable by either party under the law of contracts. Therefore, it must be definite.in its terms and conditions, since it directly affects the satisfaction of the tax liability.

5723.1

Prescribed Form

A taxpayer seeking to compromise a tax liability based on doubt as to collectibility must submit Form 433, Statement of Financial Condition and Other Information. This form includes questions geared to develop a full and complete description of the taxpayer's financial situation.

5723.3

Refusal To Submit Financial Statement

If a taxpayer professing inability to pay refuses to submit the required Form 433, the offer will be immediately rejected since the Service cannot determine whether the amount offered is also the maximum amount collectible.

5725.1

Liability of Husband and Wife

(1) Under IRC 6013(d)(3), the liability for income tax on a joint return by husband and wife is expressly made "joint and several." Either or both of the spouses are liable for the entire amount of the tax shown on a joint return. When the liability of both parties is sought to be compromised, the offer should be submitted in the names of

and signed by both spouses in order to make the waiver and other provisions of the offer form effective against both parties.

(2) An "innocent spouse" may be relieved of liability in certain cases under IRC 6013(e) and IRC 6653(b). In the event that one of the jointly liable taxpayers claims to be an "innocent spouse," the question should be referred to the district Examination function for determination.

   (a) Should the offer be acceptable, the report should not be prepared until after the district Examination function has made its determination. Since a favorable decision for the party claiming "innocent spouse" will change the amount of the liability sought to be compromised, any recommendation for acceptance must reflect the redetermined liability.

5740

Investigation of Offers

5741.1

General

(1) Once an offer in compromise is received in Special Procedures function, a determination whether the offer merits further consideration must be made. SPf should use all information contained in the offer file and may consult with the revenue officer assigned the TDAs [tax deficiency assessments] to obtain additional financial information or verify existing information.

(2) Summary rejection in SPf can be made on the grounds that the offer is frivolous, was filed merely to delay collection, or where there is no basis for compromise. A desk review of the offer can result in this determination. Although not all-inclusive, the following list provides guidelines on the criteria for summary rejection most often encountered:

   (a) Taxpayer has equity in assets subject to the Federal tax lien clearly in excess of the total liability sought to be compromised,

   (b) The total liability is extremely large and the taxpayer has offered only a minimum sum well below his/her equity and earning potential (e.g., offering $100 to compromise a $50,000 tax liability). Although the taxpayer could be persuaded to raise the offer, the fact that this initial amount offered was so low indicates bad faith and the desire to delay collection,

(c) The taxpayer is not current in his/her filing or payment requirements for periods not included in the offer,

(d) The taxpayer refuses to submit a complete financial statement (Form 433),

(e) Acceptance of the offer would adversely affect the image of the government,

(f) Taxpayer has submitted a subsequent offer which is not significantly different from a previously rejected offer and the taxpayer's financial condition has not changed,

(g) In cases involving doubt as to liability for the 100-percent penalty, the liability is clearly established and the taxpayer has offered no new evidence to cast doubt on its validity.

5741.2

Public Policy

(1) An accepted offer, like any contract, is an agreement between two parties resulting from a "meeting of the minds." It is incumbent upon each party to negotiate the best terms possible. Normally, the offer and subsequent negotiations are of a private nature. However, when accepting an offer, the Service is in a unique position since it represents the government's interest in the negotiations and the accepted offer becomes part of public record. Therefore, public policy dictates that an offer can be rejected if public knowledge of the agreement is detrimental to the government's interest. The offer may be rejected even though it can be shown conclusively that the amounts offered are greater than could reasonably be collected in any other manner. Because the Government would be in the position of foregoing revenue, the circumstances in which public policy considerations could be used to reject the offer must be construed very strictly. The following may be used as a guideline for instances where public policy issues are most often encountered:

(a) Taxpayer's notoriety is such that acceptance of an offer will hamper future Service collection and/or compliance efforts. However, simply because the taxpayer is famous or well-known is not a basis in and of itself for rejecting the offer on public policy grounds.

(b) There is a possibility of establishing a precedent which might lead to numerous offers being submitted on liabilities incurred as a result of occupational drives to enforce tax compliance.

(c)   Taxpayer has been recently convicted of tax related crimes. Again, the notoriety of the individual should be considered when making a public policy determination. The publicity surrounding the case, taxpayer's compliance since the case was concluded, or the taxpayer's position in the community should all be considered prior to rejecting an otherwise acceptable offer.

(d)   Situations where it is suspected that the financial benefits of criminal activity are concealed or the criminal activity is continuing would normally preclude acceptance of the offer for public policy reasons. Criminal Investigation function should be contacted to coordinate the Government's action in these cases.

Publication 594

Understanding The Collection Process

Mission

The purpose of the Internal Revenue Service is to collect the proper amount of tax revenue at the least cost; serve the public by continually improving the quality of our products and services; and perform in a manner warranting the highest degree of public confidence in our integrity, efficiency and fairness.

Existe una versión de esta publicación en español, la Publicación 594S, que puede obtener en la oficina local del Servicio de Impuestos Internos

KEEP THIS PUBLICATION FOR A REFERENCE

Department of the Treasury
Internal Revenue Service
Publication 594 (Rev. 10-96)
Catalog Number 46596B

Introduction

This publication explains your rights and responsibilities regarding payment of Federal tax. This information applies to all taxpayers, including individuals who owe income tax and taxpayers who owe employment tax. Special rules that apply only to employers are covered in separate sections of this publication.

Although this publication discusses the legal authority that allows the Internal Revenue Service (IRS) to collect taxes, it is not intended as a precise and technical analysis of the law.

Do not ignore your tax bill. **If you owe the tax shown on a bill, you should make arrangements to pay it.** If you believe it is incorrect, contact the IRS immediately to suspend action until the mistake is corrected. See the following discussion titled "If you believe your bill is wrong," on page 3.

Important reminder about child support. By law, the IRS can collect certified child support obligations. The collection and payment of these debts, with certain exceptions, follow the same process as the collection of unpaid taxes.

Highlights

The answers to the following questions are found in this publication. After each question, you will find the appropriate heading where the topic is explained. These commonly-asked questions relate to the bill you received for your unpaid taxes.

- What if I disagree with the amount of tax that IRS says I owe?

  See "If you believe your bill is wrong," on page 3.

- What is the best way to contact the IRS and explain my situation (why I haven't paid)?

  See "Numbers to Call for Assistance," on this page.

- What do I do if I disagree with the IRS employee and want to appeal?

  See "When you do not agree with decisions of IRS employees," on page 2.

- What are my rights to appeal if I disagree with an IRS decision?

  See "When you do not agree with decisions of IRS employees," "Administrative review," and "Your Appeal Rights," on pages 2, 7, and 8.

- I have tried to get the IRS to resolve my tax problems but can't.

  See "Problem Resolution Program," on page 2.

- Can I make monthly payments on my account?

  See "Making installment payments for individuals or businesses," and "Simplified installment agreements" on page 3.

- Can I settle my tax account for less than what I owe?

  See "Offer in Compromise," on page 4.

- What if; I can't pay any amount? Will you take money out of my wages?

  See "What Happens When You Take No Action to Pay," and "Levy on wages," on pages 5 and 6.

- Can I postpone paying my taxes until my financial condition improves?

  See "Delaying collection if you cannot pay," on page 3.

- I'm an employer. What happens if I cannot pay my employment taxes?

  See "What Happens When You Take No Action to Pay," and "Trust Fund Recovery Penalty Assessments for Employers," on pages 5 and 8.

- How do I make a tax deposit if I do not have tax deposit coupons for employment taxes?

  See "Paying employment taxes," on page 4.

- What happens to my tax refund if I owe taxes for prior years?

  See "If your current Federal and State tax return shows a tax refund and you owe back taxes," on page 4.

- Does owing taxes have an effect on my credit?

  See "Lien," on page 5.

Numbers to Call

Tax Information & Assistance
  Call Specific number if listed,
  otherwise call toll free
  1-800-829-1040

Tax Forms and Publications
  1-800-829-3676
    1-800-829-4059 for TDD users)

  FAX: 703-487-4160

Internet: World Wide Web-
http://www.irs.ustreas.gov
FTP-ftp.irs.ustreas.gov
Telnet-iris.irs.ustreas.gov

■■■■■■■
■■■■■■■
■■■■■■■

▶ *What do I do if I disagree with an IRS employee's decision and want to appeal?*

See "When you do not agree with decisions of IRS employees."

▶ *How can I have my case transferred to another IRS office?*

See "Transferring the location of your tax case."

▶ *How can I get help on unresolved tax problems?*

See "Problem Resolution Program."

Your Rights

When dealing with the IRS, you have the right to be treated fairly, professionally, promptly, and courteously by IRS employees.

Publication 1, Your Rights As A Taxpayer. This publication explains some of your most important rights as a taxpayer. It also explains the Examination, Appeal, Collection and Refund processes.

You received a copy of Publication 1 with your initial bill, which is also called a *"Notice of Tax Due and Demand for Payment."* You may also request a copy of Publication 1 from an IRS employee at or before your first in-person interview with an IRS employee.

▶ *When you do not agree with decisions of IRS employees.* If at any step of the Collection process you do not agree with the decision of an IRS employee, you have the right to an administrative review with the employee's manager. You also have a right to appeal many collection actions including Liens, Levies and Seizures to the Appeals Office and effective January 1997 the termination of installment agreements. At your request, the employee will either arrange for you to meet with the manager or tell you the manager's name and where to contact him or her. Publication 1660, Collection Appeal Rights for Liens, Levies, Seizures, and Installment Agreements), explains how to request an appeal and your rights to appeal liens, levies, seizures, and termination of installment agreements.

Who can represent you in IRS matters. You may represent yourself or you may have an attorney, certified public accountant, enrolled agent or any person enrolled to practice before the Internal Revenue Service represent you. For example you may want your tax preparer to respond to a tax bill that you believe is not correct.

To authorize another person to have access to your Federal tax information, you can use Form 2848, *Power of Attorney and Declaration of Representative,* or Form 8821, *Tax Information Authorization,* or any other properly written power of attorney or authorization. You can get copies of these forms from your local IRS office or by calling the toll-free number shown on page 1.

Sharing your tax information. Under the law, we can share your tax information with city and state tax agencies, and in some cases, the Department of Justice, other federal agencies, and persons you authorize. We can also share it with certain foreign governments under tax treaty provisions.

▶ *Transferring the location of your tax case.* You have the right to request that we transfer your tax case to another IRS office. Generally, we will transfer your case if you have a valid reason for making the request, such as a change of address.

If you move, send Form 8822, *Change of Address,* to any IRS office, so you will receive any notices sent to you.

Receiving receipts for payments you made to IRS. IRS must provide you with a receipt (Form 809) when you pay in cash. You have the right to ask for and receive a receipt for all payments you make. You should ask for a receipt at the time you make a payment. You also have the right to receive copies or confirmation of all contractual arrangements (such as an installment agreement) that you make with us.

▶ **Problem Resolution Program (PRP)**

PRP is a program designed to help taxpayers who have been unable to resolve their tax problems after repeated attempts to do so with another IRS department.

Before contacting PRP, you should first request assistance from an employee or manager in an IRS Collection office. If the problem is still not resolved, you should contact your local IRS district office and ask for PRP.

PRP provides an avenue to help resolve your problem when you believe that: 1) your account information is incorrect, 2) a significant matter or event is not being considered in your case, or 3) your rights as a taxpayer have been violated.

If you suffer a significant hardship. If you have or are about to have a significant hardship because of the collection of your tax debt, additional assistance is available. A significant hardship may occur if you cannot maintain necessities such as food, clothing, shelter, transportation, and medical treatment.

To apply for relief, you can submit Form 911, *Application For Taxpayer Assistance Order (ATAO) to Relieve Hardship,* or contact the district PRP office if the employee assigned to your case cannot or will not take action to relieve your hardship. Any IRS employee can help you apply for ATAO handling. We can help you obtain and complete the form, take the information by telephone, or you can contact the district PRP office in order to obtain and complete the form and submit it to PRP.

The Taxpayer Advocate or a Problem Resolution Officer will review your application and if appropriate, take steps to relieve your hardship.

When You Have Not Paid Enough Tax

If you do not pay the full amount of tax you owe, you will receive a tax bill. This bill begins the collection process. The length of the process depends on how soon you respond and pay the bill. We encourage you to pay your bill by check or money order.

Understanding your tax bill. When you file your tax return with the IRS, we check it to make sure the math is accurate and to see if you have paid the correct amount of tax. If you owe tax and have not paid all of it, we will send you a bill which is called a *Notice of Tax Due and Demand for Payment.* The bill will include the tax due, plus penalties and interest that we have charged on the unpaid balance of your account from the date you should have paid your taxes.

What you can do to avoid having overdue taxes. If you owe taxes because not enough tax was withheld from your wages, you should file a new Form W-4, *Employee's Withholding Allowance Certificate,* with your employer(s) to claim a lower number of withholding allowances. If you need help computing the correct number of withholding allowances, see Publication 919, *Is My Withholding Correct?*

If you are self-employed and owe tax, you should increase your estimated tax payments. These payments are explained in Publication 505, *Tax Withholding and Estimated Tax,* and are reported on Form 1040ES, *Estimated Tax for Individuals.*

If you are an employer, see "Paying employment taxes," discussed on page 4 of this publication. For other types of taxes, see the tax instruction booklet that was mailed with your tax forms.

If you believe your bill is wrong. If you believe your bill is wrong, please let us know, as soon as possible, by calling the telephone number identified on the bill or by writing to the IRS office that sent you this bill. You may also call the IRS or visit the IRS office nearest you.

To help us correct the problem, please include in your correspondence explaining the problem: 1) a copy of the bill, and 2) copies of any records, canceled checks, etc., that will help us understand what you believe is wrong.

Here is a sample format you can use for a letter:

Date

Internal Revenue Service
Address
- Your name, address, and daytime telephone number.
- Taxpayer identification number (social security number or employer identification number) as stated on bill.
- Tax form number as stated on bill.
- Tax period as stated on bill.

State your reason(s) why you believe your bill is wrong. Enclose copies of any information supporting your statement, such as copies of canceled checks or a copy of your tax return and a copy of the tax bill.

Your signature

If we find that you are correct, we will adjust your account, and if necessary, we will send you a corrected bill.

Making Arrangements to Pay Your Bill

This section explains what happens if you are unable to pay your bill in full. All taxpayers are expected to pay their taxes in full; however, if you cannot pay your tax bill in full, we will analyze your ability to pay and then try to find the best way for you to pay the bill.

We will consider different methods of payment, such as paying in installments.

Note: The first part of this section applies primarily to individuals. However, many of the procedures also apply to employers. The last part of this section explains the rules that apply only to employers and payment of employment taxes.

When you pay your tax bill or send us correspondence, please do the following:

1) Include a copy of the most recent tax bill,
2) Identify the tax form number, the tax year or period, and your taxpayer identification number, as shown on your bill, in all your correspondence with us.
3) Also, write your taxpayer identification number (social security number or employer identification number, as appropriate) on your check, and
4) Enclose your payment if you owe tax.

If you can pay only part of your bill. If you cannot pay your bill in full, you should pay as much as you can and immediately call us, write us, or visit your nearest IRS office to explain your circumstances. Whenever you write, be sure to enclose a copy of your tax bill and on your letter, print your name, taxpayer identification number, and the tax form and period shown on your bill.

After we receive your explanation, we will try to find the best way for you to pay your tax bill.

1) We may ask you to complete a Collection Information Statement. We use this form to review your financial condition to determine how you can pay the amount due.

2) We can ask you to sell or mortgage any assets to secure funds to pay the taxes.
3) We will ask you to secure a commercial loan if we determine that you are able to do so. A benefit of obtaining a loan is that you will avoid penalties and interest that we will continue to charge on your unpaid balance until all tax, penalties, and interest are paid.
4) We may take enforced collection action, such as issue a levy on your bank account, levy your wages, or take your other income or assets if you neglect or refuse to pay or make other arrangements to satisfy your bill in full.

Making installment payments for individuals or businesses. We will help you complete a *Collection Information Statement,* Form 433A or 433F for individuals, or Form 433B, for businesses. We use these forms to help us compare your monthly income with your expenses, determine if you qualify for an installment agreement, and the amount you can pay.

You can use these methods to make installment payments:

1) Personal checks, business checks, money orders, or certified funds,
2) Payroll deductions that your employer agrees to take from your salary and send to the IRS in regular payments, or
3) Electronic transfers from your bank account or other similar means.

If you have an installment agreement, you must make each payment on time. If you cannot pay on time, let us know why immediately.

Caution: You will be charged a fee if your installment agreement is approved or needs to be reinstated. Also, while you are making installment payments, we will continue to charge your account with interest and penalties on the unpaid balance of taxes you owe plus interest on the unpaid balance of penalties and interest you owe.

Other actions that we may take include:

- Filing a Notice of Federal Tax Lien to secure the Government's interest until you make the final payment (See the section on "Liens" on pages 5-6),
- Requiring you to provide current information on your financial condition to determine any change in your ability to pay, and
- Ending the installment agreement if you do not provide financial information when requested or if you do not meet the terms of the agreement, such as paying late, missing a payment, or not filing or paying all required tax returns. If this happens, we may take enforced collection action. See "What Happens When You Take No Action To Pay," on page 5.

Note: Because your agreement is based on your financial circumstances, it could change. However, you will receive a letter 30 days in advance of any change we would make to your plan.

Simplified installment agreements. A simplified process enables many taxpayers to qualify for a streamlined installment agreement. In most cases, applying requires little paperwork and a Federal tax lien may not be required. To apply, call or visit your local IRS office for details about completing Form 9465, *Installment Agreement Request.*

Delaying collection if you cannot pay. If we determine that you cannot pay any amount of your tax debt, we may temporarily delay collection until

▶ *What if I disagree with the amount of tax that IRS says I owe?*

See "If you believe your bill is wrong."

▶ *Can I make monthly payments on my account?*

See "Making installment payments for individuals or businesses," and "Simplified installment agreements."

▶ *Can I postpone paying my taxes until my financial condition improves?*

See "Delaying collection if you cannot pay."

3

your financial condition improves. If we delay collection, the amount of your debt will increase because we will continue to charge a penalty for late payment and interest on your debt. During a delay, we will review your ability to pay. We may also file a Notice of Federal Tax Lien (explained on page 5) to protect the Government's interest in your assets and send you a reminder to pay.

If your current Federal and State tax return shows a tax refund and you owe back taxes. If you are entitled to receive a tax refund while you still owe unpaid taxes, we will automatically apply the refund to pay the unpaid tax debt and refund the remaining balance to you.

If you are bankrupt. If you are involved in an ongoing bankruptcy proceeding, contact your local IRS office. While the bankruptcy proceeding may not eliminate your tax debt, it will temporarily stop IRS enforcement action to collect a debt related to the bankruptcy.

▶ ***Offer in Compromise.*** The Service may accept an offer in compromise to settle unpaid tax accounts for less than the full amount of the balance due when the facts support the liklihood that the Service will be unable to collect the debt in full. This applies to all taxes, including any interest and penalty or additional amount(s), arising under the Internal Revenue laws. The amount you offer must reflect your maximum ability to pay, taking into consideration the total value of your equity in all your assets and future income.

How to file an Offer in Compromise. You can get Form 656, *Offer in Compromise*, and Form 433A, *Collection Information Statement for Individuals*, Publication 1854, How to Prepare a Collection Information statement (Form 433A), or Form 433B, *Collection Information Statement for Business*, plus additional information regarding the filing procedure, at any IRS office. You may also call the toll-free numbers listed on page 1 for assistance or to receive tax forms or publications.

Additional Payment Procedures for Employers

Throughout this publication, we will refer to Employer's Quarterly Federal Taxes as employment taxes. This tax is reported on Form 941, *Employer's Quarterly Tax Return. Form 940, Employer's Annual Federal Unemployment Tax Return*, is used by employers to report Federal unemployment tax.

Note: If your business receives funds from the Small Business Administration or a Small Business Investment Company, you should notify that organization about your unpaid taxes.

General information. Employment taxes are:
- The amounts you withhold from your employees for income tax and social security tax, plus
- The amount of social security tax you pay as an employer on behalf of each employee.

Although your bill includes all of the amounts above, the amounts that you have withheld from your employee's earnings are referred to as "trust fund taxes." They are called "trust fund taxes" because they are actually the employee's money which you hold in trust until you make a Federal tax deposit in that amount.

Degree of taxpayer cooperation. When we collect these unpaid taxes, we distinguish between those taxpayers who show a sincere effort to meet their tax obligations and those taxpayers who show little or no evidence of cooperation. We make this distinction because we believe that taxpayers who are making an effort to comply should be given an opportunity to resolve their bill, over a short period of time.

On the other hand, we believe that "repeater" or "chronic delinquent" trust fund cases require a swift and decisive IRS response for the following reasons:

1) The taxpayer (employer) is using "trust fund" monies as operating capital and thereby gains an unfair competitive advantage over other businesses who are complying, and
2) The taxpayer has been warned and yet continues to divert the "trust fund" monies.

Caution: The amount owed can increase dramatically if the taxpayer ignores the federal tax deposit and/or filing requirements, thus making it increasingly difficult to recover from the tax debt.

▶ ***Paying employment taxes.*** You should pre-pay your taxes by using Federal Tax Deposit coupons (Form 8109). If you do not have preprinted tax deposit coupons, call or visit the IRS and request a Federal Tax Deposit coupon (Form 8109-B). You should make your deposits directly to the Federal Reserve Bank in your area or to any financial institution authorized to accept Federal tax deposits.

Caution: Do not make Federal tax deposits to an IRS office. A deposit to an IRS office will not be considered as a deposit of the taxes and will subject you to a penalty. However, you may file Form 941, *Employer's Quarterly Federal Tax Return*, at an IRS office.

If any of the preprinted information on your Form 8109 is incorrect, follow the instructions in the coupon book for correcting it.

Reordering forms. You will receive a new Federal tax deposit coupon booklet automatically when you use coupon number 6 or 7 from your current book. However, if for some reason you do not receive your coupons automatically, you can call or visit your nearest IRS office and we will place the order for you.

More information on Form 8109. For more information about making federal tax deposits, you can obtain a copy of Circular E, *Employer's Tax Guide*, or Notice 109, *Information About Depositing Employment and Excise Taxes*, from any IRS office.

If you do not deposit taxes on time. If you do not timely pre-pay your tax using deposit coupons or if you were not required to make any deposit and/or did not include your payment when you filed your return, we will charge you interest and penalties on any unpaid balance.

We may charge you penalties for not depositing employment taxes timely up to 15% of the amount not deposited, depending upon how many days late you make the deposit.

If you do not pay withheld trust fund taxes, we may take additional collection action.

- We can require you to file and pay your taxes on a monthly rather than quarterly basis.
- We can also require you to open a special bank account and deposit the amounts required to be withheld within two banking days after you pay wages to your employees. If, after you are required to do so, you do not open a special account and make timely deposits, you may be found guilty of a misdemeanor.

▶ **7** *Can I settle my tax account for less than what I owe?*

See "Offer in Compromise."

▶ **8** *How do I make a tax deposit if I do not have tax deposit coupons for employment taxes?*

See "Paying employment taxes."

What Happens When You Take No Action to Pay

You will not need to read this section if you have already paid your tax. Please note that before we take any of the actions explained in this section, we try to contact you and give you the opportunity to pay voluntarily.

If you do not take some action to pay your tax bill, we may take any of the following actions:

- File a Notice of Federal Tax Lien,
- Serve a Notice of Levy,
- Seize and sell your property (personal, real estate, and business property),
- Notify payers of your interest and dividend income to begin backup withholding, or
- Assess a trust fund recovery penalty, if you owe employment taxes. (See "Trust Fund Recovery Penalty Assessments for Employers," discussed on page 8).

Some of these actions are referred to as "enforced collection actions" because they are the means by which the IRS can enforce the notice and demand for tax.

Lien

This section gives information to help you understand what a lien is, how it affects your credit rating, and how it is released.

Before the IRS files a Notice of Federal Tax Lien, three requirements must be met:

1) The IRS must assess the liability,
2) The IRS must send you a notice and demand for payment, and
3) You must neglect or refuse to fully pay the liability within 10 days of notice and demand. Entering into an installment agreement does not preclude the filing of a notice of lien.

Once these requirements are met, a lien is created for the amount of your tax debt. This lien attaches to all your property (such as your house or car) and to all your rights to property (such as your accounts receivable).

A lien is not valid against the claims of other creditors until the IRS files a Notice of Federal Tax Lien with an appropriate official to establish priority status among these creditors. An example of this is filing a lien in the county where you own property or in the state where you conduct business. By filing a Notice of Federal Tax Lien, the Government is providing a public notice to your creditors that the Government has a claim against all your property, including property that you acquire after the lien was filed.

Caution: Once filed, a lien may harm your credit rating.

Releasing a Lien

The IRS will issue a Release of the Notice of Federal Tax Lien:

1) Within 30 days after you satisfy the tax due (including interest and other additions to the tax) by payment or adjustment, or
2) Within 30 days after we accept a bond that you submit guaranteeing payment of the debt.

In addition, you must pay all fees charged by a state or other jurisdiction for both filing and releasing the lien. These fees will be added to the balance you owe.

Publication 1450, *Request for Release of Federal Tax Lien,* describes how to request a release of a Federal tax lien.

Automatic release of a Federal Tax Lien. A lien will release automatically if we have not refiled it before the time expires to legally collect the tax. This is usually a period of 10 years.

What you can do if IRS does not release a lien. If the IRS knowingly or negligently does not release a Notice of Federal Tax Lien when it should be released, you may sue the Federal government, but not IRS employees, for damages.

Before you file a lawsuit, you must first exhaust all administrative appeals. Also, you must file the suit within 2 years from the date when the IRS should have released the lien.

If you win a civil lawsuit, you may be awarded payment for any losses that you had because the IRS did not release the lien. You may also be paid for your share of the costs of the lawsuit. However, any costs that you could have reasonably reduced will be subtracted from that payment.

Special Release of Tax Lien — Application for a Discharge of a Federal Tax Lien against Property

Each application for a discharge of a tax lien releases the effects of the lien against one specific piece of property. If you are giving up ownership of property, such as when you sell your home, you may apply for a Certificate of Discharge.

You may receive a Certificate of Discharge if any of the following circumstances apply:

- You have other property, subject to the lien, that is worth at least two times the total of the tax you owe, plus any additions to the tax you owe and any other debts you owe on the property, such as a mortgage.
- The IRS receives the value of the government's interest in the property and you are giving up ownership.
- The IRS determines that the government's interest in the property has no value at the time you are giving up ownership.
- The property in question is being sold, and there is a dispute as to who is entitled to the sale proceeds, and the proceeds are placed in escrow while the dispute is being resolved.

When applying for a discharge, you must send your written application in duplicate to the IRS district director where your property is located.

For assistance in requesting a discharge of a Federal Tax Lien, see Publication 783, *Instructions on How to Apply for a Certificate of Discharge of Property From the Federal Tax Lien.*

When the IRS Lien Is Secondary to Another Lien — Subordination

Subordination is made at the discretion of the IRS. It means that the IRS has allowed its lien to take a lower place than someone else's lien.

The IRS may let its lien take a lower place than a "junior lienor" (someone whose lien originally had a lower place then the IRS lien) if it receives the dollar value of the lien in the property that the junior lienor is acquiring, for example, a second mortgage.

We may also subordinate a lien if we believe that doing so would speed collection of the tax. For example, we may subordinate a lien that would allow a farmer to receive a loan to harvest a crop.

I'm an employer. What happens if I cannot pay my employment taxes?

See "What Happens When You Take No Action To Pay" (this page) and "Trust Fund Recovery Penalty Assessments for Employers" (page 8).

Does owing taxes have an effect on my credit?

See "Lien."

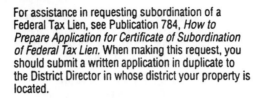

For assistance in requesting subordination of a Federal Tax Lien, see Publication 784, *How to Prepare Application for Certificate of Subordination of Federal Tax Lien.* When making this request, you should submit a written application in duplicate to the District Director in whose district your property is located.

Withdrawal of Liens —Internal Revenue Code 6323(j) and Taxpayers Bill of Rights 2 allows the withdrawal of a filed notice of tax lien if:

- the notice was filed prematurely or not in accordance with IRS procedures,
- the taxpayer has entered into an installment agreement to satisfy the liability on the notice of lien unless the agreement provides otherwise),
- the withdrawal will facilitate collection of the tax, or
- the withdrawal would be in the best interests of both the taxpayer (as determined by the Taxpayer Advocate) and the Government

The IRS must provide a copy of the withdrawal to the taxpayer and, upon written request of the taxpayer, to other specified institutions.

Incorrect Lien — Your Administrative Appeal

You may appeal the filing of a Notice of Federal Tax Lien if you believe we filed the lien in error. A lien is incorrect if:

- You paid the entire amount you owed the IRS before we filed the lien,
- We assessed the tax and filed the lien when you were in bankruptcy and subject to the automatic stay during bankruptcy,
- We made a procedural error in making an assessment, or
- The time to collect the tax (called the statute of limitations) expired before we filed the lien.

Note: You may not appeal this Notice of Federal Tax Lien if you are challenging the underlying debt that generated the filing of the lien.

If we agree with your appeal, we will release the lien within 14 days after we determine that the lien was filed incorrectly. we will issue a certificate of release of an incorrect lien that includes a statement that we filed the Notice of Federal Tax Lien in error.

▶ *What effect can a levy have on my salary and bank accounts?*

See "Levy."

▶ *What must happen to release a levy?*

See "Releasing a levy."

▶ Levy

A levy is one method the IRS uses to collect tax that you have not paid voluntarily. It means we can, by legal authority, take property to satisfy a tax debt. Levies can be made on property that you hold (such as your vehicle, boat, or house) or on property that is yours, but is held by third parties (such as wages or funds on deposit at a bank).

For example, IRS may levy your wages (salary), commissions, the cash value of life insurance, licenses or franchises, securities, contracts, demand notes, accounts receivables, rental income, dividends, retirement accounts, etc.

Also, in most states that have state income taxes, the IRS can levy a state refund check and apply the state refund to a federal tax debt.

A levy is different from a lien. A lien is a claim used as security for the tax debt, while a levy is used to actually take the property to satisfy the tax debt.

Authority to levy. Generally, the IRS does not need court authorization to take levy action.

However, we are required to have court authorization to enter private premises, if this is necessary, to seize property.

Generally, before IRS takes levy action, three legal requirements must be met:

1) The IRS must assess the tax and send you a "Notice and Demand" for payment,
2) You must neglect or refuse to pay the tax, and
3) The IRS must send you a Final Notice of Intent to Levy at least 30 days in advance of the levy.

We may give you this notice in person, leave it at your dwelling or usual place of business, or send it by certified or registered mail to your last known address. The bill that usually accompanies this publication is such a notice.

Caution: If we conclude that collection of your tax is threatened, we may take immediate collection action before all three requirements have been met. For example, if a taxpayer is planning to quickly leave the country, we may believe that collection is threatened or in jeopardy.

If we make a decision that collection of your tax is threatened or in jeopardy, you may seek IRS managerial or court review, or both. These procedures are explained in the letter you will receive when the demand for payment is made.

Levy on wages. If the IRS levies your salary or wages, the levy will end when one of the following occurs:

- The levy is released,
- You pay your tax debt, or
- The time expires for legally collecting the tax.

If we levy your salary or wages, contact the specific person or call the telephone number listed on the Notice of Levy for assistance.

Levy on your bank account. If the IRS levies your bank account, your bank is required to hold funds you have on deposit, up to the amount you owe, for 21 days. This period allows you time to resolve any problems about the levy or make other arrangements to pay. The bank is then required to send the money, plus interest if it applies, to the IRS.

To discuss your account, you should contact the IRS by calling the person whose name is shown on the Notice of Levy.

▶ ***Releasing a levy.*** We must release your levy if any of the following occur:

- You pay the tax, penalty, and interest that you owe.
- The time for collection (statute of limitations) expires before the levy is served.
- You provide documentation for the IRS to determine that releasing the levy will help collect the tax.
- You have, or entered into, an approved, current installment agreement for the tax on the levy. (However, If you and the IRS have agreed that a current levy will continue while installment payments are made, we will not release it.)
- The IRS determines that the levy is creating an economic hardship.
- The fair market value of the property exceeds the levy and releasing part of the seized property would not hinder the collection of tax.

Property that cannot be levied. Certain types of property are exempt from seizure (levy) by Federal law. They include all of the following items:

- Wearing apparel and school books. (However, expensive items of wearing apparel, such as furs, are luxuries and are not exempt from levy).

- Fuel, provisions, furniture, and personal effects for a head of household, that total up to $2,500 (index for inflation after 1996).
- Books and tools you use in your trade, business, or profession, that total up to $1,250 (index for inflation after 1996).
- Unemployment benefits.
- Undelivered mail.
- Certain annuity and pension benefits.
- Certain service-connected disability payments.
- Workmen's compensation.
- Salary, wages, or other income that have been included in a judgment for court-ordered child support payments.
- Certain public assistance payments.
- Assistance under the Job Training Partnership Act.
- Deposits to the special Treasury fund made by members of the armed forces and Public Health Service employees who are on permanent duty assigned outside the United States or its possessions.
- A minimum weekly exemption for wages, salary, and other income based on the standard deduction plus the number of allowable personal exemptions divided by 52. In the case of no response to the certification of exemptions, the exempt amount will be computed as if you were married filing separately with one exemption.

Publication 1494, *Table of Figuring Amount Exempt from Levy on Wages, Salary and Other Income* (Forms 668-W and 668-W(c)), can be used to determine the amount of earned income exempt from levy.

Returning levied property. We can consider returning property that has been levied if:

- We levy before the two required notices are sent to you or before your time for responding to them has passed (10 days for the Notice and Demand; 30 days for the Notice of Intent to levy).
- We do not follow our procedures.
- We agree to let you pay in installments, but we still levy, and the agreement does not say that we can do this.
- Returning the property will help get the tax paid.
- Returning the property is both in you best interest and the government's.

How to file a claim for reimbursement when IRS made a mistake in levying your account or misplaced your check. You may be entitled to be reimbursed for fees your bank charged you because IRS made a mistake when we levied your account.

To receive this reimbursement, you must file a claim with the IRS within one year after the bank charged you with the fee. To file your claim, use Form 8546, *Claim for Reimbursement of Bank Charges Incurred Due to Erroneous Service Levy or Misplaced Payment Check.*

▶ Seizures and Sales

If you do not pay (or make arrangements to resolve) your tax debt, we may seize and sell any type of real or personal property that you own or have an interest in (including residential and business property) to satisfy your tax bill. Seizure of a primary residence requires the approval from an IRS district director or assistant district director except if the collection of the tax is in jeopardy.

If we seize or levy your property, you should contact the IRS employee who made the seizure or levy for assistance.

When property cannot be seized or levied. We may not seize any of your property when the estimated cost to seize and sell the property is more than the fair market value of the property to be seized. In addition, we may not seize or levy your property on the day you attend a collection interview because of a summons.

However, we can seize or levy your property on this date if collection of the tax is in jeopardy. You may contact the IRS employee who made the seizure or levy if you have any questions.

Administrative review. You have the right to an administrative review of our seizure action when we have taken your personal property that you need to maintain your business. See "When you do not agree with decisions of IRS employees," on page 2 for information about how to apply for this review.

Notice of proposed sale. After we seize your property, we must give public notice of a pending sale. Public notice usually appears in a newspaper that is published or circulated in the county where the sale will be held. We will personally deliver the original notice of sale to you or send it to you by certified mail. After we give notice, we must wait at least 10 days before conducting the sale.

However, if the property is perishable and must be sold immediately, we are not required to wait 10 days before holding the sale.

Minimum bid. Before the sale, we will compute a "minimum bid price." This is the lowest amount that we will accept for the sale of the property to protect your interest in that property. We will tell you the minimum bid price we set, which is usually 80% or more of the forced sale value of the property, after any liens are subtracted.

If you disagree with this minimum bid price, you can appeal it by requesting that the price be recomputed by either an IRS valuation engineer or a private appraiser who can assist the IRS engineer. If you still disagree with the revised appraisal, you may obtain a second appraisal.

▶ ***Release of property.*** Before the date of sale, we may release the property that we seized from you if you:

1) Pay us the amount of the Government's interest in the property,
2) Enter into an escrow arrangement,
3) Furnish an acceptable bond, or
4) Make an acceptable agreement for payment of the tax.

Your right to "buy back" the property. You have the right to "buy back" your personal property at any time before the sale. To do this, you must pay the tax due, including interest and penalties, and pay the expenses of seizure.

For real estate, you (or anyone with an interest in the property) may redeem it at any time within 180 days after the sale by paying the purchaser the amount paid for the property plus interest at 20% annually.

Sale procedures. You may request that we sell the seized property within 60 days. For information on how to make this request, you should contact the IRS employee who made the seizure. We will grant your request unless it is in the Government's best interest to retain the property. We will inform you in writing of our decision whether or not we are able to grant your request.

After the sale, we use the proceeds first to pay the expenses of the levy and sale. We then use any remaining amount to pay the tax bill.

If the sale proceeds are less than the total of the tax bill and the expenses of levy and sale, you will still have to pay the remaining unpaid tax.

If the sale proceeds are more than the total of the tax bill and the expenses of the levy and sale, we will notify you about the surplus money and provide you with instructions about how to request a refund. However, if a person, such as a mortgagee or other lienholder, submits a claim superior to yours, we will pay that claim before we refund any remaining funds to you based on your request.

▶ *What types of property can the IRS seize?*

See "Seizures and Sales."

▶ *How can I obtain a release of the seized property?*

See "Release of Property."

► *My business is closed. Can I be held responsible for unpaid "trust fund" taxes?*

See "Who is a responsible person for trust fund tax."

Backup Withholding

You are legally required to report your interest, dividend, or patronage dividend income on your individual income tax return. You must report the correct amounts, and these amounts must match the amounts that the payers report to IRS. You are also required to provide your correct taxpayer identification number to all payers of interest, dividends and miscellaneous income.

Usually, there is no withholding of tax on interest and dividend payments. However, if you do not report this interest and dividend income or provide the correct taxpayer identification number as required, you may be subject to backup withholding. This occurs when we notify all those who pay you interest or dividends to begin withholding income tax on these payments. You may also be subject to backup withholding if you do not provide your correct taxpayer identification number.

How to prevent backup withholding from starting. Before we notify your payers to withhold, we will send you at least four notices over a period of at least 120 days to give you a chance to correct the underreporting and pay any additional tax to avoid backup withholding.

Stopping backup withholding. Once backup withholding begins, we will stop it when:

1) The income is properly reported,
2) The income tax is paid in full,
3) You furnish the correct taxpayer identification number, and
4) The IRS notifies the payer to stop withholding.

Generally, we will notify payers to stop withholding at the end of the year if we receive full payment of the tax by October 15. If we receive full payment after October 15, they will continue withholding through the following year.

While you are subject to backup withholding, you must certify to any new payers that you are subject to backup withholding. If you falsely certify that you are not subject to backup withholding, you will be liable for a penalty of $1,000 or imprisonment for up to one year, or both. For additional information, see Publications 1281 and 1679 which contain information about backup withholding and taxpayer identification numbers.

Trust Fund Recovery Penalty Assessments for Employers

To encourage prompt payment of withheld income and employment taxes, including social security and railroad retirement taxes or collected excise taxes, Congress passed a law that provides for the trust fund recovery penalty. This penalty is used as a tool for collection of unpaid employment taxes. The penalty also applies to those excise taxes which are commonly referred to as "collected" excise taxes.

If you are a "responsible person," we can apply this penalty against you immediately after you do not pay trust fund taxes in response to a notice and demand for payment. Also, we can apply this penalty regardless of whether you are out of business or without assets.

Caution: Once we assert the penalty, we can take collection action against your individual assets, such as filing a Federal tax lien if you are the responsible person(s).

Figuring the penalty amount. The amount of the penalty is equal to the unpaid trust fund tax. The penalty is computed based on two amounts which constitute trust fund tax:

1) The unpaid income taxes withheld, plus
2) The employee's portion of the FICA taxes withheld.

For collected taxes, the penalty is based on the unpaid amount of collected excise taxes.

Who Is Subject to the Penalty

We may impose the penalty against any person who is responsible for collecting or paying withheld income and employment taxes or for paying collected excise taxes AND who willfully fails to collect or pay them. Therefore, the two key elements that support this penalty assessment are **responsibility** and **willfulness**.

► *Who is a responsible person for trust fund tax.* A responsible person is one who has the duty to perform and the power to direct the collecting, accounting, and paying of trust fund taxes. Therefore, responsibility involves status, duty, and authority.

This person may be:

- An officer or an employee of a corporation,
- A member or employee of a partnership,
- A corporate director or shareholder,
- A member of a board of trustees of a nonprofit organization, or
- Another person with sufficient authority and control over funds to direct their disbursement.

In some situations the responsible person may be a person who is not directly affiliated with the delinquent business. For example, the penalty may be assessed against an official or employee of a bank or other financial institution who has the authority to direct the financial affairs of the business and:

- Furnishes funds to a business and directs how the funds are to be distributed, or
- Directs the business not to pay the taxes.

Proof of willfulness. By willful, we mean conduct that is intentional, deliberate, voluntary, and knowing — as opposed to accidental conduct. YOU are considered to have a willful attitude if you have free will or choice and yet either intentionally disregard the law or are plainly indifferent to legal requirements.

For willfulness to exist, the responsible person must:

1) Have known about the unpaid taxes, and
2) Have used the funds to keep the business going or allowed available funds to be paid to other creditors.

Willfulness does not imply that you had acted for personal gain. For example, the courts ruled in one case that the actions of a corporate officer, in permitting withheld taxes to be used for operating expenses of the business (whether at the officer's direction or with his tacit approval) is sufficient evidence of willfulness that the trust fund recovery penalty can be charged to that officer.

In addition, If an employer meets payrolls, we can infer that sufficient funds were available to pay the tax, regardless of whether the funds were actually set aside or otherwise specifically identified for tax purposes.

Your Appeal Rights

The appeal process is outlined clearly in Publication 5, *Appeal Rights and Preparation of Protests for Unagreed Cases.* If we recommend that you pay the trust fund recovery penalty amount, you can attempt to resolve the matter informally through a discussion with the group manager of the IRS employee in your district. If you disagree with the decision of the group manager, you may request a conference before the Regional Director of Appeals.

☆ **U.S. GOVERNMENT PRINTING OFFICE: 1996 416-402**

Quick and Easy Access to Tax Help and Forms:

 ## PERSONAL COMPUTER

Why not use a personal computer and modem to get the forms and information you need?

Here is a sample of what you will find when you visit the IRS's Internet Web Site at — http://www.irs.ustreas.gov

- Forms and Instructions
- Publications
- Educational Materials
- IRS Press Releases and Fact Sheets
- Tele-Tax Topics on About 150 Tax Topics
- Answers to Frequently Asked Questions

You can also reach us using:

- Telnet at **iris.irs.ustreas.gov**
- File Transfer Protocol at **ftp.irs.ustreas.gov**
- Direct Dial (by modem)—You can also dial direct to the Internal Revenue Information Services (IRIS) by calling **703-321-8020** using your modem. IRIS is an on-line information service on FedWorld. FedWorld's help desk (703-487-4608) offers technical assistance on accessing IRIS (not tax help) during normal business hours.

 ## PHONE

You can also get information and forms by phone. Just call 1-800-829-1040 for free information.

Forms and Publications

You can order forms, instructions, and publications by phone. Just call 1-800-TAX-FORM (1-800-829-3676) between 7:30 a.m. and 5:30 p.m. on weekdays. The best time to call is before 9 a.m. or after 2 p.m. Thursdays and Fridays are the best days to contact us. (The hours are Pacific time in Alaska and Hawaii, Eastern time in Puerto Rico.) You should receive your order or notification of its status within 7 to 15 workdays.

Tele-Tax Topics

You can listen to pre-recorded messages covering about 150 tax topics.

 ## FAX

*Just call **703-487-4160** from the telephone connected to your fax machine to get the following:*

Forms and Instructions

We can fax you over 100 of the most requested forms and instructions.

Tele-Tax Topics

We can also fax you Tele-Tax topics covering about 150 tax topics.

 ## MAIL

You can order forms, instructions, and publications by completing the order blank.

 ## WALK-IN

You can pick up certain forms, instructions, and publications at many post offices, libraries, and IRS offices. See page 40 for a partial listing of products. You can also photocopy, or print out from a CD-ROM or the Internet, many other products at participating libraries.

 ## CD-ROM

To order the CD-ROM, contact Supt. Docs. at 202-512-1800 (select Option #1), or by computer through GPO's Internet Web Site (http://www.access.gpo.gov/su_docs).

For small businesses, return preparers, or others who may frequently need tax forms or publications, a CD-ROM containing over 2,000 products can be purchased for $25 from the Government Printing Office (GPO), Superintendent of Documents (Supt. Docs.). Current tax year materials, and tax forms from 1991 and publications from 1994, are included on the disc.

What Is Tele-Tax?

Tele-Tax allows you to get:

Refund Information. *Check the status of your 1996 refund.*

Recorded Tax Information. *There are about 150 topics that answer many Federal tax questions. You can listen to up to three topics on each call you make.*

How Do I Use Tele-Tax?

Refund Information

Be sure to have a copy of your 1996 tax return available because you will need to know the first social security number shown on your return, the filing status, and the exact whole-dollar amount of your refund. Then, call the appropriate phone number listed on this page and follow the recorded instructions.

 The IRS updates refund information every 7 days. If you call to check the status of your refund and are not given the date it will be issued, please wait 7 days before calling back.

Touch-tone service is generally available Monday through Friday from 7:00 a.m. to 11:30 p.m. Rotary or pulse service is generally available Monday through Friday from 7:30 a.m. to 5:30 p.m. (Hours may vary in your area.)

Recorded Tax Information

Touch-tone service is available 24 hours a day, 7 days a week. Rotary or pulse service is generally available Monday through Friday from 7:30 a.m. to 5:30 p.m. (Hours in Alaska and Hawaii may vary.)

Select the number of the topic you want to hear. Then, call the appropriate phone number listed on this page. Have paper and pencil handy to take notes.

Choosing the Right Number

- If a number is listed below that is a local call for you, please use that number.
- If a number is not listed below for your local calling area, please call **1-800-829-4477.**

Arizona
Phoenix, 602-640-3933

California
Oakland, 510-839-4245

Colorado
Denver, 303-592-1118

District of Columbia
202-628-2929

Florida
Jacksonville, 904-355-2000

Georgia
Atlanta, 404-331-6572

Illinois
Chicago, 312-886-9614

Indiana
Indianapolis, 317-377-0001

Maryland
Baltimore, 410-244-7306

Massachusetts
Boston, 617-536-0709

Missouri
St. Louis, 314-241-4700

New York
Buffalo, 716-685-5533

Ohio
Cincinnati, 513-421-0329
Cleveland, 216-522-3037

Oregon
Portland, 503-294-5363

Pennsylvania
Philadelphia, 215-627-1040
Pittsburgh, 412-261-1040

Tennessee
Nashville, 615-781-5040

Texas
Dallas, 214-767-1792
Houston, 713-541-3400

Virginia
Richmond, 804-783-1569

Washington
Seattle, 206-343-7221

Topics by Fax or Personal Computer

Tele-Tax topics are also available by a fax machine or a personal computer and modem.

Tele-Tax Topics

Topic No.	Subject
	IRS Help Available
101	IRS services—Volunteer tax assistance, toll-free telephone, walk-in assistance, and outreach programs
102	Tax assistance for individuals with disabilities and the hearing impaired
103	Small Business Tax Education Program (STEP)—Tax help for small businesses
104	Problem Resolution Program—Help for problem situations
105	Public libraries—Tax information tapes and reproducible tax forms
	IRS Procedures
151	Your appeal rights
152	Refunds—How long they should take
153	What to do if you haven't filed your tax return (Nonfilers)

Topic No.	Subject
154	Form W-2—What to do if not received
155	Forms and Publications—How to order
156	Copy of your tax return—How to get one
157	Change of address—How to notify the IRS
911	Hardship assistance applications
	Collection
201	The collection process
202	What to do if you can't pay your tax
203	Failure to pay child support and other Federal obligations
204	Offers in compromise
	Alternative Filing Methods
251	Form 1040PC tax return
252	Electronic filing
253	Substitute tax forms

Topic No.	Subject
254	How to choose a tax preparer
255	TeleFile
	General Information
301	When, where, and how to file
302	Highlights of tax changes
303	Checklist of common errors when preparing your tax return
304	Extensions of time to file your tax return
305	Recordkeeping
306	Penalty for underpayment of estimated tax
307	Backup withholding
308	Amended returns
309	Tax fraud—How to report
310	Power of attorney information
999	Local information

Tele-Tax Topics

(Continued)

Topic numbers are effective January 1, 1997.

Order Blank for Forms and Publications

The most frequently ordered forms and publications are listed on the next page. We will mail you two copies of each form and one copy of each publication or set of instructions you order. To help reduce waste, please order only the items you need to prepare your return.

How To Use the Order Blank

Circle the items you need on the order blank below. Use the blank spaces to order items not listed. If you need more space, attach a separate sheet of paper.

Print or type your name and address accurately in the space provided below. Cut the order blank on the dotted line. Enclose the order blank in your own envelope and address it to the IRS address shown on this page that applies to you. You should receive your order or notification of its status within 7 to 15 workdays after we receive your request.

Do not send your tax return to any of the addresses listed on this page. Instead, see **Where Do I File?** on the back cover.

Where To Mail Your Order Blank for Free Forms and Publications

If you live in:	Mail to:	Other locations:
Alaska, Arizona, California, Colorado, Hawaii, Idaho, Montana, Nevada, New Mexico, Oregon, Utah, Washington, Wyoming, Guam, Northern Marianas, American Samoa	Western Area Distribution Center Rancho Cordova, CA 95743-0001	**Foreign Addresses—** If your mailing address is in a foreign country, mail the order blank to either: Eastern Area Distribution Center (EADC), P.O. Box 25866, Richmond, VA 23286-8107; or Western Area Distribution Center, Rancho Cordova, CA 95743-0001, whichever is closer. Mail letter requests for other forms and publications to: EADC, P.O. Box 25866, Richmond, VA 23286-8107.
Alabama, Arkansas, Illinois, Indiana, Iowa, Kansas, Kentucky, Louisiana, Michigan, Minnesota, Mississippi, Missouri, Nebraska, North Dakota, Ohio, Oklahoma, South Dakota, Tennessee, Texas, Wisconsin	Central Area Distribution Center P.O. Box 8903 Bloomington, IL 61702-8903	**Puerto Rico—**EADC, P.O. Box 25866, Richmond, VA 23286-8107
Connecticut, Delaware, District of Columbia, Florida, Georgia, Maine, Maryland, Massachusetts, New Hampshire, New Jersey, New York, North Carolina, Pennsylvania, Rhode Island, South Carolina, Vermont, Virginia, West Virginia	Eastern Area Distribution Center P.O. Box 85074 Richmond, VA 23261-5074	**Virgin Islands—**V.I. Bureau of Internal Revenue, 9601 Estate Thomas, Charlotte Amalie, St. Thomas, VI 00802

---------------------------------- *Detach at this line* ----------------------------------

Order Blank

Fill in your name and address

Name

Number, street, and apt. number

City, town or post office, state, and ZIP code

Circle the Forms, Instructions, and Publications You Need

The items in bold may be picked up at many post offices and libraries.

1040	Schedule F (1040)	Schedule 3 (1040A) & instructions	2119 & instructions	8582 & instructions	Pub. 501	Pub. 529	Pub. 929
Instructions for 1040 & Schedules	Schedule H (1040) & instructions	**1040EZ**	2210 & instructions	8606 & instructions	Pub. 502	Pub. 550	Pub. 936
Schedules A&B (1040)	Schedule R (1040) & instructions	**Instructions for 1040EZ**	2441 & instructions	8822 & instructions	Pub. 505	Pub. 554	
Schedule C (1040)	Schedule SE (1040)	1040-ES & instructions (1997)	3903 & instructions	8829 & instructions	Pub. 508	Pub. 575	
Schedule C-EZ (1040)	**1040A**	1040-V & instructions	4562 & instructions	Pub. 1	Pub. 521	Pub. 590	
Schedule D (1040)	**Instructions for 1040A & Schedules**	1040X & instructions	4868 & instructions	Pub. 17	Pub. 523	Pub. 596	
Schedule E (1040)	**Schedule 1 (1040A)**	2106 & instructions	5329 & instructions	Pub. 334	Pub. 525	Pub. 910	
Schedule EIC (1040A or 1040)	**Schedule 2 (1040A)**	2106-EZ & instructions	8283 & instructions	Pub. 463	Pub. 527	Pub. 926	

N

Forms

Form 1040

Instructions for Form 1040 and Schedules

Schedule A, Itemized Deductions

Schedule B, Interest and Dividend Income

Schedule C, Profit or Loss From Business

Schedule C-EZ, Net Profit From Business

Schedule D, Capital Gains and Losses

Schedule E, Supplemental Income and Loss

Schedule EIC, Earned Income Credit (Qualifying Child Information)

Schedule F, Profit or Loss From Farming

Schedule H, Household Employment Taxes

Schedule R, Credit for the Elderly or the Disabled

Schedule SE, Self-Employment Tax

Form 1040A

Instructions for Form 1040A and Schedules

Schedule 1, Interest and Dividend Income for Form 1040A Filers

Schedule 2, Child and Dependent Care Expenses for Form 1040A Filers

Schedule 3, Credit for the Elderly or the Disabled for Form 1040A Filers

Form 1040EZ

Instructions for Form 1040EZ

Form 1040-ES, Estimated Tax for Individuals

Form 1040-V, Payment Voucher

Form 1040X, Amended U.S. Individual Income Tax Return

Form 2106, Employee Business Expenses

Form 2106-EZ, Unreimbursed Employee Business Expenses

Form 2119, Sale of Your Home

Form 2210, Underpayment of Estimated Tax by Individuals, Estates, and Trusts

Form 2441, Child and Dependent Care Expenses

Form 3903, Moving Expenses

Form 4562, Depreciation and Amortization

Form 4868, Application for Automatic Extension of Time To File U.S. Individual Income Tax Return

Form 5329, Additional Taxes Attributable to Qualified Retirement Plans (Including IRAs), Annuities, and Modified Endowment Contracts

Form 8283, Noncash Charitable Contributions

Form 8582, Passive Activity Loss Limitations

Form 8606, Nondeductible IRAs (Contributions, Distributions, and Basis)

Form 8822, Change of Address

Form 8829, Expenses for Business Use of Your Home

Publications

See **Pub. 910** for a complete list of available publications.

  1 Your Rights as a Taxpayer
 17 Your Federal Income Tax
334 Tax Guide for Small Business
463 Travel, Entertainment, Gift, and Car Expenses
501 Exemptions, Standard Deduction, and Filing Information
502 Medical and Dental Expenses
505 Tax Withholding and Estimated Tax
508 Educational Expenses
521 Moving Expenses
523 Selling Your Home
525 Taxable and Nontaxable Income
527 Residential Rental Property (Including Rental of Vacation Homes)
529 Miscellaneous Deductions
550 Investment Income and Expenses
554 Older Americans' Tax Guide
575 Pension and Annuity Income
590 Individual Retirement Arrangements (IRAs)
596 Earned Income Credit
910 Guide to Free Tax Services
926 Household Employer's Tax Guide
929 Tax Rules for Children and Dependents
936 Home Mortgage Interest Deduction

Mailing Addresses of Internal Revenue Service Centers

Alabama—Memphis, TN 37501
Alaska—Ogden, UT 84201
Arizona—Ogden, UT 84201
Arkansas—Memphis, TN 37501
California—*Counties of Alpine, Amador, Butte, Calaveras, Colusa, Contra Costa, Del Norte, El Dorado, Glenn, Humboldt, Lake, Lassen, Marin, Mendocino, Modoc, Napa, Nevada, Placer, Plumas, Sacramento, San Joaquin, Shasta, Sierra, Siskiyou, Solano, Sonoma, Sutter, Tehama, Trinity, Yolo, and Yuba*—
Ogden, UT 84201
All other counties—
Fresno, CA 93888
Colorado—Ogden, UT 84201
Connecticut—Andover, MA 05501
Delaware—Philadelphia, PA 19255
District of Columbia—
Philadelphia, PA 19255
Florida—Atlanta, GA 39901
Georgia—Atlanta, GA 39901
Hawaii—Fresno, CA 93888
Idaho—Ogden, UT 84201
Illinois—Kansas City, MO 64999
Indiana—Cincinnati, OH 45999
Iowa—Kansas City, MO 64999
Kansas—Austin, TX 73301
Kentucky—Cincinnati, OH 45999
Louisiana—Memphis, TN 37501
Maine—Andover, MA 05501
Maryland—Philadelphia, PA 19255
Massachusetts—
Andover, MA 05501
Michigan—Cincinnati, OH 45999
Minnesota—Kansas City, MO 64999
Mississippi—Memphis, TN 37501
Missouri—Kansas City, MO 64999
Montana—Ogden, UT 84201
Nebraska—Ogden, UT 84201
Nevada—Ogden, UT 84201
New Hampshire—
Andover, MA 05501
New Jersey—Holtsville, NY 00501
New Mexico—Austin, TX 73301

New York—*New York City and counties of Nassau, Rockland, Suffolk, and Westchester*—
Holtsville, NY 00501
All other counties—
Andover, MA 05501
North Carolina—
Memphis, TN 37501
North Dakota—Ogden, UT 84201
Ohio—Cincinnati, OH 45999
Oklahoma—Austin, TX 73301
Oregon—Ogden, UT 84201
Pennsylvania—
Philadelphia, PA 19255
Rhode Island—Andover, MA 05501
South Carolina—Atlanta, GA 39901
South Dakota—Ogden, UT 84201
Tennessee—Memphis, TN 37501
Texas—Austin, TX 73301
Utah—Ogden, UT 84201
Vermont— Andover, MA 05501
Virginia— Philadelphia, PA 19255
Washington—Ogden, UT 84201
West Virginia—
Cincinnati, OH 45999
Wisconsin—
Kansas City, MO 64999
Wyoming—Ogden, UT 84201
American Samoa—
Philadelphia, PA 19255

Guam:
Nonpermanent residents—
Philadelphia, PA 19255
Permanent residents—
Department of Revenue
and Taxation
Government of Guam
PO Box 23607
GMF, GU 96921
Puerto Rico—
Philadelphia, PA 19255
Virgin Islands:
Nonpermanent residents—
Philadelphia, PA 19255
Permanent residents—
V.I. Bureau of Internal Revenue
9601 Estate Thomas
Charlotte Amalie
St. Thomas, VI 00802
Foreign country: *U.S. citizens and those filing Form 2555, Form 2555-EZ, or Form 4563*—
Philadelphia, PA 19255
All A.P.O. and F.P.O. addresses—
Philadelphia, PA 19255

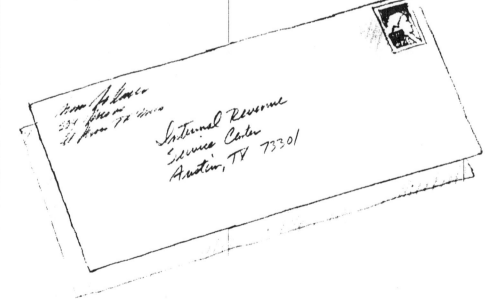

Taxpayer Assistance Programs

The IRS has programs that offer free assistance with tax return preparation and tax counseling using volunteers trained by the IRS. Call the IRS office in your area and ask for the Taxpayer Education Coordinator or the Public Affairs Officer for more information on these programs. They can provide you with times and locations of services and information on becoming a volunteer.

Volunteer Income Tax Assistance (VITA)

VITA provides free tax help to people with a low to moderate income who cannot afford paid professional tax assistance, people with disabilities, people uncomfortable speaking and understanding English, the elderly, and others with special needs.

After completing IRS training, VITA volunteers help prepare basic tax returns, including Forms 1040, 1040A, 1040EZ, and some basic schedules.

VITA sites are generally located at community and neighborhood centers, libraries, schools, shopping malls, houses of worship, and other convenient locations.

Tax Counseling for the Elderly (TCE)

The TCE program provides free tax help to people age 60 or older. Volunteers who provide tax counseling are often retired individuals associated with non-profit organizations that receive grants from the IRS. Grant funds are used to reimburse volunteers for out-of-pocket expenses. These include transportation, meals, and other expenses incurred in training or in providing tax counseling assistance in any of the locations where the elderly are located, such as retirement homes, neighborhood sites, or private houses of the homebound.

Call your local IRS office for more information on this program and to find locations of TCE assistance in your area.

Student Tax Clinics

Student Tax Clinics are sponsored by law and graduate accounting schools. They are staffed by student volunteers who provide free tax assistance to people who would not normally obtain counsel when faced with a tax audit or examination. Students who have received special permission from the IRS may represent these people before the IRS during examination and appeal proceedings.

Bank, Post Office, and Library Program

The IRS supplies free tax preparation materials to many post offices, libraries, and reference areas in technical schools, military bases, prisons, and community colleges. Participating libraries have tax forms available for distribution or copying, reference sets of IRS publications on preparing Forms 1040, 1040A, 1040EZ, and general tax information. Post offices stock Forms 1040, 1040A, 1040EZ, and the instructions and related schedules.

Banks are no longer tax forms distribution outlets. However, banks that participate in the electronic filing program may distribute tax forms.

Problem Resolution Program (PRP)

If you have a tax problem with the IRS and have been unable to resolve it through normal IRS procedures, you may qualify for PRP assistance.

When IRS employees recognize persistent problems, they can refer them to PRP, which has the authority to cut through red tape. They will keep you informed of your case's progress. PRP can usually help with delayed refunds, unanswered inquiries, and incorrect billing notices. However, PRP cannot help when there is an administrative or formal appeals procedure available or when an inquiry only questions the constitutionality of the tax system.

PRP may also be able to help if you are suffering or about to suffer a significant hardship because of your tax problem. Request Form 911, *Application for Taxpayer Assistance Order (ATAO) to Relieve Hardship*, at your local IRS office or by calling 1-800-829-1040. A significant hardship usually means being unable to provide the necessities of life, such as food, shelter, clothing, or medical care for you or your family. The Problem Resolution Officer (PRO) or other official will review your case and advise you of action taken.

Call your local IRS office, write your local PRO, or call 1-800-829-1040 for PRP assistance. Deaf and hearing-impaired people who have access to teletypewriter/telecommunication device for the deaf (TTY/TDD) equipment may call 1-800-829-4059.

For more information about PRP and for a list of PRP addresses download Publication 1546, *How to Use the Problem Resolution Program of the IRS*, via the Internet or order by calling 1-800-829-3676.

Taxpayer Education Programs

The IRS has year-round education programs designed to help you understand the tax laws and IRS procedures. Volunteers trained by the IRS are an important part of these programs. For times and locations of available services in your community, or to become a volunteer, call the IRS office in your area and ask for the Taxpayer Education Coordinator or the Public Affairs Officer.

Community Outreach Tax Education

Groups of people with common tax concerns, such as retirees, farmers, small business owners, and employees, can get free tax help from IRS staff or trained volunteers at convenient community locations.

This program offers two kinds of assistance. One provides line-by-line self-help income tax return preparation for people who want to prepare their own returns. The other provides tax seminars on various tax topics. Outreach sessions may be co-sponsored by community organizations and other government agencies.

Understanding Taxes Program for Students

Understanding Taxes consists of three separate tax education courses designed to teach students about their federal tax rights and responsibilities and the economics and history on which our tax system is based.

- The eighth grade program, *Taxes in U.S. History*, details the roles that taxes have played in our nation's history. It is designed for U.S. history classes. Students learn how tax policies of the past have contributed to tax policies in effect today. Teachers can integrate the program into standard curricula.
- The high school program, *Understanding Taxes*, explains how to prepare and file a simple tax return and teaches about the history, politics, and economics of our tax system. The variety of topics covered in the modular format allow the course to be used in a number of different classes, such as history, economics, consumer education, social studies, government, civics, and business education.
- The post-secondary program, *Taxes and You*, is designed to assist adult learners in becoming responsible participants in the tax system.

Students will learn how taxes affect people and the economy and how to interpret and prepare tax forms. By learning how to pay only what is owed, managing personal finances will become a lot easier.

Practitioner Education

Practitioner Education provides training to people who prepare tax returns for a fee. As part of this program, practitioner institutes are held in every state in cooperation with colleges, state bureaus of revenue, and professional associations. Tax professionals can learn about recent tax law changes at these institutes, which will enhance the professional quality of the services they provide.

Taxpayer Bill of Rights 2

The Taxpayer Bill of Rights 2 preserves the balance between safeguarding the rights of individual taxpayers and enabling the Internal Revenue Service to administer the tax laws efficiently, fairly, and with the least amount of burden to the taxpayer. It is the culmination of a cooperative effort among the IRS, the Treasury Department, and the Congress. This bill was signed on July 30, 1996.

The law established the Office of Taxpayer Advocate (within the IRS) to help taxpayers resolve tax issues. For example, the advocate could direct the IRS to immediately pay a refund to a taxpayer to relieve severe hardship; or temporarily halt a collection until the IRS reviews the appropriateness of its action.

Other Taxpayer Bill of Rights 2 provisions include:

- extending the interest free period for tax liabilities from 10 days to 21 days.
- allowing the IRS to inform a divorced or separated spouse of any IRS actions against the other spouse. This would help protect the first spouse from joint tax liability.
- requiring the IRS to notify a taxpayer 30 days before altering or ending an installment agreement.

Publication 1, *Your Rights As a Taxpayer*, explains some of the most important rights as a taxpayer and also discusses examination, appeal, collection, and refund processes. This publication can be downloaded from the Internet or ordered through the IRS at 1-800-829-3676.

Your Rights as a Taxpayer

THE FIRST PART OF THIS PUBLICATION EXPLAINS SOME OF YOUR MOST IMPORTANT RIGHTS AS A TAXPAYER.

THE SECOND PART EXPLAINS THE EXAMINATION, APPEAL, COLLECTION, AND REFUND PROCESSES.

DECLARATION OF TAXPAYER RIGHTS

I. Protection of Your Rights

IRS employees will explain and protect your rights as a taxpayer throughout your contact with us.

II. Privacy and Confidentiality

The IRS will not disclose to anyone the information you give us, except as authorized by law. You have the right to know why we are asking you for information, how we will use it, and what happens if you do not provide requested information.

III. Professional and Courteous Service

If you believe that an IRS employee has not treated you in a professional manner, you should tell that employee's supervisor. If the supervisor's response is not satisfactory, you should write to your IRS District Director or Service Center Director.

IV. Representation

You may either represent yourself, or with proper written authorization, have someone else represent you in your place. You can have someone accompany you at an interview. You may make sound recordings of any meetings with our examination or collection personnel, provided you tell us in writing 10 days before the meeting.

V. Payment of Only The Correct Amount of Tax

You are responsible for paying only the correct amount of tax due under the law—no more, no less.

VI. Help From The Problem Resolution Office

Problem Resolution Officers can help you with unresolved tax problems and can offer you special help if you have a significant hardship as a result of a tax problem. For more information, write to the Problem Resolution Office at the District Office or Service Center where you have the problem, or call 1-800-829-1040 (1-800-829-4059 for TDD users).

VII. Appeals and Judicial Review

If you disagree with us about the amount of your tax liability or certain collection actions, you have the right to ask the IRS Appeals Office to review your case. You may also ask a court to review your case.

VIII. Relief From Certain Penalties

The IRS will waive penalties when allowed by law if you can show you acted reasonably and in good faith or relied on the incorrect advice of an IRS employee.

EXAMINATIONS, APPEALS, COLLECTIONS, AND REFUNDS

Examinations (Audits)

We accept most taxpayer's returns as filed. If we inquire about your return or select it for examination, it does not suggest that you are dishonest. The inquiry or examination may or may not result in more tax. We may close your case without change; or, you may receive a refund.

By Mail

We handle many examinations and inquiries by mail. We will send you a letter with either a request for more information or a reason why we believe a change to your return may be needed. If you give us the requested information or provide an explanation, we may or may not agree with you, and we will explain the reasons for any changes. Please do not hesitate to write to us about anything you do not understand. If you cannot resolve a question through the mail, you can request a personal interview with an examiner.

By Interview

If we notify you that we will conduct your examination through a personal interview, or you request such an interview, you have the right to ask that the examination take place at a reasonable time and place that is convenient for both you and the IRS. At the end of your examination, the examiner will give you a report if there are any proposed changes to your tax return. If you do not agree with the report, you may meet with the examiner's supervisor.

Repeat Examinations

If we examined your tax return for the same items in either of the 2 previous years and proposed no change to your tax liability, please contact us as soon as possible so we can determine if we should discontinue the repeat examination. Publication 556, *Examination of Returns, Appeal Rights, and Claims for Refund,* will give you more information about the rules and procedures of an IRS examination.

Appeals

If you do not agree with the examiner's findings, you can appeal them to our Appeals Office. Most differences can be settled without expensive and time-consuming court trials. Your appeal rights are explained in detail in Publication 5, *Appeal Rights and Preparation of Protests for Unagreed Cases.*

If you do not wish to use our Appeals Office or disagree with its findings, you can take your case to the U.S. Tax Court, U.S. Court of Federal Claims, or the U.S. District Court where you live. If the court agrees with you on most issues in your case, and finds that our position was largely unjustified, you may be able to recover some of your administrative and litigation costs. You will not be eligible to recover these costs unless you tried to resolve your case administratively, including going through our appeals system, and you gave us all the information necessary to resolve the case.

Collections

Publication 594, *Understanding The Collection Process,* explains your rights and responsibilities regarding payment of federal taxes. It is divided into several sections that explain the procedures in plain language. The sections include:

1. *When you have not paid enough tax.* This section describes tax bills and explains what to do if you think your bill is wrong.

2. *Making arrangements to pay your bill.* This covers making installment payments, delaying collection action, and submitting an offer in compromise.

3. *What happens when you take no action to pay.* This covers liens, releasing a lien, levies, releasing a levy, seizures and sales, and release of property. Publication 1660, *Collection Appeal Rights (for Liens, Levies and Seizures),* explains your rights to appeal liens, levies and seizures and how to request these appeals.

Refunds

You may file a claim for refund if you think you paid too much tax. You must generally file the claim within 3 years from the date you filed your return or 2 years from the date you paid the tax, whichever is later. The law generally provides for interest on your refund if it is not paid within 45 days of the date you filed your return or claim for refund. Publication 556, *Examination of Returns, Appeal Rights, and Claims for Refund,* has more information on refunds.

Tax Information

The IRS provides a great deal of free information. The following are sources for forms, publications and additional information:

- **Tax Information:**
  1-800-829-1040

- **Forms and Publications:**
  1-800-829-3676
  (1-800-829-4059 for TDD users)

- **IRS FAX Forms:** From your FAX machine dial **703-487-4160**

- **Internet:** World Wide Web - http://www.irs.ustreas.gov
  FTP - ftp.irs.ustreas.gov
  Telnet - iris.irs.ustreas.gov

Department of the Treasury
Internal Revenue Service
Publication 1 (Rev. 5-96)
Catalog Number 64731W

IRS FORMS

APPENDIX B

Form **2848**
(Rev. December 1995)
Department of the Treasury
Internal Revenue Service

Power of Attorney
and Declaration of Representative
▶ For Paperwork Reduction and Privacy Act Notice, see the instructions.

OMB No. 1545-0150

For IRS Use Only
Received by:
Name _____
Telephone ( )_____
Function _____
Date ___/___/___

| **Part I** | **Power of Attorney** (Please type or print.) |

1 **Taxpayer Information** (Taxpayer(s) must sign and date this form on page 2, line 9.)

Taxpayer name(s) and address

Social security number(s)	Employer identification number
Daytime telephone number ( )	Plan number (if applicable)

hereby appoint(s) the following representative(s) as attorney(s)-in-fact:

2 **Representative(s)** (Representative(s) must sign and date this form on page 2, Part II.)

Name and address	CAF No. .... Telephone No. ( ) .... Fax No. ( ) .... Check if new: Address ☐ Telephone No. ☐
Name and address	CAF No. .... Telephone No. ( ) .... Fax No. ( ) .... Check if new: Address ☐ Telephone No. ☐
Name and address	CAF No. .... Telephone No. ( ) .... Fax No. ( ) .... Check if new: Address ☐ Telephone No. ☐

to represent the taxpayer(s) before the Internal Revenue Service for the following tax matters:

3 **Tax Matters**

Type of Tax (Income, Employment, Excise, etc.)	Tax Form Number (1040, 941, 720, etc.)	Year(s) or Period(s)

4 **Specific Use Not Recorded on Centralized Authorization File (CAF).**—If the power of attorney is for a specific use not recorded on CAF, check this box. (See **Line 4—Specific uses not recorded on CAF** on page 3.) . . . . ▶ ☐

5 **Acts Authorized.**—The representatives are authorized to receive and inspect confidential tax information and to perform any and all acts that I (we) can perform with respect to the tax matters described on line 3, for example, the authority to sign any agreements, consents, or other documents. The authority does not include the power to receive refund checks (see line 6 below), the power to substitute another representative unless specifically added below, or the power to sign certain returns (see **Line 5—Acts authorized** on page 4).

List any specific additions or deletions to the acts otherwise authorized in this power of attorney: ....
....
....

Note: In general, an unenrolled preparer of tax returns cannot sign any document for a taxpayer. See Revenue Procedure 81-38, printed as Pub. 470, for more information.
Note: The tax matters partner/person of a partnership or S corporation is not permitted to authorize representatives to perform certain acts. See the instructions for more information.

6 **Receipt of Refund Checks.**—If you want to authorize a representative named on line 2 to receive, **BUT NOT TO ENDORSE OR CASH,** refund checks, initial here _____ and list the name of that representative below.

Name of representative to receive refund check(s) ▶

Form **2848** (Rev. 12-95)

7 Notices and Communications.—Original notices and other written communications will be sent to you and a copy to the first representative listed on line 2 unless you check one or more of the boxes below.

a If you want the first representative listed on line 2 to receive the original, and yourself a copy, of such notices or communications, check this box . . . . ▶ ☐

b If you also want the second representative listed to receive a copy of such notices and communications, check this box . . . . ▶ ☐

c If you do not want any notices or communications sent to your representative, check this box . . . . ▶ ☐

8 Retention/Revocation of Prior Power(s) of Attorney.—The filing of this power of attorney automatically revokes all earlier power(s) of attorney on file with the Internal Revenue Service for the same tax matters and years or periods covered by this document. If you do not want to revoke a prior power of attorney, check here . . . . ▶ ☐
YOU MUST ATTACH A COPY OF ANY POWER OF ATTORNEY YOU WANT TO REMAIN IN EFFECT.

9 Signature of Taxpayer(s).—If a tax matter concerns a joint return, **both** husband and wife must sign if joint representation is requested, otherwise, see the instructions. If signed by a corporate officer, partner, guardian, tax matters partner/person, executor, receiver, administrator, or trustee on behalf of the taxpayer, I certify that I have the authority to execute this form on behalf of the taxpayer.

▶ **IF NOT SIGNED AND DATED, THIS POWER OF ATTORNEY WILL BE RETURNED.**

Signature	Date	Title (if applicable)

Print Name

Signature	Date	Title (if applicable)

Print Name

Part II　Declaration of Representative

Under penalties of perjury, I declare that:

- I am not currently under suspension or disbarment from practice before the Internal Revenue Service;
- I am aware of regulations contained in Treasury Department Circular No. 230 (31 CFR, Part 10), as amended, concerning the practice of attorneys, certified public accountants, enrolled agents, enrolled actuaries, and others;
- I am authorized to represent the taxpayer(s) identified in Part I for the tax matter(s) specified there; and
- I am one of the following:

  a Attorney—a member in good standing of the bar of the highest court of the jurisdiction shown below.

  b Certified Public Accountant—duly qualified to practice as a certified public accountant in the jurisdiction shown below.

  c Enrolled Agent—enrolled as an agent under the requirements of Treasury Department Circular No. 230.

  d Officer—a bona fide officer of the taxpayer's organization.

  e Full-Time Employee—a full-time employee of the taxpayer.

  f Family Member—a member of the taxpayer's immediate family (i.e., spouse, parent, child, brother, or sister).

  g Enrolled Actuary—enrolled as an actuary by the Joint Board for the Enrollment of Actuaries under 29 U.S.C. 1242 (the authority to practice before the Service is limited by section 10.3(d)(1) of Treasury Department Circular No. 230).

  h Unenrolled Return Preparer—an unenrolled return preparer under section 10.7(a)(7) of Treasury Department Circular No. 230.

▶ **IF THIS DECLARATION OF REPRESENTATIVE IS NOT SIGNED AND DATED, THE POWER OF ATTORNEY WILL BE RETURNED.**

Designation—Insert above letter **(a–h)**	Jurisdiction (state) or Enrollment Card No.	Signature	Date

Privacy Act and Paperwork Reduction Act Notice.—We ask for the information on this form to carry out the Internal Revenue laws of the United States. Form 2848 is provided by the IRS for your convenience and its use is voluntary. If you choose to designate a representative to act on your behalf, under section 6109 you must disclose your social security number (SSN) or your employer identification number (EIN). The principal purpose of this disclosure is to secure proper identification of the taxpayer. We also need this information to gain access to your tax information in our files and properly respond to your request. If you do not disclose this information, the IRS may suspend processing the power of attorney and may not be able to fill your request until you provide the number.

The time needed to complete and file this form will vary depending on individual circumstances. The estimated average time is: **Recordkeeping, 20 min.; Learning about the law or the form, 29 min.; Preparing the form, 29 min.; Copying, assembling, and sending the form to the IRS, 35 min.**

If you have comments concerning the accuracy of these time estimates or suggestions for making this form simpler, we would be happy to hear from you. You can write to the Tax Forms Committee, Western Area Distribution Center, Rancho Cordova, CA 95743-0001. **DO NOT** send this form to this address. Instead, see **Filing the Power of Attorney** below.

General Instructions

Section references are to the Internal Revenue Code unless otherwise noted.

Purpose of form.—Use Form 2848 to grant authority to an individual to represent you before the IRS and to receive tax information. You may file this form ONLY if you want to name a person(s) to represent you and that person is a "person recognized to practice before the Service." Persons recognized to practice before the Service are listed in Part II, Declaration of Representative, items **a–h.** Any person not listed there is not authorized to practice before the IRS under the provisions of Treasury Department Circular No. 230 and cannot act as your representative. However, you can use **Form 8821,** Tax Information Authorization, to authorize any person or organization to receive and inspect confidential tax return information under the provisions of section 6103. For additional information about this or any other matter concerning practice before the IRS, get **Pub. 216,** Conference and Practice Requirements.

Fiduciaries.—A fiduciary (trustee, executor, administrator, receiver, or guardian) stands in the position of a taxpayer and acts as the taxpayer. Therefore, a fiduciary does not act as a representative and should not file a power of attorney. **Form 56,** Notice Concerning Fiduciary Relationship, should be filed to notify the IRS of the existence of a fiduciary relationship. If a fiduciary wishes to authorize an individual to represent or perform certain acts on behalf of the entity, a power of attorney must be filed and signed by the fiduciary acting in the position of the taxpayer.

Authority granted.—This power of attorney authorizes the individual(s) named to perform any and all acts you can perform, such as

signing consents extending the time to assess tax, recording the interview, or executing waivers agreeing to a tax adjustment. However, authorizing someone as your power of attorney does not relieve you of your tax obligations. Delegating authority or substituting another representative must be specifically stated on line 5. However, the authority granted to an unenrolled preparer may not exceed that allowed under Revenue Procedure 81-38, printed as **Pub. 470,** Limited Practice Without Enrollment.

The power to sign tax returns can only be granted in limited situations. See **Line 5— Acts authorized** on page 4 for more information.

Filing the power of attorney.—File the original, photocopy, or facsimile transmission (fax) of the power of attorney with each IRS office with which you deal. If the power of attorney is filed for a matter currently pending before an office of the IRS, such as an examination, file the power of attorney with that office. Otherwise, file it with the service center where the related return was, or will be, filed. Refer to the instructions for the related tax return for the service center addresses.

Substitute Form 2848.—If you want to prepare and use a substitute Form 2848, get **Pub. 1167,** Substitute Printed, Computer-Prepared, and Computer-Generated Tax Forms and Schedules. If your substitute Form 2848 is approved, the form approval number must be printed in the lower left margin of each substitute Form 2848 you file with the IRS.

Specific Instructions
Part I—Power of Attorney
Line 1—Taxpayer information

Individuals.—Enter your name, SSN (and/or EIN, if applicable), and street address in the space provided. If a joint return is involved, and you and your spouse are designating the same representative(s), also enter your spouse's name and SSN, and your spouse's address if different from yours.

Corporations, partnerships, or associations.—Enter the name, EIN, and business address. If this form is being prepared for corporations filing a consolidated tax return (Form 1120), do not attach a list of subsidiaries to this form. Only the parent corporation information is required on line 1. Also, line 3 should only list Form 1120 in the Tax Form Number column. A subsidiary must file its own Form 2848 for returns that are required to be filed separately from the consolidated return, such as **Form 720,** Quarterly Federal Excise Tax Return, and **Form 941,** Employer's Quarterly Federal Tax Return.

Employee plan.—Enter the plan name, EIN of the plan sponsor, three-digit plan number, and business address of the sponsor.

Trust.—Enter the name, title, and address of the trustee, and the name and EIN of the trust.

Estate.—Enter the name, title, and address of the decedent's executor/personal representative, and the name and identification number of the estate. The identification number for an estate includes both the EIN, if the estate has one, and the decedent's SSN.

Line 2—Representative(s).—Enter the name of your representative(s). Only individuals may be named as representatives. Use the identical name on all submissions. If you want to name more than three representatives, indicate so on this line and attach a list of additional representatives to the form.

Enter the nine-digit Centralized Authorization File (CAF) number for each representative. If a CAF number has not been assigned, enter "None," and the IRS will issue one directly to your representative. The CAF number is a unique nine-digit identification number (not the SSN, EIN, or enrollment card number) that the IRS assigns to representatives. The CAF number is not an indication of authority to practice. The representative should use the assigned CAF number on all future powers of attorney. CAF numbers will not be assigned for employee plans and exempt organizations application requests (EP/EO).

Check the appropriate box to indicate if either the address or telephone number is new since a CAF number was assigned. Enter your representative's fax telephone number, if available.

If the representative is a former employee of the Federal Government, he or she must be aware of the postemployment restrictions contained in 18 U.S.C., section 207 and in Treasury Department Circular No. 230, section 10.26. Criminal penalties are provided for violation of the statutory restrictions, and the Director of Practice is authorized to take disciplinary action against the practitioner.

Line 3—Tax matters.—You must enter the type of tax, the tax form number, and the year(s) or period(s) in order for the power of attorney to be valid. For example, you may list "income tax, Form 1040" for calendar year "1995" and "Excise tax, Form 720" for the "1st, 2nd, 3rd, and 4th quarters of 1995." A general reference to "All years," "All periods," or "All taxes" is **not** acceptable. Any power of attorney with a general reference will be returned.

You may list any tax years or periods that have already ended as of the date you sign the power of attorney. However, you may include on a power of attorney only future tax periods that end no later than 3 years after the date the power of attorney is received by the IRS. You must enter the type of tax, the tax form number, and the future year(s) or period(s).

If the matter relates to estate tax, enter the date of the taxpayer's death instead of the year or period. If the type of tax, tax form number, or years or periods does not apply to the matter (i.e., representation for a penalty or filing a ruling request or determination), specifically describe on this line the matter to which the power of attorney pertains and enter "Not Applicable" in the appropriate column(s).

Line 4—Specific uses not recorded on CAF.—Generally, the IRS records all powers of attorney on the CAF system. However, a power of attorney will not be recorded on the CAF if it does not relate to a specific tax period or it is for a specific issue. Examples of specific issues include but are not limited to the following: **(a)** civil penalty issues, **(b)** trust fund recovery penalty, **(c)** request for a private letter ruling, **(d)** application for an EIN, **(e)** claims filed on **Form 843,** Claim for

Refund and Request for Abatement, **(f)** corporation dissolutions, **(g)** a request to change accounting methods, and **(h)** a request to change accounting periods. Check the specific-use box on line 4 if the power of attorney is for a use that will not be listed on the CAF. If the box on line 4 is checked, the representative should bring a copy of the power of attorney to each meeting with the IRS. A specific-use power of attorney will not automatically revoke any prior powers of attorney.

Line 5—Acts authorized.—If you want to modify the acts that your named representative(s) can perform, describe any specific additions or deletions in the space provided. The authority to substitute another representative or delegate authority must be specifically stated on line 5.

If you want to authorize your representative to sign an income tax return, this authorization must be specifically listed and the requirements of Regulations section 1.6012-1(a)(5) must be satisfied. In general, this regulation only permits a representative to sign your return if you are unable to make the return by reason of: **(a)** disease or injury, **(b)** continuous absence from the United States (including Puerto Rico), for a period of at least 60 days prior to the date required by law for filing the return, or **(c)** specific permission is requested of and granted by the district director for other good cause.

If you want to authorize a person other than a representative (an agent) to sign an income tax return, you must:

  1. Complete the information on lines 1–3,

  2. Check the box on line 4, and

  3. Write the following on line 5:

"This power of attorney is being filed pursuant to Regulation 1.6012(a)(5), reason (a), (b), or (c), which requires a power of attorney to be attached to a return if a return is signed by an agent. No other acts on behalf of the taxpayer are authorized."

Reasons (a), (b), and (c) are defined above. The agent does not complete Part II, Declaration of Representative.

If any representative you name is an unenrolled return preparer, the acts that person can perform on your behalf are limited by Revenue Procedure 81-38 (Pub. 470). In general, an unenrolled return preparer is permitted to appear as your representative only before revenue agents and examining officers of the Examination Division and the EP/EO Division and is not permitted to represent you before other offices (i.e., Collection Division or Appeals Division) of the IRS. Also, an unenrolled return preparer is not permitted to extend the statutory period, execute waivers, delegate authority, or substitute another representative.

Tax matters partner/person.—The tax matters partner/person (TMP) (as defined in sections 6231(a)(7) and 6244) is authorized to perform various acts on behalf of the partnership or S corporation. The following are examples of acts performed by the TMP that **cannot** be delegated to the representative: **(a)** binding nonnotice partners to a settlement agreement under section 6224 and, under certain circumstances, binding all partners or shareholders to a settlement agreement under Tax Court Rule

248; **(b)** filing a petition for readjustment of partnership or subchapter S items in the Tax Court, District Court, or Claims Court, under sections 6226 and 6244, based on the issuance of a notice of final partnership administrative adjustment or notice of final S corporation administrative adjustment by the IRS; **(c)** filing a request for administrative adjustment on behalf of the partnership or S corporation under sections 6227 and 6244; **(d)** filing a petition for adjustment of partnership items with respect to an administrative request in the Tax Court, District Court, or Claims Court, under sections 6228 and 6244; and **(e)** extending the statute of limitations on assessment of any tax attributable to partnership or subchapter S items (and affected items) under sections 6229 and 6244.

Line 6—Receipt of refund checks.—If you want to authorize your representative to receive, but not endorse, refund checks on your behalf, you must initial and enter the name of that person in the space provided. Section 10.31 of Treasury Department Circular No. 230 prohibits an attorney, CPA, or enrolled agent, any of whom is an income tax return preparer, from endorsing or otherwise negotiating a tax refund check.

Line 7—Notices and communications.—Original notices and other written communications will be sent to you and a copy to the first representative listed, unless you check one or more of the boxes. If you check:

  1. Only box (a). The original will be sent to the first representative and a copy to you.

  2. Only box (b). The original will be sent to you and copies to the first two listed representatives.

  3. Both boxes (a) and (b). The original will be sent to the first representative and copies to you and the second representative listed.

  4. Only box (c). The original will be sent to you. No copies will be sent to any representatives.

Line 8—Retention/revocation of prior power(s) of attorney.—If there is any existing power(s) of attorney you do not want to revoke, check the box on this line and attach a copy of the power(s) of attorney.

If you want to revoke an existing power of attorney and do not want to name a new representative, send a copy of the previously executed power of attorney to each IRS office where the power of attorney was filed. The copy of the power of attorney must have a current signature of the taxpayer under the signature already on line 9. Write "REVOKE" across the top of the form. If you do not have a copy of the power of attorney you want to revoke, send a statement to each IRS office where you filed the power of attorney. The statement of revocation must indicate that the authority of the power of attorney is revoked and must be signed by the taxpayer. Also, the name and address of each recognized representative whose authority is revoked must be listed.

A representative can withdraw from representation by filing a statement with each office of the IRS where the power of attorney was filed. The statement must be signed by the representative and identify the name and

address of the taxpayer(s) and tax matter(s) from which the representative is withdrawing. Include your CAF No. on the statement if one has been assigned to you.

The filing of a Form 2848 will not revoke any Form 8821 that is in effect.

Line 9—Signature of taxpayer(s).

*Individuals.—*You must sign and date the power of attorney. If a joint return has been filed and both husband and wife will be represented by the same individual(s), both must sign the power of attorney unless one spouse authorizes the other, in writing, to sign for both. In that case, attach a copy of the authorization. However, if a joint return has been filed and husband and wife will be represented by different individuals, each taxpayer must execute his or her own power of attorney on a separate Form 2848.

*Corporations or associations.—*An officer having authority to bind the taxpayer must sign. However, the tax matters person may sign on behalf of an S corporation.

*Partnerships.—*All partners must sign unless one partner is authorized to act in the name of the partnership. A partner is authorized to act in the name of the partnership if, under state law, the partner has authority to bind the partnership. A copy of such authorization must be attached. For purposes of executing Form 2848, the tax matters partner is authorized to act in the name of the partnership. For dissolved partnerships, see Regulations section 601.503(c)(6).

*Other.—*If the taxpayer is a dissolved corporation, deceased, insolvent, or a person for whom or by whom a fiduciary (a trustee, guarantor, receiver, executor, or administrator) has been appointed, see Regulations section 601.503(d).

Part II—Declaration of Representative

The representative(s) you name must sign and date this declaration and enter the designation (i.e., items **a–h**) under which he or she is authorized to practice before the IRS. In addition, the representative(s) must list the following in the "Jurisdiction" column:

a Attorney—Enter the two-letter abbreviation for the state (e.g., "NY" for New York) in which admitted to practice.

b Certified Public Accountant—Enter the two-letter abbreviation for the state (e.g., "CA" for California) in which licensed to practice.

c Enrolled Agent—Enter the enrollment card number issued by the Director of Practice.

d Officer—Enter the title of the officer (i.e., President, Vice President, or Secretary).

e Full-Time Employee—Enter title or position (e.g., Comptroller or Accountant).

f Family Member—Enter the relationship to taxpayer (i.e., spouse, parent, child, brother, or sister).

g Enrolled Actuary—Enter the enrollment card number issued by the Joint Board for the Enrollment of Actuaries.

h Unenrolled Return Preparer—Enter the two-letter abbreviation for the state (e.g., "KY" for Kentucky) in which the return was prepared.

Note: *If the representation is outside the United States, conditions **a–h** do not apply.*

 Printed on recycled paper

Form **843**

(Rev. January 1997)

Department of the Treasury
Internal Revenue Service

Claim for Refund and Request for Abatement

▶ See separate instructions.

OMB No. 1545-0024

*Use Form 843 only if your claim involves **(a)** one of the taxes shown on line 3a or **(b)** a refund or abatement of interest, penalties, or additions to tax on line 4a.*

Do not *use Form 843 if your claim is for—*
- *An overpayment of income taxes;*
- *A refund of fuel taxes;*
- *An overpayment of excise taxes reported on Form 720, 730, or 2290 (see **General Instructions**).*

Please type or print		
Name of claimant		Your social security number
Address (number, street, and room or suite no.)		Spouse's social security number
City or town, state, and ZIP code		Employer identification number
Name and address shown on return if different from above		Daytime telephone number ( )

1 Period—prepare a separate Form 843 for each tax period

From , 19 , to , 19

2 Amount to be refunded or abated

$

3a Type of tax, penalty, or addition to tax:

☐ Employment ☐ Estate ☐ Gift ☐ Excise (unless reported on Form 720, 730, or 2290—see instructions.)

☐ Penalty—IRC section ▶ _____

b Type of return filed (see instructions):

☐ 706 ☐ 709 ☐ 940 ☐ 941 ☐ 943 ☐ 945 ☐ 990-PF ☐ 4720 ☐ Other (specify)

4a Request for abatement or refund of:

☐ Interest caused by IRS errors or delays (if applicable—see instructions).

☐ A penalty or addition to tax as a result of erroneous advice from the IRS.

b Dates of payment ▶

5 **Explanation and additional claims.** Explain why you believe this claim should be allowed, and show computation of tax refund or abatement of interest, penalty, or addition to tax.

Signature. If you are filing Form 843 to request a refund or abatement relating to a joint return, both you and your spouse must sign the claim. Claims filed by corporations must be signed by a corporate officer authorized to sign, and the signature must be accompanied by the officer's title.

Under penalties of perjury, I declare that I have examined this claim, including accompanying schedules and statements, and, to the best of my knowledge and belief, it is true, correct, and complete.

Signature (Title, if applicable. Claims by corporations must be signed by an officer.) Date

Signature Date

For Paperwork Reduction Act Notice, see separate instructions. Cat. No. 10180R Form **843** (Rev. 1-97)

Department of the Treasury
Internal Revenue Service

Instructions for Form 843
(Revised January 1997)
Claim for Refund and Request for Abatement

Section references are to the Internal Revenue Code.

Paperwork Reduction Act Notice

We ask for the information on this form to carry out the Internal Revenue laws of the United States. Internal Revenue Code sections 6402 and 6404 state the conditions under which you may file a claim for refund and request for abatement of certain taxes, penalties, and interest. Form 843 may be used to file your claim. Section 6109 requires that you disclose your taxpayer identification number (TIN). Routine uses of this information include providing it to the Department of Justice for civil and criminal litigation and to cities, states, and the District of Columbia for use in administering their tax laws.

You are not required to provide the information requested on a form that is subject to the Paperwork Reduction Act unless the form displays a valid OMB control number. Books or records relating to a form or its instructions must be retained as long as their contents may become material in the administration of any Internal Revenue law. Generally, tax returns and return information are confidential, as required by Code section 6103.

The time needed to complete and file this form will vary depending on individual circumstances. The estimated average time is:

Recordkeeping .... 26 min.

Learning about the law or the form .... 7 min.

Preparing the form .... 20 min.

Copying, assembling, and sending the form to the IRS ..... 28 min.

If you have comments concerning the accuracy of these time estimates or suggestions for making this form simpler, we would be happy to hear from you. You can write to the Tax Forms Committee, Western Area Distribution Center, Rancho Cordova, CA 95743-0001. **DO NOT** send Form 843 to this address. Instead, see **Where To File** below.

General Instructions

A Change To Note

New rules apply in certain cases to abatement of interest accrued on deficiencies or payments for tax years **beginning after** July 30, 1996. See **Line 4** under **Specific Instructions** for more information.

Purpose of Form.— Use Form 843 to file a claim for refund of certain overpaid taxes, interest, penalties, and additions to tax. For example, if on your employment tax return you reported and paid more Federal income tax than you actually withheld from an employee, use this form to claim a refund.

Also use Form 843 to request abatement of an overassessment (or the unpaid portion of an overassessment) if more than the correct amount of tax (except income, estate, and gift tax), interest, additions to tax, or penalties have been assessed.

Do not use Form 843 to claim:

• A refund or to request an abatement of your income tax. Individuals must use **Form 1040X**, Amended U.S. Individual Income Tax Return. Corporations that filed Form 1120 or 1120-A must use **Form 1120X**, Amended U.S. Corporation Income Tax Return. Other income tax filers should file a claim on the appropriate amended tax return.

• A refund of excise taxes reported on Form 720, 730, or 2290. You must use **Form 8849,** Claim for Refund of Excise Taxes. Form 8849 is also used to claim refunds of excise taxes imposed on fuels, chemicals, and other articles used for nontaxable purposes or for which there is a reduced rate of tax.

• A refund of the required payment under section 7519. Instead, file **Form 8752,** Required Payment or Refund Under Section 7519.

Generally, you must file a separate Form 843 for each tax period and each type of tax. Exceptions are provided for certain claims in the **Specific Instructions** below.

Who May File.— You may file Form 843 or your agent may file it for you. If your agent files, the original or a copy of **Form 2848,** Power of Attorney and Declaration of Representative, must be attached.

If you are filing as a legal representative for a decedent whose return you filed, attach to Form 843 a statement that you filed the return and you are still acting as the representative. If you did not file the decedent's return, attach certified copies of letters of testamentary, letters of administration, or similar evidence to show your authority. File **Form 1310,** Statement of Person Claiming Refund Due a Deceased Taxpayer, with Form 843 if you are the legal representative of a decedent.

Where To File.— File Form 843 with the Internal Revenue Service Center where you filed your return.

Specific Instructions

Social Security Number.— If you are filing Form 843 to request a refund or abatement relating to a joint return, enter social security numbers for both you and your spouse.

Line 3

Line 3a.— Check the appropriate box to show the type of tax, penalty, or addition to tax. If you are filing a claim for refund or request for abatement of an assessed penalty, check the box and enter the applicable Internal Revenue Code (IRC) section. Generally, you can find the IRC section on the Notice of Assessment you receive from the service center.

Line 3b.— Check the appropriate box to show the type of return, if any, that you filed.

Caution: You must attach **Form 941c,** Supporting Statement To Correct Information, or an equivalent statement, if you are claiming a refund of taxes reported on Form 941, 941-M, 941-SS, 943, or 945.

Line 4

Requesting Abatement or Refund of Interest Under Section 6404(e)

Section 6404(e) gives the IRS the authority to abate interest when the additional interest is attributable to IRS errors or delays.

Section 6404(e) applies only if there was an error or delay in performing a ministerial act (defined below) and only relates to taxes for which a notice of deficiency is required by section 6212(a). This includes income, generation-skipping, estate and gift taxes, and certain excise taxes imposed by chapter 41, 42, 43, 44, or 45. Section 6404(e) does not allow abatement of interest for employment taxes or other excise taxes. Get **Pub. 556,** Examination of Returns, Appeal Rights, and Claims of Refund, for more information.

Ministerial Act.—The term "ministerial act" means a procedural or mechanical act that **does not** involve the exercise of judgment or discretion and that occurs during the processing of your case after all prerequisites of the act, such as conferences and review by supervisors, have taken place. See Rev. Proc. 87-42, 1987-2 C.B. 589, for more information.

If you are requesting an abatement of interest, write "Request for Abatement of Interest Under Rev. Proc. 87-42" at the top of Form 843.

On line 1, state the tax period involved. Check the first box on line 4a. On line 4b, show the dates of any payment of interest or tax liability for the tax period involved.

On line 5, state the type of tax involved, when you were first contacted by the IRS in writing about the deficiency or payment, the specific period for which you are requesting abatement of interest, the circumstances of your case, and the reasons why you believe that failure to abate the interest would result in grossly unfair treatment.

Only one Form 843 is required if the interest assessment resulted from the IRS's error or delay in performing a single ministerial act affecting a tax assessment for multiple tax years or types of tax (for example, where 2 or more tax years were under examination).

Tax Years Beginning After July 30, 1996

For interest accruing on payments or deficiencies for tax years beginning after July 30, 1996, section 6404(e) will apply to certain managerial acts as well as ministerial acts, but the errors or delays must be unreasonable. Follow the instructions for line 1 through line 5 above, but **do not** refer to Rev. Proc. 87-42.

Requesting Abatement or Refund of a Penalty or Addition to Tax as a Result of Erroneous Written Advice

Section 6404(f) gives the IRS the authority to abate any portion of a penalty or addition to tax attributable to erroneous advice furnished to you in writing by an officer or employee of the IRS, acting in his or her official capacity.

The penalty or addition to tax will be abated only if:

1. You reasonably relied on the written advice;

2. The written advice was in response to a specific written request you made for advice; and

3. The penalty or addition to tax did not result from your failure to provide the IRS with adequate or accurate information.

If you are filing a request for abatement or refund of a penalty or addition to tax because of erroneous written advice, write "Request for Abatement of Penalty or Addition to Tax Pursuant to Section 6404(f)" at the top of Form 843. Complete lines 1 through 3. Check the appropriate box on line 4a. On line 4b, show the date of payment if the penalty or addition to tax has been paid.

Send Form 843 to the Internal Revenue Service Center where your return was filed. If the erroneous advice does not relate to an item on a tax return, Form 843 should be sent to the service center where your return was filed for the tax year you relied on the erroneous advice.

You must attach copies of the following information to Form 843:

1. Your written request for advice;

2. The erroneous written advice you relied on that was furnished to you by the IRS; and

3. The report, if any, of tax adjustments identifying the penalty or addition to tax, and the item(s) relating to the erroneous advice.

An abatement of any penalty or addition to tax under this section will be allowed only if you submit the request for abatement within the period allowed for collection of the penalty or addition to tax or, if you paid the penalty or addition to tax, within the period allowed for claiming a credit or refund of such penalty or addition to tax.

Line 5

Explain in detail your reasons for filing this claim and show your computation for the credit, refund, or abatement. Also attach appropriate supporting evidence.

Form **9465**	**Installment Agreement Request**	OMB No. 1545-1350

(Rev. January 1996)
Department of the Treasury
Internal Revenue Service

▶ **See instructions below and on back.**

Note: *Do not file this form if you are currently making payments on an installment agreement. You must pay your other Federal tax liabilities in full or you will be in default on your agreement.*

If you can't pay the full amount you owe, you can ask to make monthly installment payments. If we approve your request, you will be charged a $43 fee. **Do not include the fee with this form.** We will deduct the fee from your first payment after we approve your request, unless you choose **Direct Debit** (see the line 13 instructions). We will usually let you know within 30 days after we receive your request whether it is approved or denied. But if this request is for tax due on a return you filed after March 31, it may take us longer than 30 days to reply.

To ask for an installment agreement, complete this form. Attach it to the front of your return when you file. If you have already filed your return or you are filing this form in response to a notice, see **How Do I File Form 9465?** on page 2. If you have any questions about this request, call 1-800-829-1040.

Caution: *A Notice of Federal Tax Lien may be filed to protect the government's interest until you pay in full.*

1 Your first name and initial · Last name · **Your social security number**

If a joint return, spouse's first name and initial · Last name · **Spouse's social security number**

Your current address (number and street). If you have a P.O. box and no home delivery, show box number. · Apt. number

City, town or post office, state, and ZIP code. If a foreign address, show city, state or province, postal code, and full name of country.

2 If this address is new since you filed your last tax return, check here . . . . ▶ ☐

3 ( ) _____ _____
Your home phone number · Best time for us to call

4 ( ) _____ _____ _____
Your work phone number · Ext. · Best time for us to call

5 Name of your bank or other financial institution:

_____

Address

_____

City, state, and ZIP code

6 Your employer's name:

_____

Address

_____

City, state, and ZIP code

7 Enter the tax return for which you are making this request (for example, Form 1040). But if you are filing this form in response to a notice, don't complete lines 7 through 9. Instead, attach the bottom section of the notice to this form and go to line 10. . . . . ▶ _____

8 Enter the tax year for which you are making this request (for example, 1995) . . . . ▶ _____

9 Enter the total amount you owe as shown on your tax return . . . . ▶ $_____

10 Enter the amount of any payment you are making with your tax return (or notice). See instructions . ▶ $_____

11 Enter the amount you can paym each month. **Make your payments as large as possible to limit interest and penalty charges.** The charges will continue until you pay in full . . . . ▶ $_____

12 Enter the date you want to make your payment each month. Do not enter a date later than the 28th ▶ _____

13 If you would like to make your monthly payments using **Direct Debit** (automatic withdrawals from your bank account), check here. . . . . ▶ ☐

Your signature	Date	Spouse's signature. If a joint return, BOTH must sign.	Date

The time needed to complete and file this form will vary depending on individual circumstances. The estimated average time is: **Learning about the law or the form,** 2 min.; **Preparing the form,** 24 min.; and **Copying, assembling, and sending the form to the IRS,** 20 min.

If you have comments concerning the accuracy of this time estimate or suggestions for making this form simpler, we would be happy to hear from you. You can write to the Tax Forms Committee, Western Area Distribution Center, Rancho Cordova, CA 95743-0001. **DO NOT** send the form to this address. Instead, see **How Do I File Form 9465?** on this page.

General Instructions

If you cannot pay the full amount you owe shown on your tax return (or on a notice we sent you), you can ask to make monthly installment payments. But before requesting an installment agreement, you should consider other less costly alternatives, such as a bank loan.

You will be charged interest and may be charged a late payment penalty on any tax not paid by its due date, even if your request to pay in installments is granted. To limit interest and penalty charges, file your return on time and pay as much of the tax as possible with your return (or notice).

You will be charged a $43 fee if your request is approved. **Do not include the fee with this form.** We will send you a letter telling you your request has been approved, how to pay the fee, and how to make your first installment payment. After we receive each payment, we will send you a letter showing the remaining amount you owe, and the due date and amount of your next payment.

By approving your request, we agree to let you pay the tax you owe in monthly installments instead of immediately paying the amount in full. In return, you agree to make your monthly payments on time. **You also agree to meet all your future tax liabilities.** This means that you must have adequate withholding or estimated tax payments so that your tax liability for future years is paid in full when you timely file your return. If you do not make your payments on time or have an outstanding past-due amount in a future year, you will be in default on your agreement and we may take enforcement actions to collect the entire amount you owe.

Bankruptcy—Offer-in-Compromise.—If you are in bankruptcy or we have accepted your offer-in-compromise, **do not** file this form. Instead, call your local IRS District Office Special Procedures function. You can get the number by calling 1-800-829-1040.

Specific Instructions

Line 1

If you are making this request for a joint tax return, show the names and SSNs in the same order as on your tax return.

Line 10

Even if you can't pay the full amount you owe now, you should pay as much of it as possible to limit penalty and interest charges. If you are filing this form with your tax return, make the payment with your return. If you are filing this form by itself, for example, in response to a notice, include a check or money order payable to the Internal Revenue Service with this form. **Do not** send cash. On your payment, write your name, address, social security number, daytime phone number, and the tax year and tax return for which you are making this request (for example, "1995 Form 1040").

Line 11

You should try to make your payments large enough so that your balance due will be paid off by the due date of your next tax return.

Line 12

You can choose the date your monthly payment is due. For example, if your rent or mortgage payment is due on the first of the month, you may want to make your installment payments on the 15th. When we approve your request, we will tell you the month and date that your first payment is due. If we have not replied by the date you choose for your first payment, you may send the first payment to the Internal Revenue Service Center at the address shown on this page for the place where you live. Make your check or money order payable to the Internal Revenue Service. See the instructions for line 10 for what to write on your payment.

Line 13

Check the box on line 13 if you want your monthly payments automatically deducted **(Direct Debit)** from your bank account. If your installment agreement request is approved, we will send you the required Direct Debit enrollment form and you must include the $43 fee when you return it.

How Do I File Form 9465?

● If you haven't filed your return, attach Form 9465 to the front of your return.

● If you have already filed your return, you are filing your return electronically, or you are filing this form in response to a notice, mail it to the **Internal Revenue Service Center** at the address shown below for the place where you live. No street address is needed.

If you live in:	Use this address:
Florida, Georgia, South Carolina	Atlanta, GA 39901
New Jersey, New York (New York City and counties of Nassau, Rockland, Suffolk, and Westchester)	Holtsville, NY 00501
New York (all other counties), Connecticut, Maine, Massachusetts, New Hampshire, Rhode Island, Vermont	Andover, MA 05501
Illinois, Iowa, Minnesota, Missouri, Wisconsin	Kansas City, MO 64999
Delaware, District of Columbia, Maryland, Pennsylvania, Virginia	Philadelphia, PA 19255
Indiana, Kentucky, Michigan, Ohio, West Virginia	Cincinnati, OH 45999
Kansas, New Mexico, Oklahoma, Texas	Austin, TX 73301
Alaska, Arizona, California (counties of Alpine, Amador, Butte, Calaveras, Colusa, Contra Costa, Del Norte, El Dorado, Glenn, Humboldt, Lake, Lassen, Marin, Mendocino, Modoc, Napa, Nevada, Placer, Plumas, Sacramento, San Joaquin, Shasta, Sierra, Siskiyou, Solano, Sonoma, Sutter, Tehama, Trinity, Yolo, and Yuba), Colorado, Idaho, Montana, Nebraska, Nevada, North Dakota, Oregon, South Dakota, Utah, Washington, Wyoming	Ogden, UT 84201
California (all other counties), Hawaii	Fresno, CA 93888
Alabama, Arkansas, Louisiana, Mississippi, North Carolina, Tennessee	Memphis, TN 37501
American Samoa Guam: Nonpermanent residents only* Puerto Rico (or if excluding income under section 933) Virgin Islands: Nonpermanent residents only* Foreign country (or if a dual-status alien): U.S. citizens and those filing Form 2555, 2555-EZ, or 4563 All APO and FPO addresses	Philadelphia, PA 19255

*Permanent residents of Guam and the Virgin Islands cannot use Form 9465.

 Printed on recycled paper

Form **911** (Rev. January 1994)	Department of the Treasury – Internal Revenue Service **Application for Taxpayer Assistance Order (ATAO)** **(Taxpayer's Application for Relief from Hardship)**	If sending Form 911 with another form or letter, put Form 911 on top.

Note: If you have not tried to obtain relief from the IRS office that contacted you, use of this form may not be necessary. Use this form only after reading the instructions for **When To Use This Form.** Filing this application may affect the statutory period of limitations. (See instructions for line 14.)

Section I.   Taxpayer Information

1. Name(s) as shown on tax return	2. Your Social Security Number
	4. Tax form
	3. Social Security of Spouse Shown in 1.
	5. Tax period ended
6. Current mailing address (number & street). For P.O. Box, see instructions Apt. No.	8. Employer identification number, if applicable.
7. City, town or post office, state and ZIP Code	9. Person to contact
If the above address is different from that shown on latest filed tax return and you want us to update our records with this new address, check here .... ☐	10. Daytime telephone number ( ) 11. Best time to call

12. Description of significant hardship (If more space is needed, attach additional sheets.)

13. Description of relief requested (If more space is needed, attach additional sheets.)

ATAO

14. Signature of taxpayer or Corporate Officer (See instructions.)	15. Date	16. Signature of spouse shown in block 1	17. Date

Section II.   Representative Information (If applicable)

18. Name of authorized representative (Must be same as on Form 2848 or 8821)	22. Firm name
19. Centralized Authorization File (CAF) number	23. Mailing address
20. Daytime telephone number ( ) 21. Best time to call	
24. Representative Signature	25. Date

Section III.   (For Internal Revenue Service only)

26. Name of initiating employee	27. ☐ IRS Identified ☐ Taxpayer request	28. Telephone ( )	29. Function	30. Office	31. Date

Cat. No. 16965S   Form **911** (Rev. 1-94)

Instructions

When To Use This Form: Use this form to apply for relief from a **significant hardship** which may have already occurred or is about to occur if the IRS takes or fails to take certain actions. A significant hardship normally means not being able to provide the necessities of life for you or your family. Examples of such necessities include, but are not limited to: food, shelter, clothing, or medical care. You may use this form at any time. Instead of using this form, **however, the IRS prefers that requests for relief first be made with the IRS office that most recently contacted you.** In most cases, the relief needed can be secured directly from the appropriate IRS employee. For example, Collection employees handle requests for payment arrangements on late taxes or releases of levy on wages, salaries, or bank accounts; Taxpayer Service employees handle requests for immediate refunds of overpaid taxes; Examination employees handle requests for review of additional tax assessments when the taxpayer has had no opportunity to present proof of claimed deductions.

If an IRS office will not grant the relief requested, or will not grant the relief in time to avoid the significant hardship, you may submit this form. No enforcement action will be taken while we are reviewing your application.

Note: Do not use this application to change the amount of any tax you owe. If you disagree with the amount of tax assessed, see **Publication 1, Your Rights as a Taxpayer.**

Where To Submit This Form: Submit this application to the Internal Revenue Service, Problem Resolution Office, in the district where you live. For the address of the Problem Resolution Office in your district or for more information, call the local Taxpayer Assistance number in your local telephone directory or 1-800-829-1040.

Overseas Taxpayers: Taxpayers residing overseas should submit this application to the Internal Revenue Service., Problem Resolution Office, Assistant Commissioner (International), P.O. Box 44817, L'Enfant Plaza Station, Washington, D.C. 20026-4817.

Caution: Incomplete applications or applications submitted to the incorrect office may result in delays. If you do not hear from us within one week of submitting Form 911, please contact the Problem Resolution Office where you sent your application.

Section I. Taxpayer Information

1. Name(s) as shown on tax return. Enter your name as it appeared on the tax return for each period you are asking for help even if your name has changed since the return was submitted. If you filed a joint return, enter both names.

4. Tax form. Enter the tax form number of the form for which you are requesting assistance. For example, if you are requesting assistance for a problem involving an individual income tax return, enter "1040." If your problem involves more than one tax form, include the information in block 12.

5. Tax period ended. If you are requesting assistance on an annually filed return, enter the calendar year or the ending date of the fiscal year for that return. If the problem concerns a return filed quarterly, enter the ending date of the quarter involved. File only one Form 911 even if multiple tax periods are involved. If the problem involves more than one tax period, include the information in block 12.

6. Current mailing address (number and street). If your post office does not deliver mail to your street address and you have a P.O. box, show your box number instead of your street address.

8. Employer Identification Number. Enter the employer identification number (*EIN)* of the business, corporation, trust, etc., for the name you showed in block 1.

9. Person to contact. Enter the name of the person to contact about the problem. In the case of businesses, corporations, trusts, estates, etc., enter the name of a responsible official.

10. Daytime telephone number. Enter the daytime telephone number, including area code, of the person to contact.

12. Description of significant hardship. Describe the action(s) being taken (or not being taken) by the Internal Revenue Service that are causing you significant hardship. If you know it, include the name of the person, office, telephone number, and/or address of the last contact you had with IRS regarding this problem.

13. Description of relief requested. Be specific. If your remaining income after paying expenses is too little to meet an IRS payment, give the details. Describe the action you want the IRS to take.

14. and 16. Signature(s) If you filed a joint return it is not necessary for both you and your spouse to sign this application for your account to be reviewed. If you sign the application the IRS **may** suspend applicable statutory periods of limitations for the assessment of additional taxes and for the collection of taxes. If the taxpayer is your dependent child who cannot sign this application because of age, **or someone incapable of signing the application because of some other reason,** you may sign the taxpayer's name in the space provided followed by the words "By (your signature), parent (or guardian)." If the application is being made for other than the individual taxpayer, a person having authority to sign the return should sign this form. Enter the date Form 911 is signed.

Section II. Representative Information

Taxpayers: If you wish to have a representative act in your behalf, you must give your representative power of attorney or tax information authorization for the tax form(s) and period(s) involved. (*See Form 2848, Power of Attorney and Declaration of Representative and Instructions or Form 8821, Tax Information Authorization, for more information.*)

Representatives: If you are an authorized representative submitting this request on behalf of the taxpayer identified in Section I, complete blocks 18 through 25, attach a copy of Form 2848, Form 8821, or the power of attorney. Enter your Centralized Authorization File (*CAF*) number in block 19. The CAF number is the unique number that Internal Revenue Service assigns to a representative after a valid Form 2848 or Form 8821 is filed with an IRS office.

(For IRS Use Only)

ATAO Code	How recevied	Date of Determination	PRO signature

Form **911** (Rev. 1-94)

Form **433-F**
(Rev. August 1995)

Department of the Treasury — Internal Revenue Service

Collection Information Statement

Your name(s) and address	Your Social Security Number
	Your Spouse's Social Security Number
	Area Code and Phone Numbers
	Home: ( )
	Your Work: ( )
(County _____)	Your Spouse's Work: ( )
Your Employer or Business (name and address)	Your Spouse's Employer or Business (name and address)

A. ACCOUNTS (Include banks, S&Ls, Credit Unions, CDs, IRAs, Keogh, SEPs, mutual funds, stock brokerage accounts)

Name of Institution	Address	Type of Account	Balance

B REAL ESTATE (home and other real estate)

County/Description	Value	Balance Owed	Equity	Monthly Payment

C. OTHER ASSETS (cars, boats, RV's, whole life policies, etc.)

County/Description	Value	Balance Owed	Equity	Monthly Payment

D. CREDIT CARDS

Type (e.g., VISA/Nations Bank)	Credit Limit	Balance Owed	Minimum Monthly Payment

E. MONTHLY INCOME

Your Gross Pay: _____	Spouse's Gross Pay _____	Your Available Income: _____
Federal Tax Withholding: _____	Federal Tax Withholding: _____	
State and Local Taxes: _____	State and Local Taxes: _____	Spouse's Avail. Income: _____
Social Security Taxes: _____	Social Security Taxes: _____	
Retirement/Medicare: _____	Retirement/Medicare: _____	Total Available Income: _____
Court Ordered payments: _____	Court Ordered Payments: _____	
Your Net Pay: _____	Spouse's Net Pay: _____	
Other Income: _____	Other Income: _____	
Your Available Income: _____	Spouse's Available Income: _____	

F. MONTHLY EXPENSES

	Amount	IRS USE
Rent (do not show mortgage here)		
NATIONAL STANDARDS: food, household/ personal needs, miscellaneous *(See Instructions)*		
Utilities (electric, gas., water, phone)		
Transportation (gas, bus fare, insurance, etc.)		
Medical (Insurance, drugs, doctor bills)		
Child Care/Dependent Care		
Quarterly Est. Tax Payments (Form 1040ES)		
Life Insurance (NOT listed in Section C)		
Other Deductions or Expenses NOT Listed		
1. _____		
2. _____		
3. _____		
TOTAL EXPENSES		

G. ADDITIONAL INFORMATION

Total Number of Dependents (include yourself and spouse): _____

Expected Changes To Income, Health Expenses, ETC.

AMOUNT YOU PROPOSE TO PAY IRS EACH MONTH FOR TAXES YOU OWE:	$

FOR IRS USE ONLY (Sections B, C, D, and F)

TOTAL ALLOWABLE EXPENSES

MONTHLY PAYMENT AMOUNT:

Under penalties of perjury, I declare that to the best of my knowledge and belief this statement of assets, liabilities, and other information is true, correct. and complete.

Your Signature	Spouse's Signature	Date

Cat. No. 62053J

Form **433-F** (Rev. 8-95)

How to prepare a
Collection Information Statement (Form 433-F)

How to prepare a

Collection Information Statement (Form 433-F)

Complete all blocks, except shaded areas. Write "N/A" (Not Applicable) in those blocks that do not apply to you. If you don't complete the form, we won't be able to help determine the best method for you to pay the amount due. The areas explained below are the ones we have found to be the most confusing to people completing the form.

Section A - Accounts

Include banks, S&Ls, credit unions, CDs, IRAs, Keogh, SEPS, mutual funds, stock brokerage accounts, etc. Enter all accounts even if there is currently no balance. Do not enter bank loans.

Section B - Real Estate

Home and other real estate. List all real estate that you own or are purchasing. Include address and county description along with the current market value and amount owed on the loan, mortgage, etc. Subtract amount owed from current market value to determine equity.

Section C - Other Assets

List cars, boats, RVs, whole life policies, etc. (Complete the same as Section B above.

Section D - Credit Cards

Enter credit cards issued by a bank, credit union, or savings and loan (MasterCard, Visa, overdraft protection, etc.). List other charge accounts such as, department stores and oil companies.

Section E - Monthly Income

Enter your gross monthly wages and/or salary. Under Gross pay, list amounts withheld for the item listed. Do not include allotments you elect to take out of your pay such as, insurance payments, credit union deductions, car payments, etc. List these expenses in Section C and Section F.

Section F - Monthly Expenses

Rent
Enter your monthly rent payment. If you are a homeowner, write N/A.

National Standard Expenses (See expense chart)
This category includes clothing and services, food, housekeeping supplies, personal care products and services, and miscellaneous. Enter the amount you are allowed, based on your total monthly gross income and the size of your family, from the chart on the back of these instructions. If you claim a higher amount, each expense item must be substantiated. Explain why the amount is higher.

Transportation
Enter your average monthly transportation expenses. Transportation expenses include: insurance, registration fees, regular maintenance, fuel, parking and tolls or public transportation.

Medical
Show recurring medical expenses only. Do not include an occasional medical expense.

Child Care/Dependent Care
Enter monthly amount paid for care of a dependent child or adult.

Quarterly Estimated Tax Payments (Form 1040ES)
Enter the monthly average you pay on your estimated tax.

Life Insurance
Show term life or other insurance not listed in Section C.

Other Expenses
List other expenses or deductions not shown in any other section.

Total all expenses listed in Section F.

Section G - Additional Information

Show total number of dependents in the household that can be claimed on your tax return.

Enter the maximum amount you propose to pay each month for taxes you owe.

Certification

For joint income tax liabilities, both husband and wife should sign the statement.

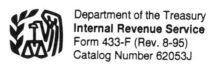

Department of the Treasury
Internal Revenue Service
Form 433-F (Rev. 8-95)
Catalog Number 62053J

National Standard Expenses

Total Monthly Income	Number of Persons in Household				
	One	Two	Three	Four	Over Four
Less than $830	315	509	553	714	+120
$830 to $1,249	383	517	624	723	+130
$1,250 to $1,669	448	569	670	803	+140
$1,670 to $2,499	511	651	731	839	+150
$2,500 to $3,329	551	707	809	905	+160
$3,330 to $4,169	590	840	948	1,053	+170
$4,170 to $5,829	665	913	1,019	1,177	+180
$5,830 and over	923	1,179	1,329	1,397	+190

Expenses include: Housekeeping supplies
Clothing and clothing services
Personal care products and services
Food
Miscellaneous

To find the amount you are allowed, read down the Total Gross Monthly Income Column until you find your income, then read across to the column for the number of persons in your family.

If there are more than four persons in your family, multiply the number of additional persons by the amount in the "Over Four" column and add the result to the amount in the "Four" column. (For example total monthly income of $830 to $1,249 for six persons would equal a monthly national standard of 723 + 130 + 130, or 983.

Normally, expenses should be allowed only for persons who can be claimed as exemptions on your income tax return.

Dollar amounts are derived from Bureau of Labor Statistics (BLS) Consumer Expenditure Survey, 1992-93, Tables 1, 3, 4, and 5.

Form **433-A**
(Rev. September 1995)
Department of the Treasury
Internal Revenue Service

Collection Information Statement for Individuals

Note: **Complete all blocks, except shaded areas. Write "N/A"** *(not applicable)* **in those blocks that do not apply.**
Instructions for certain line items are in Publication 1854.

1 Taxpayer(s) name(s) and address	2 Home phone number ( )	3 Marital status
County	4a Taxpayer's social security number	4b Spouse's social security number

Section I — Employment Information

5 Taxpayer's employer or business *(name and address)*

a How long employed	b Business phone number ( )	c Occupation

d Number of exemptions claimed on Form W-4	e Pay period: ☐ Weekly ☐ Monthly ☐ Bi-weekly ☐ .... Payday: .... (Mon–Sun)	f (Check appropriate box) ☐ Wage earner ☐ Sole proprietor ☐ Partner

6 Spouse's employer or business *(name and address)*

a How long employed	b Business phone number ( )	c Occupation

d Number of exemptions claimed on Form W-4	e Pay period: ☐ Weekly ☐ Monthly ☐ Bi-weekly ☐ .... Payday: .... (Mon–Sun)	f (Check appropriate box) ☐ Wage earner ☐ Sole proprietor ☐ Partner

Section II — Personal Information

7 Name, address and telephone number of next of kin or other reference	8 Other names or aliases	9 Previous address(es)

10 Age and relationship of dependents living in your household *(exclude yourself and spouse)*

11 Date of Birth ▶	a Taxpayer	b Spouse	12 Latest filed income tax return *(tax year)*	a Number of exemptions claimed	b Adjusted Gross Income

Section III — General Financial Information

13 Bank accounts *(include savings and loans, credit unions, IRA and retirement plans, certificates of deposit, etc.)* Enter bank **loans** in item 28.

Name of Institution	Address	Type of Account	Account No.	Balance

Total *(Enter in item 21)* . . . . ▶

Cat. No. 20312N

Form **433-A** (Rev. 9-95)

Section III (continued)   General Financial Information

14   Charge cards and lines of credit from banks, credit unions, and savings and loans. List all other charge accounts in item 28.

Type of Account or Card	Name and Address of Financial Institution	Monthly Payment	Credit Limit	Amount Owed	Credit Available
Totals (Enter in item 27) ▶					

15   Safe deposit boxes rented or accessed (List all locations, box numbers, and contents)

16   **Real Property** (Brief description and type of ownership) | **Physical Address**

a

County ....

b

County ....

c

County ....

17 Life Insurance (Name of Company)	Policy Number	Type	Face Amount	Available Loan Value
		☐ Whole ☐ Term		
		☐ Whole ☐ Term		
		☐ Whole ☐ Term		
Total (Enter in item 23) ▶				

18   Securities (stocks, bonds, mutual funds, money market funds, government securities, etc.):

Kind	Quantity or Denomination	Current Value	Where Located	Owner of Record

19   Other information relating to your financial condition. If you check the **"Yes"** box, please give dates and explain on page 4, Additional Information or Comments:

a Court proceedings	☐ Yes ☐ No	**b** Bankruptcies	☐ Yes ☐ No
c Repossessions	☐ Yes ☐ No	**d** Recent sale or other transfer of assets for less than full value	☐ Yes ☐ No
e Anticipated increase in income	☐ Yes ☐ No	**f** Participant or beneficiary to trust, estate, profit sharing, etc.	☐ Yes ☐ No

Section IV — Assets and Liabilities

Description	Current Market Value	Current Amount Owed	Equity in Asset	Amount of Monthly Payment	Name and Address of Lien/Note Holder/Lender	Date Pledged	Date of Final Payment
20 Cash							
21 Bank accounts (from item 13)							
22 Securities (from item 18)							
23 Cash or loan value of insurance							
24 Vehicles (model, year, license, tag #)							
a							
b							
c							
25 Real property (from Section III, item 16) a							
b							
c							
26 Other assets							
a							
b							
c							
d							
e							
27 Bank revolving credit (from item 14)							
28 Other liabilities (including bank loans, judgments, notes, and charge accounts not entered in item 13) a							
b							
c							
d							
e							
f							
g							
29 Federal taxes owed (prior years)							
30 Totals			$	$			

Internal Revenue Service Use Only Below This Line

Financial Verification/Analysis

Item	Date Information or Encumbrance Verified	Date Property Inspected	Estimated Forced Sale Equity
Personal residence			
Other real property			
Vehicles			
Other personal property			
State employment (husband and wife)			
Income tax return			
Wage statements (husband and wife)			
Sources of income/credit (D&B report)			
Expenses			
Other assets/liabilities			

Section V   Monthly Income and Expense Analysis

Total Income			Necessary Living Expenses		
Source	**Gross**			**Claimed**	*(IRS use only)* **Allowed**
31 Wages/salaries *(taxpayer)*	$		42 National Standard Expenses [1]	$	$
32 Wages/salaries *(spouse)*			43 Housing and utilities [2]		
33 Interest, dividends			44 Transportation [3]		
34 Net business income from Form 433-B)			45 Health care		
35 Rental income			46 Taxes *(income and FICA)*		
36 Pension *(taxpayer)*			47 Court ordered payments		
37 Pension *(spouse)*			48 Child/dependent care		
38 Child support			49 Life insurance		
39 Alimony			50 Secured or legally-perfected debts *(specify)*		
40 Other			51 Other expenses *(specify)*		
41 Total income	$		**52 Total expenses**	$	$
			53 *(IRS use only)* Net difference *(income less necessary living expenses)*	$	

Certification   **Under penalties of perjury, I declare that to the best of my knowledge and belief this statement of assets, liabilities, and other information is true, correct, and complete.**

54 Your signature	55 Spouse's signature *(if joint return was filed)*	56 Date

Notes

1 Clothing and clothing services, food, housekeeping supplies, personal care products and services, and miscellaneous.

2 Rent or mortgage payment for the taxpayer's principal residence. Add the average monthly payment for the following expenses if they are **not** included in the rent or mortgage payment: property taxes, homeowner's or renter's insurance, parking, necessary maintenance and repair, homeowner dues, condominium fees and utilities. Utilities include gas, electricity, water, fuel oil, coal, bottled gas, trash and garbage collection, wood and other fuels, septic cleaning, and telephone.

3 Lease or purchase payments, insurance, registration fees, normal maintenance, fuel, public transportation, parking, and tolls.

Additional information or comments:

Internal Revenue Service Use Only Below This Line

Explain any difference between Item 53 and the installment agreement payment amount:

Name of originator and IDRS assignment number: Date

How to prepare a Collection Information Statement (Form 433-A)

Complete all blocks, except shaded areas. Write "N/A" (Not Applicable) in those blocks that do not apply to you. *If you don't complete the form, we won't be able to help determine the best method for you to pay the amount due.* The areas explained below are the ones we have found to be the most confusing to people completing the form.

Section III

Item 13—Bank Accounts
Enter all accounts even if there is currently no balance. *Do Not* enter bank loans.

Item 14—Bank Charge Cards, Lines of Credit, etc.
Enter only credit issued by a bank, credit union, or savings and loan (MasterCard, Visa, overdraft protection, etc.). List other charge accounts such as oil companies and department stores in Item 28.

Item 16—Real Property Description and Ownership
List all real property that you own or are purchasing. Include the address, county, and type of buildings on the property. List the names of all owners and type of ownership (such as joint tenants, tenant in common, etc.)

Section IV

Items 24 thru 26—Vehicles, Real Property, and Other Assets

Current Market Value - Indicate the amount you could sell the asset for today.

Equity in Asset - Subtract liability (current amount owned) from current market value.

Date Pledged - Enter the date the loan was originally taken out or property given as security.

Date of Final Payment - Enter the date the loan will be fully paid. If you are behind in payments, enter "Behind."

List other assets you own such as campers, boats, jewelry, antiques, etc. in item 26.

Item 28—Other Liabilities
List all other liabilities, including charge accounts, bank loans and notes, personal loans, medical bills, etc.

Section V

If only one spouse has a tax liability, but both have income, list the total household income and expenses.

Items 31 and 32—Wages and Salaries
Enter your *gross* monthly wages and/or salaries. Do not deduct withholding, or allotments you elect to take out of your pay such as insurance payments, credit union deductions, car payments, etc. List these expenses in Section IV and Section V.

Item 34—Net Business Income
Enter your monthly *net* business income, that is, what you earn after you have paid your ordinary and necessary monthly business expenses.

Necessary Living Expenses

To be necessary, expenses must provide for the health and welfare of you and your family and/or provide for the production of income, and must be reasonable in amount. You may be asked to provide substantiation of certain expenses.

Item 42—National Standard Expenses
This category includes clothing and clothing services, food, housekeeping supplies, personal care products and services, and miscellaneous. Enter the amount you are allowed, based on your total monthly gross income and the size of your family, from the chart on the back of these instructions. If you claim a higher amount, you must substantiate why a higher amount is necessary for each item included in this category.

Item 43—Housing and Utilities
Enter the monthly rent or mortgage payment for your principal residence. Add the average monthly payment for the following expenses if they are *not* included in your rent or mortgage payment: property taxes, homeowner's or renter's insurance, parking, necessary maintenance and repair, homeowner dues, condominium fees, and utilities. Utilities includes gas, electricity, water, fuel oil, coal, bottled gas, trash and garbage collection, wood and other fuels, septic cleaning and telephone.

Item 44—Transportation
Enter your average monthly transportation expenses. Transportation expenses include: lease or purchase payments, insurance, registration fees, normal maintenance, fuel, public transportation, parking and tolls.

Item 50—Secured or Legally-perfected Debts
Do not enter mortgage payment entered in Item 43, or lease or purchase payments entered in Item 44.

Item 51—Other Expenses
Enter your average monthly payments for any other *necessary* expenses.

Item 53—Net Difference
Do not show an entry in this space. IRS use only.

Certification

For joint income tax liabilities, both husband and wife should sign the statement.

Department of the Treasury
Internal Revenue Service
Publication 1854 (Rev. 9-95)
Catalog No. 21563Q

National Standard Expenses
(Item 42)

Total Monthly Income	Number of Persons in Household				
	One	Two	Three	Four	Over Four
Less than $830	315	509	553	714	+120
$830 to $1,249	383	517	624	723	+130
$1,250 to $1,669	448	569	670	803	+140
$1,670 to $2,499	511	651	731	839	+150
$2,500 to $3,329	551	707	809	905	+160
$3,330 to $4,169	590	840	948	1,053	+170
$4,170 to $5,829	665	913	1,019	1,177	+180
$5,830 and over	923	1,179	1,329	1,397	+190

Expenses include: Housekeeping supplies
Clothing and clothing services
Personal care products and services
Food
Miscellaneous

To find the amount you are allowed, read down the Total Gross Monthly Income Column until you find your income, then read across to the column for the number of persons in your family.

If there are more than four persons in your family, multiply the number of additional persons by the amount in the "Over Four" column and add the result to the amount in the "Four" column. (For example total monthly income of $830 to $1,249 for six persons would equal a monthly national standard of 723 + 130 + 130, or 983.

Normally, expenses should be allowed only for persons who can be claimed as exemptions on your income tax return.

Dollar amounts are derived from Bureau of Labor Statistics (BLS) Consumer Expenditure Survey, 1992-93, Tables 1, 3, 4, and 5.

*U.S. Government Printing Office: 1995 — 387-109/21884

Form **433-B**
(Rev. June 1991)
Department of the Treasury
Internal Revenue Service

Collection Information Statement for Businesses

(If you need additional space, please attach a separate sheet.)

Note: Complete all blocks, except shaded areas. Write "N/A" *(not applicable)* in those blocks that do not apply.

1 Name and address of business	2 Business phone number ( )

3 (Check appropriate box)
- ☐ Sole proprietor
- ☐ Partnership
- ☐ Corporation
- ☐ Other *(specify)*
....
....

County ....

4 Name and title of person being interviewed	5 Employer identification number	6 Type of business

7 Information about owner, partners, officers, major shareholder, etc.

Name and Title	Effective Date	Home Address	Phone Number	Social Security Number	Total Shares or Interest

Section I General Financial Information

8 Latest filed income tax return ▶

Form	Tax year ended	Net income before taxes

9 Bank accounts *(List all types of accounts including payroll and general, savings, certificates of deposit, etc.)*

Name of Institution	Address	Type of Account	Account Number	Balance
			Total *(Enter in item 17)* . . . . ▶	

10 Bank credit available *(Lines of credit, etc.)*

Name of Institution	Address	Credit Limit	Amount Owed	Credit Available	Monthly Payments
Totals *(Enter in items 24 or 25 as appropriate)* . . . . ▶					

11 Location, box number, and contents of all safe deposit boxes rented or accessed

Section I (continued)　　　　　General Financial Information

12　Real property

Brief Description and Type of Ownership	Physical Address
a	
	County ....
b	
	County ....
c	
	County ....
d	
	County ....

13　Life insurance policies owned with business as beneficiary

Name Insured	Company	Policy Number	Type	Face Amount	Available Loan Value
Total (Enter in item 19) . . . . ▶					

14a Additional information regarding financial condition (*Court proceedings, bankruptcies filed or anticipated, transfers of assets for less than full value, changes in market conditions, etc. Include information regarding company participation in trusts, estates, profit-sharing plans, etc.*)

b If you know of any person or organization that borrowed or otherwise provided funds to pay net payrolls:

(i) Who borrowed funds?

(ii) Who supplied funds?

15 Accounts/notes receivable (*Include current contract jobs, loans to stockholders, officers, partners, etc.*)

Name	Address	Amount Due	Date Due	Status
		$		
Total (Enter in item 18) . . . . ▶		$		

Section II — Asset and Liability Analysis

(a) Description		(b) Cur. Mkt. Value	(c) Liabilities Bal. Due	(d) Equity in Asset	(e) Amt. of Mo. Pymt	(f) Name and Address of Lien/Note Holder/Obligee	(g) Date Pledged	(h) Date of Final Pymt.
16 Cash on hand								
17 Bank accounts								
18 Accounts/Notes receivable								
19 Life insurance loan value								
20 Real property (from item 12)	a							
	b							
	c							
	d							
21 Vehicles (model, year, and license)	a							
	b							
	c							
22 Machinery and equipment (specify)	a							
	b							
	c							
23 Merchandise inventory (specify)	a							
	b							
24 Other assets (specify)	a							
	b							
25 Other liabilities (including notes and judgments)	a							
	b							
	c							
	d							
	e							
	f							
	g							
	h							
26 Federal taxes owed								
27 Total								

Section III   Income and Expense Analysis

The following information applies to income and expenses during the period _____ to _____	Accounting method used

Income		**Expenses**	
28 Gross receipts from sales, services, etc.	$	34 Materials purchased	$
29 Gross rental income		(Number of employees ....) 35 Net wages and salaries	
30 Interest		36 Rent	
31 Dividends		*(IRS use only)* 37 Allowable installment payments	
32 Other income *(specify)*		38 Supplies	
		39 Utilities/telephone	
		40 Gasoline/oil	
		41 Repairs and maintenance	
		42 Insurance	
		43 Current taxes	
		44 Other *(specify)*	
33 **Total income** ▶	$	45 **Total expenses** *(IRS use only)* ▶	$
		46 **Net difference** *(IRS use only)* ▶	$

Certification: Under penalties of perjury, I declare that to the best of my knowledge and belief this statement of assets, liabilities, and other information is true, correct, and complete.

47 Signature	48 Date

Internal Revenue Service Use Only Below This Line

Financial Verification/Analysis

Item	Date Information or Encumbrance Verified	Date Property Inspected	Estimated Forced Sale Equity
Sources of income/credit (D&B report)			
Expenses			
Real property			
Vehicles			
Machinery and equipment			
Merchandise			
Accounts/notes receivable			
Corporate information, if applicable			
U.C.C.: senior/junior lienholder			
Other assets/liabilities			

Explain any difference between item 46 (or P&L) and the installment agreement payment amount:

Name of originator and IDRS assignment number	Date

Department of Treasury
Internal Revenue Service

Form 656 (Rev. 1-97)
Catalog Number 16728N

Form 656

Offer in Compromise

■ What you should know before submitting an offer in compromise

■ Worksheets to calculate an acceptable offer amount using
Form 433-A and/or 433-B and Publication 1854*

■ How to correctly complete Form 656, Offer in Compromise

■ Two copies of Form 656

*Required forms can be obtained by calling 1-800-829-1040

What You Should Know Before Preparing an Offer in Compromise

Legal Limitations on Compromise	IRS *may* legally compromise a tax liability owed based only on: ■ **Collectibility**—doubt that IRS can collect the full amount owed and/or ■ **Liability**—doubt as to whether you owe the amount	IRS *cannot* legally accept a compromise based solely on hardship.
Are You an Offer Candidate?	*Do not* submit an offer if: ■ The entire amount you owe can be collected through liquidation of your assets or through a monthly install-ment plan. ■ IRS can collect more from your assets and/or future income than you are offering.	IRS *will not* decide that "something is better than nothing" and accept the offer because you currently have no assets or income.
Additional Agreements	The IRS may require additional agreements which would require you to:	■ Pay a percentage of future earnings ■ Give up certain present or potential tax benefits
Suspending Collection	Submitting an offer does not automatically suspend collection activity. ■ If there is an indication that you filed the offer to delay collection of the tax or if delay of collection would inter-fere with the Service's ability to collect the tax, then IRS will continue collection efforts.	■ If you have an installment agreement prior to submit-ting the offer, you must continue making those payments while the offer is being considered.
Substitute Form 656	Offer in Compromise Form 656 is the official Offer in Compromise agreement. If you are using a substitute Form 656 that is a computer generated or photocopied substitute Form 656 be aware that:	■ By signing the substitute Form 656 you affirm: 1. That this form is a verbatim duplicate of the official Form 656; 2. That you agree to be bound by all terms and condi-tions set forth in the official Form 656.
Can We Process Your Form 656?	IRS will return your offer to you and ask for clarification if you do not fill in every line item on the form. Refer to "How To Correctly Complete Form 656", page 6 that explains how to fill out the form. IRS cannot process your offer if it contains any of these problems: ■ Substitute Form 656 is not a verbatim duplicate of the official Form 656 ■ Pre-printed terms of the offer form are altered ■ Taxpayer is not identified ■ Taxpayer Identification Number is not included	■ An amount is not offered and/or payment terms are not stated ■ Appropriate signatures are not present ■ Forms 433-A and/or 433-B, if required, are missing or are incomplete ■ IRS determines that the amount you offered is less than the equity and available income indicated on the attached Form 433-A and/or 433-B

Financial Information

Only applies when submitting an offer based on doubt as to collectibility.

You must file Form 433-A, Collection Information Statement for individuals, and/or Form 433-B for businesses with Form 656. You must use Publication 1854 "How to Prepare a Collection Information Statement (Form 433-A)".

■ If you do not submit your financial statements or you submit incomplete financial statements, IRS will return the entire offer package to you. The information you provide must be current and reflect activity within the 6 months prior to the date you submit the offer. IRS uses this information to evaluate the offer.

■ *Do not* include information relating to unsecured creditors (See Form 433-A—line 28 and Form 433-B—line 25). For example, do not include amounts you owe on credit cards or loans made without pledging assets as security.

■ If you owe personal income tax and you are also self employed *you must* submit both Forms 433-A and 433-B.

■ If only one spouse has a liability but both have income, prepare the form using only the liable spouse's income and expense information unless state community property laws allow collection from a non-liable spouse. Where community property laws do not apply, IRS will require disclosure of financial information on the non-liable spouse during the investigation.

■ Complete all the items on the form that apply to you.

■ *Assets or income that is available to you but may not be available to IRS* for direct collection action, should be included on the financial statement. Even if the IRS may not collect directly from the assets, those assets are available to raise funds and those funds should be included in the offer.

How Do I Compute the Offer Amount?

To aid you in calculating an acceptable offer amount use the "Work Sheet To Calculate An Acceptable Offer Amount" on page 4. Enter this amount on Line 7 of Form 656.

Investigation of the Offer

In determining the amount that would be acceptable to compromise your liability, an offer examiner will review your offer package to insure that:

■ You accurately included all assets and income available to you.

■ You only claimed the necessary expenses allowable for the health and welfare of you and your family and/or that provide for the production of income.

■ IRS receives any requested documentation. If IRS does not receive the requested documentation, we cannot recommend the offer for acceptance and the offer will be rejected.

If financial changes are made, the examiner will recompute the amount necessary for an acceptable offer.

If Your Offer Is Accepted

■ We will send confirmation of acceptance by mail.

■ You should promptly pay any unpaid offered amounts plus any required interest according to the terms of the offer.

■ You must comply with all contractual terms and conditions of the offer.

■ We will release all Notice of Federal Tax Lien(s) when the offer amount and any additional owed interest is paid in full.

■ Failure to adhere to the 5 year compliance requirement to file all returns and pay all amounts due may result in default of your offer. If this occurs the unpaid compromised tax liability will be reinstated, any released Notice of Federal Tax Lien will be reinstated and the collection process will resume.

Public Disclosure of Your Offer

The law requires that all accepted offers in compromise be made available for review by the general public. Therefore, it is possible that the details of the offer in compromise may become publicly known.

Worksheet to Calculate an Acceptable Offer Amount Using Forms 433-A or 433-B

Read the terms and definitions below before preparing Forms 433-A or 433-B. You must use the National Standard expense amounts found in Publication 1854 to prepare Form 433-A.

Terms and Definitions

Current Market Value—The amount you could reasonably expect to be paid for the asset if you sold it. Do not guess at the value of an asset. Find out the value from realtors, used car dealers, publications, furniture dealers, or other experts on specific types of assets. If you get a written estimate, please include a copy with your financial statement.

Present and Future Income—Generally the amount collectible is your income minus necessary living expenses. We usually consider what we can collect over 5 years.

Necessary Expenses—*(Not for business entities)* Expenses needed to provide for you and your family's health and welfare and the production of income. All expenses must be reasonable in amount. IRS expense amounts are determined from the Bureau of Labor Statistics (BLS) Consumer Expenditure Survey. IRS also developed local standards for housing (includes utilities) from information received from the Bureau of Census.

Note: If the amount of your necessary expenses is unreasonable based on the BLS and local standards, IRS will not allow these expenses.

Expenses Not Generally Allowed—Tuition for private elementary and secondary schools, public or private college expenses, charitable contributions, voluntary retirement benefits, unsecured debts, cable television charges and any other expense that does not meet the "necessary expense" test.

Worksheet Instructions

Follow the steps in the appropriate worksheet below to compute the offer amount.

1. Use Form 433-A if you are an individual wage earner (go to worksheet 1)

2. Use Forms 433-A and 433-B if you are self-employed or if you are both self-employed and a wage earner (go to worksheet 2)

3. Use Form 433-B if the offer is for a business entity (go to worksheet 3)

Note: The offer investigator will review the form and compute an amount acceptable to compromise your liability. The amount you offered may have to be increased based on the investigator's review.

Worksheet 1: Individual Wage Earners

Step 1: Equity in Assets	Enter the dollar amount from line 30, Form 433-A		$
Step 2: Present and Future Income	(a) Enter the amount from line 41, Form 433-A	$	
	(b) Necessary Expenses (Total lines 42-51)	$	
	Line (a) minus line (b) =	$	
	Multiply by 60 months =		$
Step 3: Offer Amount	Add total of steps 1 and 2 above = offer amount		$
	Note: If the offer amount is more than your total liability, you are not an offer candidate. Contact your local IRS office to resolve your liabilities.		
Step 4: Form 656	Enter the total amount from step 3 above in item 7 of Form 656.		

Worksheet 2:
Self-Employed or Self-Employed and Wage Earners

Step 1: **Equity in Assets**	(a) Enter the dollar amount from line 30, Form 433-A	$_____	
	(b) Enter the dollar amount from line 27, Form 433-B.	$_____	
	Enter total of lines (a) and (b)		$_____
Step 2: **Present and** **Future Income**	Enter the amount from line 33, Form 433-B on line 34, Form 433-A. Include line 34 in total on line 41, Form 433A		
	(a) Enter the amount from line 41, Form 433-A	$_____	
	(b) Enter expenses (Total lines 42-51, Form 433-A)	$_____	
	Line (a) minus line (b) =	$_____	
	Multiply by 60 months =		$_____
Step 3: **Offer Amount**	Add total of steps 1 and 2 above = offer amount		$_____
	Note: If the offer amount is more than your total liability, you are not an offer candidate. Contact your local IRS office to resolve your liabilities.		
Step 4: **Form 656**	Enter the total amount from step 3 above in item 7 of Form 656.		

Worksheet 3:
Business Entities

Step 1: **Equity in Assets**	Enter the dollar amount from line 27, Form 433-B		$_____
Step 2: **Present and** **Future Income**	(a) Enter the amount from line 33, Form 433-B	$_____	
	(b) Enter expenses (Total lines 34-44)	$_____	
	Line (a) minus line (b) =	$_____	
	Multiply by 60 months =		$_____
Step 3: **Offer Amount**	Add total of steps 1 and 2 above = offer amount		$_____
	Note: If the offer amount is more than your total liability, you are not an offer candidate. Contact your local IRS office to resolve your liabilities.		
Step 4: **Form 656**	Enter the total amount from step 3 above in item 7 of Form 656.		

How to Correctly Complete Form 656

Two Forms 656 are provided. Use one form to submit your offer in compromise. The other form may be used as a worksheet and retained for your personal records.

Failure to read and follow these instructions could result in IRS returning your offer. Questions may be directed to your local IRS office.

Item 1

Enter the taxpayer's name and home or business address. You should also include a mailing address, if different.

If the tax liability is owed jointly by a husband and wife and both wish to make an offer, show both names. If you owe one amount by yourself (such as employment taxes), and other amounts jointly (such as income taxes), but only one person is submitting an offer, list all tax liabilities on one Form 656. If you owe one amount yourself and another amount jointly, and both parties submit an offer, you *must complete two Forms 656*, one for the amount you owe individually and one for the joint amount.

Item 2

Enter the social security number for the person submitting the offer. For example, if both husband and wife are submitting an offer on a joint income tax liability, the social security number of both persons should be entered. However, if only the husband is submitting the offer, only his social security number should be entered.

Item 3

If the liability being compromised is owed by a business, enter the employer identification number.

Item 4

Show the employer identification numbers for all other businesses (excluding corporate entities) which you own. Under the terms of the offer in compromise, you are required to comply with the filing and paying requirements of the tax laws for a period of 5 years for all the businesses that you own.

Item 5

Check the blocks that identify your tax liability and enter the tax year or period of the liability. If you owe a type of tax not preprinted, list it in the "other" block, specifying the type of tax and tax year and/or period. Tax periods related to Trust Fund Recovery assessments can be found on copies of notices and from the Notice of Federal Tax Lien.

Item 6

Check the applicable block describing the basis for your offer.

■ If **Doubt as to Liability** you must submit a written statement describing in detail why you do not believe you owe the liability. *You must complete item 7.*

■ If **Doubt as to Collectibility** you must submit Collection Information Statement, Form 433-A for individual and/or Form 433-B for businesses. *You must complete item 7.*

■ If you are submitting an offer on **both Doubt as to Liability and Doubt as to Collectibility,** please be advised that IRS will first determine whether your offer is acceptable based on Doubt as to Collectibility. If your offer is acceptable based on Doubt as to Collectibility, the liability issue will not be considered.

Item 7

■ Enter the total amount of your offer from the worksheet. Do not include amounts you have already paid, IRS has already physically collected or is due to receive.

■ Enter the amount of your deposit. A deposit is not required, however IRS encourages deposits because it reflects your good faith effort to reach an acceptable compromise. However, the law requires that your deposit go into a special fund. IRS will not pay you interest whether the deposit is applied to an accepted offer, applied to your tax liability, or refunded to you. *When the IRS cashes your check it does not mean your offer is accepted.*

■ Enter how and when you will pay the remainder of your offer. We have provided some specific time periods; 10 days, 30 days, 60 days, or 90 days. You should pay the full amount of the offer as soon as possible. If we determine that you can pay in a shorter time frame, we will require earlier payment or we will reject your offer.

■ Enter other proposed payment terms if you cannot pay the offer amount within 90 days or if you intend to make more than one payment within the specific time frames above. Include the specific dates and payment amount that we will receive. For example, $1000.00 to be paid on 12-31-97. When IRS reviews your financial statement, if we determine that you can pay in a shorter time frame, we will require earlier payment or we will reject your offer.

Item 8

It is important that you thoroughly read and understand the contractual requirements listed in this section.

Item 9

All persons submitting the offer should sign and date Form 656. Where applicable, include titles of authorized corporate officers, executors, trustees, Powers of Attorney, etc.

If you are using a substitute Form 656 be aware that:

■ By signing the substitute Form 656 you affirm:

1) That this form is a verbatim duplicate of the official Form 656.

2) That you agree to be bound by all the terms and conditions set forth in the official Form 656.

■ If the substitute form is two single sided pages, the taxpayer(s) must initial and date the first page in addition to signing and dating the second page.

Where to File

File your offer in compromise in the IRS district office in your area. If you have been working with a specific IRS employee, file the offer with that employee.

Review your offer form to ensure that all line items are entered correctly.

Department of Treasury
Internal Revenue Service

Form 656 (Rev. 1-97)
Catalog Number 16728N

Form 656

Offer in Compromise

(If you need more space, use another sheet titled "Attachment to Form 656", and sign and date it.)

Item 1

Taxpayer's Name and Home or Business Address

Name _____

Street Address _____

City _____ State _____ Zip Code _____

Mailing Address (if different from above) _____

City _____ State _____ Zip Code _____

Item 2

Social Security Numbers

(a) Primary_____

(b) Secondary_____

Item 3

Employer Identification Number (Included in offer)

_____

Item 4

Other Employer Identification Numbers (Not included in offer)

_____

_____

_____

Item 5

To: Commissioner of Internal Revenue Service

I/we (includes all types of taxpayers) submit this offer to compromise the tax liabilities plus any interest, penalties, additions to tax, and additional amounts required by law (tax liability) for the tax type and period marked below: (Please mark an "X" for the correct description and fill-in the correct tax periods(s), adding additional periods if needed.)

☐ **1040/1120 Income tax**—Year(s) _____

_____

☐ **941 Employer's Quarterly Federal Tax Return**—Quarterly Period(s) _____

_____

☐ **940 Employer's Annual Federal Unemployment (FUTA) Tax Return**—Year(s) _____

_____

☐ **Trust Fund Recovery Penalty** as a responsible person of (enter corporation name) _____

for failure to pay withholding and Federal Insurance Contributions Act Taxes (Social Security taxes)—Period(s) _____

_____

☐ **Other Federal taxes** (specify type and periods(s), _____

_____

Item 6

I/we submit this offer for the reason(s) checked below:

☐ **Doubt as to Liability**— "I do not believe I owe this amount." You *must* include a detailed explanation of the reasons you believe you do not owe the tax.

☐ **Doubt as to Collectibility**—"I have insufficient assets and income to pay the full amount." You *must* include a complete financial statement (Form 433-A and/ or Form 433-B).

Item 7

I/We offer to pay $ _____

☐ **Paid in full with this offer.**

☐ **Deposit of $_____ with this offer.**

☐ **No deposit.**

Check one of the following boxes.

☐ Balance to be paid in ☐ 10, ☐ 30, ☐ 60, or ☐ 90 days from notice of acceptance of the offer. If more than one payment will be paid during the time frame checked, provide the amount of the payment and date to be paid on the line below.

_____

☐ Other proposed payment terms. Enter the specific dates (mm/dd/yy format) and dollar amounts of the the payment terms you propose on the lines below.

_____

In addition to the above amount, IRS will add interest from the date IRS accepts the offer until the date you completely pay the amount offered, as required by section 6621 of the Internal Revenue Code, IRS compounds interest daily, as required by section 6622 of the Internal Revenue Code.

Item 8

By submitting this offer, I/we understand and agree to the following conditions:

(a) I/we voluntarily submit all payments made on this offer.

(b) IRS will apply payments made under the terms of this offer in the best interest of the government.

(c) If IRS rejects the offer or I/we withdraw the offer, IRS will return any amount paid with the offer. If I/we agree in writing, IRS will apply the amount paid with the offer to the amount owed. If I/we agree to apply the payment, the date the offer is rejected or withdrawn will be considered the date of payment. I/we understand that IRS will not pay interest on any amount I/we submit with the offer.

(d) I/we will comply with all provisions of the Internal Revenue Code relating to filing my/our returns and paying my/our required taxes for 5 years from the date IRS accepts the offer. This condition does not apply to offers based on Doubt as to Liability.

(e) I/we waive and agree to the suspension of any statutory periods of limitation (time limits provided for by law) for IRS assessment and collection of the tax liability for the tax periods identified in item (5).

(f) IRS will keep all payments and credits made, received, or applied to the amount being compromised before this offer was submitted. IRS may keep any proceeds from a levy served prior to submission of the offer, but not received at the time the offer is submitted. If I/we have an installment agreement prior to submitting the offer, I/we must continue to make the payments as agreed while this offer is pending. Installment agreement payments will not be applied against the amount offered.

(g) IRS will keep any refund, including interest, due to me/us because of overpayment of any tax or other liability, for tax periods extending through the calendar year that IRS accepts the offer. *I/we may not designate a refund, to which the IRS is entitled, to be applied to estimated tax payments for the following year.* This condition doesn't apply if the offer is based only on Doubt as to Liability.

(h) I/we will return to IRS any refund identified in (g) received after submission of this offer. This condition doesn't apply if the offer is based only on Doubt as to Liability.

(i) The total amount IRS can collect under this offer can not be more than the full amount of the tax liability.

(j) I/we understand that I/we remain responsible for the full amount of the tax liability, unless and until IRS accepts the offer in writing and I/we have met all the terms and conditions of the offer. IRS won't remove the original amount of the tax liability from its records until I/we have met all the terms of the offer.

(k) I/we understand that the tax I/we offer to compromise is and will remain a tax liability until I/we meet all the terms and conditions of this offer. If I/we file bankruptcy before the terms and conditions of this offer are completed, any claim the IRS files in the bankruptcy proceeding will be a tax claim.

(l) Once IRS accepts the offer in writing, I/we have no right to contest, in court or otherwise, the amount of the tax liability.

(m) The offer is pending starting with the date an authorized IRS official signs this form and accepts my/our waiver of the statutory periods of limitation. The offer remains pending until an authorized IRS official accepts, rejects or acknowledges withdrawal of the offer in writing. If I/we appeal the IRS decision on the offer, IRS will continue to treat the offer as pending until the Appeals Office accepts or rejects the offer in writing. If I/we don't file a protest within 30 days of the date IRS notifies me/us of the right to protest the decision, I/we waive the right to a hearing before the Appeals office about the offer in compromise.

(n) The waiver and suspension of any statutory periods of limitation for assessment and collection of the amount of the tax liability described in item (5), continues to apply: while the offer is pending (see (m) above), during the time I/we have not paid all of the amount offered, during the time I/we have not completed all terms and conditions of the offer, and for one additional year beyond each of the time periods identified in this paragraph.

(o) If I/we fail to meet any of the terms and conditions of the offer, the offer is in default, then IRS may: immediately file suit to collect the entire unpaid balance of the offer; immediately file suit to collect an amount equal to the original amount of the tax liability as liquidating damages, minus any payments already received under the terms of this offer; disregard the amount of the offer and apply all amounts already paid under the offer against the original amount of tax liability; or file suit or levy to collect the original amount of the tax liability, without further notice of any kind.

IRS will continue to add interest as required by section 6621 of the Internal Revenue Code, on the amount IRS determines is due after default. IRS will add interest from the date the offer is defaulted until I/we completely satisfy the amount owed.

Item 9

If I/we submit this offer on a substitute form, I/we affirm that this form is a verbatim duplicate of the official Form 656, and I/we agree to be bound by all the terms and conditions set forth in the official Form 656.

Under penalties of perjury, I declare that I have examined this offer, including accompanying schedules and statements, and to the best of my knowledge and belief, it is true, correct and complete.

_____
(9a) Signature of Taxpayer-proponent

_____
Date

_____
(9b) Signature of Taxpayer-proponent

_____
Date

For Official Use Only

I accept waiver of the statutory period of limitations for the Internal Revenue Service.

Signature of authorized Internal Revenue Service Official

_____
Title

_____
Date

Department of Treasury
Internal Revenue Service

Form 656 (Rev. 1-97)
Catalog Number 16728N

Form 656
Offer in Compromise

Item 1

Taxpayer's Name and Home or Business Address

_____

Name
_____

Street Address

City	State	Zip Code

_____

Mailing Address (if different from above)

_____

City	State	Zip Code

Item 2

Social Security Numbers

(a) Primary_____

(b) Secondary_____

Item 3

Employer Identification Number (Included in offer)

_____

Item 4

Other Employer Identification Numbers (Not included in offer)

_____

_____

_____

Item 5

To: Commissioner of Internal Revenue Service

I/we (includes all types of taxpayers) submit this offer to compromise the tax liabilities plus any interest, penalties, additions to tax, and additional amounts required by law (tax liability) for the tax type and period marked below: (Please mark an "X" for the correct description and fill-in the correct tax periods(s), adding additional periods if needed.)

☐ **1040/1120 Income tax**—Year(s) _____

_____

☐ **941 Employer's Quarterly Federal Tax Return**—Quarterly Period(s) _____

_____

☐ **940 Employer's Annual Federal Unemployment (FUTA) Tax Return**—Year(s) _____

_____

☐ **Trust Fund Recovery Penalty** as a
responsible person of (enter corporation name) _____

for failure to pay withholding and Federal Insurance Contributions Act Taxes (Social Security taxes)—Period(s) _____

☐ **Other Federal taxes** (specify type and periods(s),_____

_____

Item 6

I/we submit this offer for the reason(s) checked below:

☐ **Doubt as to Liability**— "I do not believe I owe this amount." You *must* include a detailed explanation of the reasons you believe you do not owe the tax.

☐ **Doubt as to Collectibility**—"I have insufficient assets and income to pay the full amount." You *must* include a complete financial statement (Form 433-A and/ or Form 433-B).

Item 7

I/We offer to pay $ _____

☐ **Paid in full with this offer.**

☐ **Deposit of $_____ with this offer.**

☐ **No deposit.**

Check one of the following boxes.

☐ Balance to be paid in ☐ 10, ☐ 30, ☐ 60, or ☐ 90 days from notice of acceptance of the offer. If more than one payment will be paid during the time frame checked, provide the amount of the payment and date to be paid on the line below.

_____

☐ Other proposed payment terms. Enter the specific dates (mm/dd/yy format) and dollar amounts of the the payment terms you propose on the lines below.

_____

In addition to the above amount, IRS will add interest from the date IRS accepts the offer until the date you completely pay the amount offered, as required by section 6621 of the Internal Revenue Code, IRS compounds interest daily, as required by section 6622 of the Internal Revenue Code.

Item 8

By submitting this offer, I/we understand and agree to the following conditions:

(a) I/we voluntarily submit all payments made on this offer.

(b) IRS will apply payments made under the terms of this offer in the best interest of the government.

(c) If IRS rejects the offer or I/we withdraw the offer, IRS will return any amount paid with the offer. If I/we agree in writing, IRS will apply the amount paid with the offer to the amount owed. If I/we agree to apply the payment, the date the offer is rejected or withdrawn will be considered the date of payment. I/we understand that IRS will not pay interest on any amount I/we submit with the offer.

(d) I/we will comply with all provisions of the Internal Revenue Code relating to filing my/our returns and paying my/our required taxes for 5 years from the date IRS accepts the offer. This condition does not apply to offers based on Doubt as to Liability.

(e) I/we waive and agree to the suspension of any statutory periods of limitation (time limits provided for by law) for IRS assessment and collection of the tax liability for the tax periods identified in item (5).

(f) IRS will keep all payments and credits made, received, or applied to the amount being compromised before this offer was submitted. IRS may keep any proceeds from a levy served prior to submission of the offer, but not received at the time the offer is submitted. If I/we have an installment agreement prior to submitting the offer, I/we must continue to make the payments as agreed while this offer is pending. Installment agreement payments will not be applied against the amount offered.

(g) IRS will keep any refund, including interest, due to me/us because of overpayment of any tax or other liability, for tax periods extending through the calendar year that IRS accepts the offer. I/we may not designate a refund, to which the IRS is entitled, to be applied to estimated tax payments for the following year. This condition doesn't apply if the offer is based only on Doubt as to Liability.

(h) I/we will return to IRS any refund identified in (g) received after submission of this offer. This condition doesn't apply if the offer is based only on Doubt as to Liability.

(i) The total amount IRS can collect under this offer can not be more than the full amount of the tax liability.

(j) I/we understand that I/we remain responsible for the full amount of the tax liability, unless and until IRS accepts the offer in writing and I/we have met all the terms and conditions of the offer. IRS won't remove the original amount of the tax liability from its records until I/we have met all the terms of the offer.

(k) I/we understand that the tax I/we offer to compromise is and will remain a tax liability until I/we meet all the terms and conditions of this offer. If I/we file bankruptcy before the terms and conditions of this offer are completed, any claim the IRS files in the bankruptcy proceeding will be a tax claim.

(l) Once IRS accepts the offer in writing, I/we have no right to contest, in court or otherwise, the amount of the tax liability.

(m) The offer is pending starting with the date an authorized IRS official signs this form and accepts my/our waiver of the statutory periods of limitation. The offer remains pending until an authorized IRS official accepts, rejects or acknowledges withdrawal of the offer in writing. If I/we appeal the IRS decision on the offer, IRS will continue to treat the offer as pending until the Appeals Office accepts or rejects the offer in writing. If I/we don't file a protest within 30 days of the date IRS notifies me/us of the right to protest the decision, I/we waive the right to a hearing before the Appeals office about the offer in compromise.

(n) The waiver and suspension of any statutory periods of limitation for assessment and collection of the amount of the tax liability described in item (5), continues to apply: while the offer is pending (see (m) above), during the time I/we have not paid all of the amount offered, during the time I/we have not completed all terms and conditions of the offer, and for one additional year beyond each of the time periods identified in this paragraph.

(o) If I/we fail to meet any of the terms and conditions of the offer, the offer is in default, then IRS may: immediately file suit to collect the entire unpaid balance of the offer; immediately file suit to collect an amount equal to the original amount of the tax liability as liquidating damages, minus any payments already received under the terms of this offer; disregard the amount of the offer and apply all amounts already paid under the offer against the original amount of tax liability; or file suit or levy to collect the original amount of the tax liability, without further notice of any kind.

IRS will continue to add interest as required by section 6621 of the Internal Revenue Code, on the amount IRS determines is due after default. IRS will add interest from the date the offer is defaulted until I/we completely satisfy the amount owed.

Item 9

If I/we submit this offer on a substitute form, I/we affirm that this form is a verbatim duplicate of the official Form 656, and I/we agree to be bound by all the terms and conditions set forth in the official Form 656.

Under penalties of perjury, I declare that I have examined this offer, including accompanying schedules and statements, and to the best of my knowledge and belief, it is true, correct and complete.

_____
(9a) Signature of Taxpayer-proponent

_____
Date

_____
(9b) Signature of Taxpayer-proponent

_____
Date

For Official Use Only

I accept waiver of the statutory period of limitations for the Internal Revenue Service.

Signature of authorized Internal Revenue Service Official

_____
Title

_____
Date